Boosting Your Emotional Intelligence and Social Skills

Discover How High Performing Leaders Use EQ To Close Sales Deals and Boost Relationships in Life with the 2.0 Practical Guide

Robin Samuel Dean

© Copyright 2019 - All rights reserved.

The content contained within this book may not be reproduced, duplicated or transmitted without direct written permission from the author or the publisher.

Under no circumstances will any blame or legal responsibility be held against the publisher, or author, for any damages, reparation, or monetary loss due to the information contained within this book. Either directly or indirectly.

Legal Notice

This book is copyright protected. This book is only for personal use. You cannot amend, distribute, sell, use, quote or paraphrase any part, or the content within this book, without the consent of the author or publisher.

Disclaimer Notice

Please note the information contained within this document is for educational and entertainment purposes only. All effort has been executed to present accurate, up to date, and reliable, complete information. No warranties of any kind are declared or implied. Readers acknowledge that the author is not engaging in the rendering of legal, financial, medical or professional advice. The content within this book has been derived from various sources. Please consult a licensed professional before attempting any techniques outlined in this book.

By reading this document, the reader agrees that under no circumstances is the author responsible for any losses, direct or indirect, which are incurred as a result of the use of information contained within this document, including, but not limited to, — errors, omissions, or inaccuracies.

Contents

How Quiet Introverts Thrive in An Extrovert World ... 1

Chapter 1: Nothing Wrong with Being an Introvert ... 2

Chapter 2: Introvert Myths Debunked ... 11

Chapter 3: Dominate Life Even When Quiet and Shy ... 17

Chapter 4: What Your Competitive Edge Is ... 24

Chapter 5: Creating Chatter and Small Talk Without Being Awkward ... 34

Chapter 6: Leverage Charisma on Command ... 42

Chapter 7: Tips for Networking and Making Friends ... 49

Chapter 8: Survival Guide for Social Events ... 57

Chapter 9: Outsell the Extroverts ... 65

Chapter 10: Crush Your Competitors ... 73

Chapter 11: Make Yourself Known ... 80

Chapter 12: Persuade People Even When You're Nervous ... 87

Chapter 13: Understanding Other People's Emotions and Thrive ... 94

Chapter 14: Tips for the Sensitive and Shy ... 101

Emotional Intelligence Primal Leadership 2.0 ... 108

Introduction ... 109

Chapter 1: What is Emotional Intelligence ... 111

Chapter 2: Emotional Intelligence Basics ... 133

Chapter 3: Signs of Low Emotional Intelligence _____ 140

Chapter 4: Boost Self-Awareness _____ 145

Chapter 5: The Need to Manage Emotions _____ 153

Chapter 6: Self-Motivation to Thrive _____ 158

Chapter 7: Learn to Understand Others and Develop Empathy _____ 167

Chapter 8: Handling Relationships for Success _____ 173

Chapter 9: Leading with Emotional Intelligence in Social Settings _____ 190

Chapter 10: How to Handle Conflicts the Right Way _____ 200

Chapter 11: Learn to Forgive _____ 211

Chapter 12: Emotional Intelligence in Leaders _____ 215

Chapter 13: Myths Debunked _____ 227

Conclusion _____ 231

The Social Anxiety and Shyness Solution _____ **232**

Chapter 1: Eliminate Social Anxiety in Less Than 60 Seconds _____ 233

Chapter 2: Make A Kickass First Impression _____ 245

Chapter 3: Start A Conversation with Anyone _____ 263

Chapter 4: Building Massive Confidence _____ 278

Chapter 5: Charisma on Demand _____ 299

Chapter 6: Instantly Persuade People _____ 308

Chapter 7: Get Respect Immediately _____ 317

Chapter 8: How to Analyze People _____ 327

Chapter 9: How to Think Under Pressure and Crush It _____ 338

Chapter 10: How to Sell Anything to Anyone All the Time _____ 344

Chapter 11: Use Psychology to Get What You Want _____ 358

How Quiet Introverts Thrive in An Extrovert World

Learn How the Shy can Outsell Anyone, succeed as an Entrepreneur, and Take Advantage to Win & Influence People & Friends - Improve Your Social Skills

Chapter 1:
Nothing Wrong with Being an Introvert

Being an introvert is not easy. People often misunderstand you and make an opinion about you even before they get to know who you truly are. There is a lot of pressure on introverts to become more outgoing and change the way they live only because society will not accept who they truly are. If you are an introvert and you are having a lot of problems dealing with it, then you need to read on. Just because you find staying in the confinement of your cubicle more comforting than talking loudly at your office meeting doesn't mean that something is wrong with you. An introvert can be just as productive and successful as an extrovert as long as they learn to prove themselves by taking the right steps.

You do not have to worry about changing your personality in order to fit in. Remember, some people were born to stand out and if being quiet makes you that person, accept it and learn how to make the most of it.

The Extrovert Expectation
One of the major problems of being an introvert is that you are normally surrounded by outgoing people who are social and have a certain expectation from you. Whether it's your work environment or the people you socialize with, there are certain expectations everyone has and they believe that you should live up

to them even if you are not comfortable with it. There are some people who manage to effortlessly engage with others even if they haven't gotten to know them that well. This may seem really difficult for an introvert who struggles to strike a conversation even with someone they are familiar with.

Just because you cannot hold up your end of the conversation it doesn't mean that you are someone who should be targeted. Introverts need to learn how to deal with society and let them know that, while they are a little shy in comparison to the other people they know and it does take them a little bit longer to hold a conversation, it doesn't make them socially awkward. If you are an introvert do not be shy of who you are. Instead, try to convert your weakness into your greatest strength by showing people your true self rather than trying to be somebody you aren't.

Self-Acceptance

Just because everybody does it, doesn't mean it is correct and that's exactly how you have to be. One of the biggest problems of society is that they look at an extrovert and keep them as their role model. They believe that these role models can strike conversations and be the center of attraction in every social gathering and that's exactly what everyone aspires to become. An introvert can also become a popular personality in the social circle once they learn that accepting their true nature can work in their favor.

Instead of trying to change the way you address situations and forcing yourself to get out of your comfort zone, you need to learn how to be comfortable in your own skin. It doesn't matter if you stand in one corner of a social gathering without striking a conversation with anyone. The very fact that you made an effort to get to the social gathering speaks volumes of you as a person.

How Quiet Introverts Thrive in An Extrovert World

Introverts are not people who are quiet all the time. They are those people who are quiet when they are in front of strangers or people, they are not comfortable with. If you want to overcome this awkwardness in society, all you need to do is know how to be comfortable in your own skin. This will help you go places without trying to push yourself to do things that don't bring you any happiness.

Don't be Misunderstood

Introverts are often misunderstood and believed to be people who tend to prefer spending time alone rather than socializing with the crowd. The truth is introverts are very creative and can come up with some of the best innovative solutions for various corporations and businesses by putting their mind to work in wonderful ways. Most introverts are known to think out of the box and while they do enjoy the solitude it doesn't mean that's what they represent. While an introvert enjoys spending time alone, it doesn't mean that they are alone all the time. It's just that they are comfortable with a certain amount of people whom they have known for a long time as opposed to an extrovert who finds comfort even with new people.

One of the best things about introverts is that their nature helps them to think before they take action and this is what reflects in the kind of work that they do. They are not hasty decision makers which means that there is less room for error with the kind of work that an introvert will complete. They also tend to get less distracted because small talk is something that they aren't into and they prefer privacy over openly sharing a lot of information about themselves.

Many people believe it's difficult to maintain a friendship with an introvert but the truth is the exact opposite. When you are looking for somebody to listen to you or share your secrets with, you will be able to do it a lot better with an introvert in comparison to an extrovert because introverts understand privacy and respect it. While you may think that they are a social misfit, the truth is they are quirky and their nature eventually tends to impress everybody who gets to know them. An introvert is not somebody who will be unable to discuss or hold up a conversation. While they may find it difficult to have a conversation with somebody new, once they begin having a conversation, they will be a lot of fun. An introvert is highly likely to become a very successful entrepreneur and a thoughtful leader.

Introverts Are Loners

One of the biggest problems of being an introvert is that most people believe you are a loner who does not fit into a social group. The truth is introverts are known to maintain their distance in a large gathering because it takes them a while to open up. If people were a little more considerate, an introvert wouldn't feel so uncomfortable in new situations and they would manage to get along with people just as well. We will discuss more common introvert myths in chapter 2.

Introverts Communicate Effectively

Contrary to belief, introverts manage to communicate very effectively and they put a lot of time and thought into the kind of communication they have. You an introvert will not send you an incomplete text message or have an incomplete conversation with you. If you are in a discussion with an introvert, they will give you their full attention and you can rest assured that your conversation will be one that is very meaningful and you will learn a lot. Yes, introverts do not like to engage in small talk but that doesn't mean that they don't like to have a conversation. They just don't like wasting time talking about things that are irrelevant or putting other people down. You're not going to come across an introvert who speaks ill of another person or who insults somebody. The sad part is, introverts are often put down by others just because they do not participate in negative gossiping. Introverts spend a lot of time on the positive aspects of life. They tend to grow and become more successful because negativity is not part of the agenda.

Introverts Are Highly Successful

You will be surprised to see a number of great personalities who were introverts by nature. Some of the most prominent personalities in history and on television have been introverts and the reason they manage to become so successful is because they work and observe. They are gifted personalities who use their thought process into developing something positive and insightful rather than indulge in unnecessary drama. Introverts will always take themselves away from drama because that's not who they truly are. They are the first people to arrive for the meeting and they will always be most prepared for it.

An introvert is also the one who will be the best dressed and always on time. They also know exactly how to treat people with respect. While some people tend to make fun of the nature of an introvert, it is their humble behavior that helps them to go places. There is no denying that an introvert may not flourish in every industry but they try to give it their best. Even if you try to put them in front of an audience, as uncomfortable as they are, they will still try to do as much as they can to focus on the task at hand. An introvert may not be the best person for a face-to-face sale or a marketing job, but they are definitely the kind of person who you would want to give a motivational speech to a group of employees just before they head in to do something prominent for the business.

Introverts can grow to be successful as long as they learn how to accept who they are and you need to do that if you want to become more confident. If you're an introvert there's nothing wrong with it. You don't have to worry about what society will say. All you need to do is stop pretending to be someone else and become the person you always wanted to be.

If you are an introvert then it's important for you to learn how to deal with the problems you face so that you are not socially awkward. You need to try and get comfortable even when you are in a social situation. Let's take a look at some of the problems that an introvert faces on a regular basis.

Making Excuses to Leave a Party

Introverts often feel pressured into going to parties at work or in their social circle but they always wonder when they can escape from the scenario completely. It's normal for an introvert to feel out of place in a larger social gathering or when they are around too many people that they do not know because it's not easy for them to open up to somebody they just met. If you are forced to go for a party you can't avoid, it would be best to go with somebody that you know because it makes you feel more comfortable and you will be able to talk to someone during the party. Every introvert has a circle of people that they are close to and comfortable with. So, take your time to figure out your circle and try to have them around you during social gatherings or parties.

Low on Energy After Regular Activities

One of the problems of being an introvert is that you tend to feel drained at the end of your regular routine because you always look for excuses not to spend time socializing with people outside of your social circle. While it's good to be who you are, you need to make a little effort to socialize with a few people and that means you making an effort to try to go outside and interact with people for a little while. The more you learn how to do this, the higher the energy levels will be and you will feel energized. One of the smartest ways to do this is to find yourself a hobby that you are truly passionate about. This could be anything from walking around the park or even getting yourself a dog to accompany you on your evening trails.

Being Questioned About Being Quiet

As an introvert, you are often asked questions with regards to why you are not saying anything. The truth is it is difficult for you to start a conversation with somebody you aren't familiar with or make yourself part of a conversation that doesn't excite you and that is absolutely fine. However, when you are questioned about why you are so quiet, always let them know that you are fine and you just enjoy listening to the conversation because you're getting to learn something.

Working on a Group Project

An introvert dreads working on a group project because they have to communicate with people, they might not know that well and they will need to work along with them. This can be in the form of an oral presentation or a research essay that you need to create for work, it is important for you to learn how to communicate with the people you are working with in order for you to get the project completed. If you are an introvert make sure that you find yourself a job that you truly love and you are passionate about because when you enjoy what you are doing, a group project will no longer matter to you since you will be more focused on getting the project completed successfully. It won't matter whether or not you have to communicate with new people.

Try to Avoid Crowds

Introverts always look to stay away from large crowds because they dread having to start a conversation with people they do not know. If you find it difficult going to the grocery store when it's too crowded because you do not like too many people around or you would prefer to eat your lunch alone at your office desk then there's nothing to worry about. This is a common fear of an introvert and the only thing you need to do is try to slowly make an effort to be around people who you associate with as your friends. The reason it is important for you to not spend your life in isolation is because this can have a negative impact on your health and your overall life and that's not healthy.

Having to Handle Phone Calls

Introverts normally cringe when they see the phone ringing because it means they have to pick up the phone and talk to the person on the other end. While you may avoid a call, you do not want to attend, you will also need to make a little effort to talk to people every now and then to let them know you are fine. Communicating with your close friends and family is essential for overall development and mental health so make sure you pick up the phone whenever you can. You should also surprise your friends and family by giving them a call every now and then just to check on them.

Worry About Losing Your Friend

Introverts always fear that they will lose their friends and they have to deal with life all alone. The truth is that your friends mean more than you think. Introverts are true to themselves and they do not lie about anything and hence they make good friends. Whether someone is looking to you for advice or whether they want your opinion on something you'll always be honest with them which is why your friends will never let go of you.

FOMO

If you have a fear of missing out then all you need to do is conquer your fear by addressing it. Whatever you fear you need to face it. Whether it means not being able to see your friends because you are missing out on social happenings, just make the effort to be there.

Living with an Extrovert

As strange as it may sound, most introverts tend to find love in an extrovert and while they say that opposites attract, it could be a little difficult to live with an extrovert when you like to do the opposite thing. While your partner may want to go out and have a good time at a party, you may want to sit at home with a bowl of popcorn and watch a romantic movie. The reason a relationship of an introvert and an extrovert is so amazing is because they manage to balance things out and get the best of both worlds. Don't look at your relationship as a problem in your life but rather look at it as a learning experience for both partners and try to bring out the best in each other.

Chapter 2:
Introvert Myths Debunked

People look at introverts as a different category of people and they believe that certain characteristics of introverts are true. These assumptions about introverts are usually made on the basis of their interaction with others and their behavior. However, some of these myths are not true and stereotyping introverts on the basis of these myths is just not fair. Here we bust a few myths about introverts.

Introverts Are Shy

A shy person is someone that is usually scared of interacting socially and that person is not necessarily an introvert. Yes, introverts avoid social interaction but not because they are shy. It's because it drains them of their energy. This is because of the extra effort they need to interact with people and this agitation is usually misinterpreted as being shy. A shy person usually avoids any kind of social interaction since they are afraid of people's perception about them and they are just afraid of not being accepted at all. When it comes to an introvert, there is no fear and their lack of social interaction is often misjudged. The fact remains that a number of extroverts are also shy when it comes to social interaction.

Introverts Do Not Like People

That is definitely far from the truth. Introverts, similar to extroverts, love people around them. The only difference between an introvert and an extrovert is the number of people that they socialize with. Introverts usually choose quality over quantity while an extrovert would choose the other way around. An introvert usually loves to hang out with a small group of people rather than attending a large lavish party. Their idea of a conversation is a one on one interaction rather than a group discussion. Introverts are loyalists and they will stay true to their friends. Just because an introvert does not hang out with as many people as an extrovert does, it doesn't mean that they do not like people. They just choose their company wisely.

Introverts Do Not Have Social Skills

Introverts are more than capable of having excellent social skills. Some introverts are known to be extremely charming and if you wouldn't know the other person was an introvert, you would mistake them for an extrovert. If an introvert doesn't have too much of an option but to interact socially, he or she would do so with a lot of energy. However, the time taken for an introvert to recharge once they have socialized is a lot more than an extrovert.

Introverts Are Not Able to Provide Any Ideas or Give Valuable Thoughts

This is another area about introverts that is usually wrong. Just because a person is quiet it doesn't mean that he or she has nothing to contribute. There is a very wrong misconception in society that the person that talks the most has the best ideas. However, more often than not we realize that the person that speaks a lot tends to speak unnecessary words. An introvert chooses to keep a low profile because they do not feel the need to express all their ideas and thoughts. Introverts also find it difficult to express themselves and this is the reason their ideas are usually suppressed. It takes them a lot of time to open up and speak to the person sitting opposite them. If you do not give them that time and you move very swiftly ahead with the conversation, you would assume that the person has nothing to say.

Introverts Love Being Alone

Yes, introverts do require a lot more alone time as compared to extroverts. However, that doesn't mean that they love being alone at all times. Introverts also look for intimacy and soulful conversations however that is only with a group of specific people. Introverts also go through loneliness and depression if no one approaches them or speaks with them. If you see an introverted person, do not wrongly assume that the person doesn't want to interact with you. They just choose not to because they are not comfortable with you and they have their own circle of friends and family members they would love to interact with.

Introverts Do Not Know How to Have Fun

While an extrovert may show a lot of excitement towards a certain activity, an introvert tends to feel drained by the same activity. This is because introverts do not usually enjoy big parties or extravagant outings. But that doesn't mean that they do not know how to enjoy themselves. Introverts love to travel, dance, go on adventures with close friends and drink a lot but they do it in their own way.

Introvert Often Tend to be Depressed

This is something that is related to the point of introverts being alone. Just because introverts are seen as people that want to be alone, people usually assume that they are undergoing a lot of depression. While an introvert will be withdrawn from the rest of the world and will keep in touch with a few friends and family members, it doesn't necessarily mean that they are depressed. There could be a very good possibility that they are drained and are disconnecting from the rest of the people until they regain their energy. Introverts have an excellent sense of imagination and they usually are a lot of fun when you get to know them better.

There Aren't Many Introverts Out There

If you thought that introverts made up only a very small population of the earth's surface then you are wrong. There are a lot more introverts than you can imagine and, in some places, they usually make up about 35% to 40% of the population. The reason people do not notice an introvert is because they tend to keep to themselves and usually go unnoticed. Some introverts even pose as extroverts and try to fit into society without being judged.

Introverts Always Prefer Listening

Yes, introverts do tend to listen a lot more than they speak however that doesn't mean that they do not enjoy speaking. People often misunderstand introverts and they assume that they just want to listen. Have you ever stopped and considered that an introvert may have dreams and passions of their own and they would love to speak to someone about it? An introvert has to deal with a lot of adjustment and this is the reason they usually feel drained out and choose to stay silent most of the time.

Introverts Never Get Angry When Interrupted

This is where a lot of people are wrong. You will notice that people get very aggressive when talking to an introvert and they usually try to suppress their voice. The reason introverts do not usually speak back is because it takes a lot of time before they say anything. Extroverts usually consider their silence as an invitation to speak and they make it a habit to cut off the introverts while they are speaking.

Introverts Are Very Rude

Introverts are probably the first to leave a party or the first to exit a social gathering. They do not like talking over the phone and in person, and this can usually be perceived as being rude. They usually take a lot of time to settle down and speak to a person regularly and until that happens, they will be looked upon as rude.

Introversion Can be Treated

This is the assumption that people make regarding introverts. Just because they are quiet and keep to themselves, people think that they need 'fixing'. Most people usually try to cure introverts and turn them into extroverts. They do not look at the value the introverts bring into their lives.

Introverts Are Usually Very Judgmental

The silent nature of an introvert makes others assume that they are being judged by that person. However, an introvert is just like any other normal human being and just because a person is silent it doesn't mean that they are judging you. Just like extroverts, introverts also love daydreaming and listening to music while going about their daily work. However, trying to fix introverts can be a futile attempt.

Introverts do Not Have a Lot of Emotions

While introverts may not be able to share their enthusiasm or act surprised, it doesn't mean that they do not feel these emotions. Introverts have a lot of feelings and they are just not able to express it in the way you and I would. They usually do not express their emotions because they do not trust everyone around them. An introvert would be open only with the person that he or she trusts and this is when you see an introvert bloom.

Chapter 3:
Dominate Life Even When Quiet and Shy

The ability to stay calm and not say a word even when people around you are chaotic and noisy is something only an introvert can do. People often believe that an introvert loses out on an opportunity because they are not confident enough to take a step ahead and achieve their desired goals. The truth is that when it comes to focusing on a task at hand and proving their value, an introvert manages to do it more effectively in comparison to an extrovert because of the amount of dedication they put into the task.

Attention is something that is really important when it comes to getting a job done effectively and one of the reasons why introverts are so good at whatever they do is because they do not tend to shift focus and usually pay a lot of attention to whatever it is, they are doing. Since an introvert does not pay too much attention to small talk and indulge in gossip, there is a less chance that they would be very interested in a conversation that is not going to be fruitful in any way. While most of their colleagues invest a lot of time in checking out insignificant facts about other co-workers, an introvert will not engage in that sort of conversation and would rather focus on proving to be an asset to the organization.

The ability of an introvert to manage to focus on task doesn't only show up when they are in a workplace, it is something that has been with them all their life.

How Quiet Introverts Thrive in An Extrovert World

An introvert will also manage to get their school and college homework done on time and in a precise manner because they don't have a lot of distractions to deal with. It is easy for an introvert to convert a lot of their energy into positive energy and do something significant with it. While an extrovert may waste a lot of time having a random conversation or socializing with new people, introverts focus on what actually matters and helps them to grow and become successful. While there are a number of people who believe that an introvert will not be able to make it big, the truth is the chances of an introvert becoming successful are just as high as that of an extrovert. Moreover, since they don't need to put in too much effort to avoid distractions, it makes them stronger candidates.

A lot of people believe that introverts are not dominating and they are very submissive when it comes to decision making. This is where most people go wrong. While an introvert does not speak a lot, the silence is often their weapon. Staying quiet doesn't necessarily mean that they agree with everything you have to say. When there is a relevant conversation and something that matters, they will voice their opinion. Do not give in to the idea of being able to dominate an introvert just because they work with you. You should know that they are just as strong headed as you are and they will not give in to something they do not believe is right. If you are an introvert and you often fear that you will not be able to succeed in your workplace or take your career to a higher path then here are a few tips for you to help you stay confident with who you are and use your silence and devoted attention to your benefit.

Learn More About Yourself
Introverts usually label themselves as an introvert without figuring out how introverted they actually are. There are some introverts who just find it difficult

hanging out with new people but are very comfortable talking to a group of people to socialize with on a regular basis. There are introverts who hate the idea of having a conversation with people, even those that they've known for a long time and try to avoid conversations altogether. If you want to do well in your career you have to come to terms with the fact that you cannot avoid conversations completely and it has to be a part of your regular life. While you may not be able to start a conversation initially, it's always good for you to start being a part of every conversation at work that is related to the kind of job that you do, so you know exactly what's happening and you are able to put your point of view across the table when necessary.

If you are not confident about talking to people in a conference room or during a meeting you will have to practice this skill. You are bound to be nervous and you will also get jittery just before you step into the meeting room but over a period of time, you will realize that this becomes a regular part of your routine. Eventually, it won't make you as uncomfortable as it did on the first day. Take time to understand your level of introverted behavior so you are able to rectify the places where you are a little weak. There is no denying that an introverted person will take a while to open up and start talking. However, the sooner you address this problem the easier it will be for you to deal with it and you will manage to come up with a solution that helps you grow your career and achieve success without any problems.

Appreciate Yourself

One of the biggest problems of an introvert is that they constantly underestimate what they can do and they always believe that they are destined for failure. Instead of worrying about how you will fail because of not being able to hold up your side of the conversation you should focus on improving your skills.

How Quiet Introverts Thrive in An Extrovert World

One of the best things about being an introvert is that you get to play to your strength. Every morning when you wake up you should remind yourself you need to do your job and you will try to do a lot better so you can actually move towards becoming successful.

While people believe that an introvert cannot be a strong leader the truth is when you have to work with a certain amount of people and you get familiar with them, you manage to be a more respected and stronger leader in comparison to an extrovert. This is because of your nature of being a little reserved, managing to maintain cordial respect, and a little distance which is necessary for people to learn to respect and be a little scared of you. When you take up the role of a leader you cannot be friends with your co-workers and this is something that an introvert can pull off really easily. This is the main reasons why most leaders, scientists, and innovators are introverts. If you think you will not be able to do something, look back at history, see the number of people who made a name for themselves and you will realize that they were all introverts. You have what it takes to be a strong leader, an entrepreneur, and a successful businessman so don't let your behavior or lack of social skills pull you down. You will manage to become successful in what you do when you put your heart to it.

Choose One Uncomfortable Act and Attempt it

There are different things that would put you outside your comfort zone depending on what kind of an introvert you are. Begin by making a list of things that make you feel anxious and stressed. Once you have a list of things you know will stress you out, make sure that the list includes things that are not as stressful to do. Each day pick one task you think you will manage to achieve depending on how you feel. The key is to not push yourself to do something extremely uncomfortable on days when you do not feel good because you may set yourself up for failure. Instead, each morning looks at the list and ask yourself 'Am I going to be able to achieve this today?' And if you think you can, attempt it. For example, your list might include going to a nightclub on your own and talking to strangers. While doing this suddenly may seem a bit weird, you can start by going to a local restaurant or a coffee shop and chatting with a random stranger. See how you are feeling, and then take it forward one step at a time. It is important to keep pushing your limits and don't quit at the slightest feeling of discomfort.

You will not be successful all the time and there will be moments when you experience cold feet and you completely give up the attempt and that's normal! You're human and everyone fails once in a while but that's how you start learning to improve towards success. Don't push yourself to attempt the same task for two days in a row because that would also stress you out. Give yourself a break every now and then and tell yourself that if I did not succeed at first, it doesn't mean I am not destined to do it. You need to tell yourself that you just need to try another day.

If you are looking to improve at what you do and achieve success the one thing you should never do is de-motivate yourself. Being an introvert is in your nature and it's not something you can change. Instead, what you can do is enhance your personality. Stop blaming yourself for the choices you make or the decisions you take. Instead, focus on how you will enhance your skills to be a more people's person without pushing your limits.

Reading

How Quiet Introverts Thrive in An Extrovert World

This may come as a surprise to you, but reading is a great way to help you learn and tell you what to do when you have no idea how to move forward. When you read, you learn a lot about different things and this will increase your knowledge. You need to learn more in order to talk about these topics in public and strike a conversation when necessary. If there's one thing you should always remind yourself, you need to be happy with who you are. When you accept this, you will start feeling positive and move forward on the path of becoming successful because you will stay focused at what you do and you won't let negative things come in your way. Just because you are quiet doesn't mean you can't achieve what you want. Reading self-help books and positive books can help you achieve a lot in life and that's the reason reading is so essential. For example, self-help books help you to get a rationalized answer to your behavior and offers solutions to help deal with the various problems you face on a regular basis. If you suffer from anxiety issues and you hate stepping up in front of a crowd, reading self-help books on dealing with anxiety will help you not only to deal with your issues but will also help you to understand how important it is for you to adopt a positive attitude, face the most challenging situations with a brave approach, and have a comfortable feeling. You can use the steps mentioned in the book to your advantage and learn how to deal with various situations in a better way.

No matter what phase of your life you are in, you need to always remember that you need to be comfortable in your own shoes and only then will you be able to improve yourself as a person. Overcoming shyness does not necessarily mean you have to change your personality completely. It means you have to learn to deal with social situations that are important and help you to change the kind of growth and success that you are aiming at. In case you are an anxious introvert, where you find it difficult even stepping into a room filled with people, the smart thing for you to do would be to seek assistance from a counselor or somebody who can help you overcome your anxiety. They can assist you in becoming more confident and able to deal with your anxiety.

Chapter 4:
What Your Competitive Edge Is

It is a noisy world out there and for an introvert, it often gets very intimidating because they believe that they have nowhere to go or voice themselves. If you are an introvert and you are worried about not being successful because you believe you lack a competitive edge then you should know that an introvert has as much to offer as an extrovert. Just because someone is loud, it is not necessary they will become successful. Being loud is usually not the best way to go about things. Providing results is something that an introvert can be more consistent with, considering the fact that they stay focused easily and do not drift away to indulge in socializing at the workplace. While an extrovert may believe that they are managing to do a great job at their workplace by keeping everybody involved in conversations, there are certain tasks only an introvert can be a pro at and this is why they manage to do the job a lot better. In case you are wondering what, an introvert can bring to the table, then here are a few facts about introverts that will amaze you.

Introverts are Very Inquisitive

An extrovert is generally confident in comparison to an introvert and that's the reason they don't invest a lot of time in observing what's happening around them. They are engrossed in many conversations and this would usually mean there is a lack of focus in whatever they do. Introverts, on the other hand, prefer to spend time observing what's going on and soak up as much information as they can. They are aware of a certain situation in comparison to the others at the workplace because they are usually calmer and more focused on understanding the job at hand. In a meeting room where there are a bunch of people trying to understand instructions, an introvert will manage to get the instructions perfectly sorted out because they are focused on that particular information and they are trying to get as much out of it as possible.

They are also keen observers and they focus on what's going on around them which helps them to keep track of progress at the workplace. When an introvert is leading a team, they manage to deliver instructions very precisely to the team and this helps them to get the job done on time and in a specific way that actually works out to the benefit of the organization. Their inquisitive nature helps them to focus on the minute details of the task that make it that much better. This also helps to reduce the number of mistakes that one would make while completing the task and it helps to get the job done faster, in a calm and composed manner, rather than in a rushed situation which is more common when extroverts are involved.

Introverts Shine When Put in the Spotlight

Just because someone is shy, it does not necessarily mean that they will not be able to perform well. Introverts actually excel at performing in a number of things and this includes the kind of work that they are handed. At the job, an introvert will focus to get it done precisely and in the right manner because they do not like mistakes and they have more energy to focus on the minute details that can help enhance the quality of work they deliver. Most introverts have a lot of power to impress people when it is their time to shine. Introverts know exactly what needs to be done to get the job completed well and when they have to work a little harder, they do it beautifully.

Don't underestimate your skills because when you are put to the test you will start performing like you never thought possible. In order for an introvert to do well, they only need to make sure that they get a job that they love doing and they will love working on a daily basis. When you're passionate about something you will push yourself to limits you never thought possible and you will do things you never imagined. So do not hold back because when it comes to performing not only will you do well but you will also surprise the people around you.

Introverts Have Their Boiling Point

Introverts may come across as calm people but that does not mean that you can challenge them and push their buttons too much. It is common for people to bully an introvert because they believe that they can get away with it but the truth is that if you try too much, you may end up on the wrong side of the table with an introvert and that isn't a nice place to be. An introvert may be socially awkward and may not manage to pull off a conversation in front of a group. They may even come across as soft-spoken but when they get upset and when you push them over the edge, you will see a side of them you never thought existed. This is something you need to be aware of when you are working alongside an introvert in the capacity of a team member.

One of the reasons an introvert can also be an amazing leader is because they know exactly how to balance the good with the bad and give their team members a challenge to work towards. Since introverts so not waste too much time in focusing on the unnecessary drama with the team, the team starts to be more focused as well and this automatically increases the productivity as well as the quality of work delivered by the entire team. As calm and quiet as they may look, an introvert can be an extremely tough boss to satisfy and this pushes the people under them to work that much harder. Not only do introverts focus on getting good things done in their own they also strive to make people working under them a lot better.

Introverts Are Competitive

Yes, an introvert can be much more competitive than an extrovert. Introverts just don't show their competitive streak because they are calm and they stay focused on what needs to be done rather than showing people how it's done. While everyone at the office may try to prove they are doing better than the others by trying to give out hints about the work that they got done, introverts simply wait till the end of the task and only deliver results that will shock people. Introvert sometimes obsessively focus on getting something done correctly and while this may seem like a bad thing, it works out to the benefit of the organization because they do not want to deliver anything that is short of perfect.

While introverts take a little time to blend into an organization, once they do, they have a strong stand and they prove how important and valuable they are to the organization by delivering results that are better. One of the best things about an introvert is that they spend a lot of time gathering information. This helps them to become stronger at what they know and use that information against others. While you may believe that an introvert is easy competition, the truth is that they are probably the strongest competition you have to face because they have paid a lot of attention to every little detail and they will use that to their advantage.

They Have Fun

A lot of people believe that an introvert is a boring person and they are also loners. The truth, however, is that an introvert is anything but a loner and in fact, they spend a lot of time enjoying themselves and socializing. The only difference between an introvert and extrovert is that an introvert will only show their wild side to people whom they trust and have spent a lot of time with as opposed to an extrovert who manages to deal with people they recently met. The truth is an introvert is safer because they will not go out with a random stranger and get drunk. Introverts have a comfort zone and they tend to include people inside their comfort zone in order to have fun. Once the introverts get to know others, not only do they manage to go out for adventures and do crazy stuff but they also do things that other people would never expect them to do.

The big difference between an introvert and extrovert is extroverts tend to follow a pack, but introverts make decisions because they try out new things and surprise people around them.

Introverts are actually more connected with their feelings than other people are and this is why they are amazing at a number of things that they do. If you are wondering why introverts are so amazing and why you shouldn't change who you are then you should know that there are some things that introverts do amazingly well.

Being an Amazing Listener
An introvert can spend a lot of time listening to conversations that people have and pay attention to every little detail of the conversation without getting bored. Extroverts are eager to start their end of the conversation without paying too much attention to the complete conversation but an introvert, on the other hand, chooses to listen patiently. They tend to listen to everything and only once they have understood their side of the story completely will they analyze and then come up with a solution or advice that can prove to be beneficial.

You don't need to worry about an introvert not paying attention to your conversation because they look you in your eye and understand every little word that you say. If there is something that they don't understand they will ask you and will make sure that they get all the details that are necessary for them to come up with a calculated solution or advice that will prove to be beneficial.

They Are Sensitive

An introvert is highly sensitive and they are aware of your feelings because they are intuitive people. Just because an introvert doesn't socialize does not mean that they do not understand what you are feeling. This is why it is easy to connect with them because they are aware of how to deal with tough situations and they can provide comfort.

They Are in Touch with Their Own Feelings

Introverts know exactly what they are feeling and they know when they need to move away from certain people or situations if they feel uncomfortable. An introvert is the last person to apologize for the way they feel. They are comfortable with who they are. It takes a while for an introvert to socialize and when they are not enjoying themselves when they are socializing, they will stop making an effort to stay a little longer just to please people. They have their feelings in mind and they pay attention to the need to feel good rather than try to make others feel good just because of their presence. While introverts know exactly when to leave a certain situation or person, they never hurt them while doing so. An introvert will not come out in the open and say that they are bored or that they are not happy being there. Instead, they will come up with an excuse that will make the person feel that the introvert genuinely needs to leave the scene.

Me Time

Introverts know the importance of spending time with themselves and they are comfortable being alone from time to time. While this seems like a problem, the truth is that an introvert tends to be more independent when compared to people who always depend on others to get stuff done. Whether it is something as simple as heading to work on their own or even taking a holiday alone, they tend to be more on their toes to get it done rather an extrovert who usually plans such things with a lot of people in mind. While it's all about socializing for an extrovert, for an introvert it's all about how they will feel and whether or not it will make them feel better. They prioritize tasks depending on their importance and while you may believe this is selfish, it is actually one of the best things to do because they do not have frustrations or unfulfilled wishes just because they had to depend on another person. They go ahead and get it done because they wanted to and not because somebody else wanted them to.

They Cultivate Healthy Relationships

Introverts take a long time to build a relationship with somebody they can trust and they do not just give in to someone the first time they meet them. This gives them time to analyze and observe the person they plan on getting into a relationship with and only once they are comfortable with the person will they take the next step ahead. While this may seem like a long and tedious task it proves to be highly beneficial because an introvert is less likely to have his or her heart broken as compared to an extrovert who has their heart on their sleeve. While an introvert may struggle with self-esteem, when they find somebody who understands what they need and supports them, they tend to become stronger and more confident in their own skin rather than trying to be somebody else.

They Love Animals

This may seem irrelevant but somebody who loves animals is always a good person by heart. Introverts are usually inclined towards animals and they shower a lot of love towards them for various reasons. To begin with, an animal does not need you to have a conversation with them and they will be just as comfortable by your side without saying a word as they would be to go out with you for a walk in the park. Introverts enjoy the company of an animal because they know that they will not have to worry about trusting them or getting to know them before they can be comfortable with them. If you are an animal person and you have an introvert as a friend, it is a great way to break the ice. Animals also work really well for introverts to learn how to come out of their shell because it can be a great conversation starter.

Deeper and More Meaningful Conversations

Small talk is not part of the plan when it comes to an introvert and if they start a conversation with someone it is usually a deep and meaningful conversation. While a lot of people believe that they will get bored by spending time with an introvert the truth is that they have so much to talk about and they talk about it with so much enthusiasm and passion that you can never get bored with them.

They Think Before They Speak

One of the best things about an introvert is that they will never say unnecessary things that may make you feel bad about your feelings. They take a while to decide what they want to say, planning the statements in their head before speaking it out loud. When you are in a relationship with an introvert you are less likely to break out into fights due to something that your partner has said because an introvert always makes calculated decisions and only says what is necessary in the right way. It's very unlikely for an introvert to use bad language or raise their voice and this makes it very easy to communicate with them even if the situation is difficult. Introverts usually do not enjoy drama and that's how they expect others to behave when around them. They do not encourage unhealthy gossip or foul language which makes them better people.

They Enjoy Nature

Introverts enjoy spending time outdoors and while a lot of people believe that they are loners and like to spend time inside, the truth is they enjoy going out for a trek and even sitting around in a garden or among the trees. Introverts do not enjoy socializing and are usually surrounded by people that matter a lot and they love spending time with. They also dislike going out for crowded parties and getting drunk in the middle of the night. They would love doing something a lot more meaningful such as a lunch picnic with family and close friends or a nature trail with their loved ones. While it seems boring when you are a little younger, once you reach a certain age you realize just how beautiful it is to spend your time in nature rather than attending a crowded party with drunk people.

They Are Creative

One of the best things about an introvert is that they are really creative and they can come up with ideas that are brilliant and very innovative. The reason an introvert is able to do this is because they spend so much time analyzing every situation that they cover up every nook and corner of the job. This enables them to come up with plans that are interesting and creative. They also have a lot of energy in them that they focus on the job at hand and it helps their imagination to go wild.

While people look at introverts as people who don't like to socialize and are antisocial, the truth is an introvert knows how to balance work and play a lot better in comparison to the others and they know exactly when they need to get home. Introverts are generally more rested and active during the day because they do not let unnecessary drama get the better of them. They are more mature when it comes to making decisions and they spend the time to think about what is right and wrong before they actually act upon it.

Chapter 5:
Creating Chatter and Small Talk Without Being Awkward

It's no secret that introverts try to avoid making small talk as much as possible and while this is healthy for their productivity, it isn't something that they can avoid all through their life. While you try to stay out of irrelevant conversations as much as possible, you still need to make small talk with people when you run across them in the hallway or even when you are standing in line to grab a cup of coffee.

While there are a number of introverts that manage to pull off small talk without too much struggle, there are also some who find it extremely uncomfortable to open up to people when exchanging pleasantries or asking them how the day is going. This makes it difficult for them to adjust in a professional scenario. If you are wondering what to do in order for you to start making small talk with people then here are a few tips and tricks that will help you.

Lowering Anxiety Levels
When it comes to small talk, introverts tend to get stressed and their anxiety levels start hitting the roof. While some people just find it difficult to indulge in small talk, there are others who completely avoid the situation. Being an introvert is easy as long as you learn how to deal with situations that make you feel uncomfortable and make yourself comfortable in situations that you have to face on a regular basis.

Question yourself as to why you do not want to go in front of a group of people and try and find the answer for it. If the reason you're avoiding people is that you simply do not like to have a conversation with them, then you need to tell yourself that this is part of socializing that is important. You need to learn to do it if you want to maintain a cordial relationship with everyone you work with. Indulging in small talk doesn't necessarily mean asking them about irrelevant stuff. It can simply mean greeting them and enquiring how they are doing. If you are not comfortable talking about other people or situations that do not matter to you, you can always excuse yourself after greeting somebody. It is healthy to talk to the people you work with and even if this means indulging in a little small talk; it is something that you need to learn to do. This is because it will help control your anxiety levels and this not only helps you to overcome your fear of talking to new people, it makes you a little more confident.

Be Purposeful

When someone strikes a conversation with you, do not approach the situation with a dull mood. Instant try to figure out what they are talking about and if its negative thoughts and attitude, then simply try to convert it into something more positive and fruitful. You need to start learning how to control conversations and talking about things that you would rather spend time discussing than talking about things that have no relevance in your life whatsoever. When you stop people from talking down to you or talking about negative things around you, they will eventually stop doing it completely and while you will still interact with these people, they will not waste your time bringing up a conversation you do not like. The reason it is important for you to have small talk is because you will learn to tell people what is important to discuss and you will try changing the way they think. Although this may seem like a really small step it works wonders to change the attitude of a person and when somebody begins doing things with a positive approach it turns out to be more fruitful and beneficial.

Channeling Your Curiosity

An introvert is generally a very curious person and this means that while they may not be able to strike a conversation instantly they most definitely have a ton of ideas in their head. Even when an introvert asks someone 'how are you doing?', they also want to get other information out of them such as 'how was your weekend?' and 'what is going on at the work front?'. While introverts do not like to waste time on unnecessary information, they are always curious to gather information that can benefit them. They are the kind of people who look for positive interactions to develop future conversations that will benefit a lot of people. When an introvert strikes a conversation that they are interested in, they start focusing on the conversation with enthusiasm and they also contribute towards the conversation in a very effective manner.

Ask Questions

As difficult as it may be to begin a conversation, it has to start sometime. Asking questions is a great way to begin a conversation because this helps you to get a response from the person and that helps you to get a little more comfortable with the conversation. The biggest fear of an introvert is that a conversation will not have any flow and once you ask a question you may not get an answer to it. The truth, however, is that when you ask a question, irrespective of what kind of question it is, you will definitely get a response so make an effort to ask a question as a conversation starter. Something as simple as asking them how they are doing or asking someone who has returned recently or resumed work after a sick leave whether they feel better are great ways to begin a conversation. It also helps you to create a bond with the people that you work with which is essential. When you start getting comfortable with the people around you, it becomes easier for you to work when you need to do a certain project as a team.

Increase the Kind of Information You Provide

One of the biggest mistakes an introvert makes is to try and keep their responses as short as possible. Introverts will usually respond to questions like 'how are you?' with one-word answers such as fine or good. While their response is appreciated, apart from providing one-word answers you should also try to add a little more by letting them know about your plan or reciprocating by asking them how they are doing. If you begin the conversation then try something different like asking them about their plans for the weekend or even some personal information like where they are originally from.

While all of this information may seem extremely irrelevant to you it's the kind of information people want to know about you too and when you begin a conversation, they will definitely respond by asking you the same questions. It easier for you to learn more about people and this helps you to establish a more comfortable zone at work. The sooner you learn how to get comfortable with the people you work with, the more you look forward to spending time at work and this will encourage you to focus better on the kind of things you do rather than getting anxious the minute you spot people you are not comfortable talking to.

Strengthen Conversations

Once you learn how to strike a conversation with someone and make small talk you, need to then take it to the next level by trying to increase the duration of the conversation and get more details about the person. While this is not necessary it is always better to do this because it helps you get comfortable with a high position and becoming a leader at your job. When you control people under you, you need to get to know them well and asking various questions throughout your professional life will help you do this in a better manner and will prepare you for what lies ahead. If you want to achieve success by doing what you love, you must make sure you get comfortable in the workspace so you are not in for a shock when you are required to speak to people suddenly.

The more you talk to people through one-on-one conversation, the more comfortable you will get and this will make it easier for you to speak to them. This will ensure that you are always in a room surrounded by a lot of people that you've already spoken to in the past as opposed to speaking in a room full of strangers. It also becomes easier for you to talk to people you've already spoken to because you can address them by name and start a conversation about something that relates to them. Not only does this help to grab the attention but it also makes them more focused on what you are saying.

Start Smiling Often

One of the biggest problems of being an introvert is that you are often passed off as someone who has a bad attitude. Just because you don't like talking to people don't mean you are a snob and you need to let people know that. If someone starts rolling their eyes the minute, they see you, it's only because they believe that you do not like talking to them or that they are not worth your time. When you spend a lot of time with people in the same environment it is important to get along with them. Just because they believe that you are a snob doesn't mean you should stop. It's important for you to try and make the first attempt and you can always begin by simply smiling and breaking the ice. Conversations are great when they begin with a smile and while you don't have to strike a conversation the very same day you smile at them you could try smiling when you walk past them for a few days before you strike a conversation to make things a little more comfortable.

Be Kind to Yourself

There would be a lot that goes on daily that will make you feel like you are responsible for certain situations or you could have changed things. You also need to get into the habit of never putting yourself down because it's important for you to understand just how much progress you have made, even if it is a tiny step. There will be mistakes along the way but it's all about reflecting, learning, and rectifying those mistakes as you move on. Sitting and pondering over things that you believe didn't go as planned is not going to help you in any way and the stress will take up your time and may make you feel sad.

While social conventions dictate that you have to be an extrovert in order to be a successful entrepreneur, the truth is that a number of very successful businessmen happen to be introverts. This means there's nothing that can hold you back from achieving the success you want as long as you learn the right method of effective communication when required. The biggest misconception that people have is a person who wants to be a leader needs to be talkative and constantly interact with the people around them but that's not true. If you are an introvert and you want to become successful it's all about effective communication and not the kind of communication that carries on for hours without really being beneficial to anyone.

Learn About Yourself and Your Skills

One of the most difficult things for a person is to figure out what works for them and whether or not they will manage to use it to their advantage. The most important thing for you to do is to identify your strong points and put it to the best use. While introverts enjoy having a strong conversation, they would prefer to invest their energy into looking for solutions to a problem everyone is focused on rather than talk about it.

Quality Over Quantity

While introverts prefer to have one-on-one communication or discussions in small groups, they definitely manage to deliver better results because they focus on quality conversations rather than quantity. While an introvert may not have an extremely long meeting and they would not spend too much time discussing with their team, they always make sure they get the message out there and it is done with precision.

Get Yourself Handy Tools

Introverts manage to use a lot of tools to their advantage and these tools are usually open-ended questions that guarantee them a response from the opposite person. This could be anything from asking them questions about their personal life or even work-related information that can get somebody to talk to you. Sometimes socializing can get the better of you and in such situation is always good to have certain questions ready to ask because this will help you strike a conversation in the most awkward situations and help you relax.

Invest in Communication

If you've always admired somebody who speaks really well and manages to grab the attention of a lot of people, then you need to start making the effort to become that way. You need to realize that the person you are looking at has invested a lot of time to learn to talk that way. Someone who communicates with you isn't just doing it because it comes to them naturally but it takes a lot of effort for them to do it and you need to do that too. It's not difficult to learn how to communicate effectively. All you need to do is practice it on a regular basis and you will manage to pick up techniques and tips that will help people communicate with you regularly and pay attention to what you have to say.

There is no denying that an introvert requires more time, energy, and effort to become a strong communicator but that does not mean that you can't talk just as well as an extrovert can. All you need to do is take the first step and ask somebody a simple question and you will be able to strike conversations with them on a regular basis. This not only helps to bring out the best of you but it ensures that it keeps your anxiety levels in control even when you can't control the kind of conversations going on around you.

Chapter 6:
Leverage Charisma on Command

It is very rare that introverts are considered charismatic. However, there is no reason an introvert cannot build charisma. Once you start developing charisma you will start seeing better things happening around you and the world will look at you as a different person. Some of the advantages of developing your charisma are:

- You will suddenly start finding new friends to go out with at night. People will start inviting you to parties and you will suddenly be part of the fun group.

- If you are a woman, then you will notice guys approaching you more often and asking you to join them for a couple of drinks.

- People will start sharing and opening up with you and they will be eager to strike up a conversation.

Building charisma not only helps build your confidence, it also helps to change your state of mind. Since you will start looking at everything from a positive point of view others will also look at you in the same manner. Here are a few ways that you can develop your charisma and turn your life around.

Preparing Yourself

Developing charisma requires a little bit of preparation work and it starts even before you leave the house. In order to build charisma, you need to change, physically as well as mentally. In order to connect with people, you need to stop thinking about how tired you will become or how badly you need to get out of a party. When you do not show interest in people you will not receive an interested response back. In order to build charisma, you need to get your mindset right and not allow anything to cause discomfort to you. You need to start being a little warmer and friendlier and focus on what has been handed over to you. To build your charismatic side you will have to start preparing physically and mentally and here are a few ways to get it done:

- Dress for the occasion and be comfortable in your skin.

- Rest a lot so that you do not feel drained while socializing.

- Have a small snack and hydrate yourself well before heading out. Do not overeat because you do not want to feel sick due to indigestion.

- Switch off your work life when you are heading out to socialize as this will help you focus on a single task at hand.

- If you have reached a place where you are extremely uncomfortable then try speaking to your colleagues and change the venue. Do not force yourself to be in an uncomfortable place as this will only ruin your mindset.

Developing Your Communication Skills

Now that you are physically and mentally prepared you will have to start building on your charm. Although you may be comfortable with your surroundings and with your mindset, you have got to have the right body language and say the right words in order to build on your charisma. How often have you come across a person that looks confident however he or she speaks the wrong words at the wrong time? You can change your clothes and change your mindset time and again however words once spoken cannot be taken back. Here are a few things you need to start controlling in order to start becoming charismatic.

Your Facial Expressions

You may not realize it but your facial expressions communicate more than the words that come out of your mouth. If you are not comfortable speaking in a group of people then you will have to start controlling your facial expressions as well. You may give out more negative signals than you think and this can put others down. For people that are not very witty and prefer to stay quiet in a group or in a one-on-one conversation, using the right facial expressions is critical. One glance from you can say a lot about your mindset and you need to start controlling this.

Making Eye Contact

This goes in tandem with your facial expressions. Maintaining eye contact doesn't mean you have to stare into the eyes of the person sitting across you. Your eyes need to have emotion. A blank stare will just end up creeping out the opposite person. If you do not want your eye contact to be awkward, then you have got to have emotions behind it such as:

- Excitement

- Amusement

- Curiosity

- Warmth

- Empathy

While you may feel a lot of negative emotion such as disappointment and anger, try to stay away from such emotions as they will go against your charismatic personality. If you are new to communicating via your eyes then here are a few techniques that you can use to your advantage:

Imagination

If you want to feel a sense of excitement and you are not getting anything from the conversation you are having with the people around you, try imagining an exciting situation and this will automatically start reflecting in your eyes. Think of the things that excite you such as going on a roller coaster ride or meeting your distant family members after a long time. Once you start imagining these things in your head, your eyes will start reflecting these emotions and the people around you will also see this. Like I said, avoid any negative emotions as this will definitely reflect in your eyes and it will push people further away from you.

Explore

If you are not very comfortable maintaining eye contact then you can explore the rest of the face. Rather than staring at their eyes you need to notice the other aspects of the face such as the cheeks, the nose and, in the case of a romantic date, even the lips. Although the opposite person will not be able to see you exploring their face, it will help you show your emotions through your eyes when you begin exploring the other aspects of their face. For example, if you notice that your date's lips are very beautiful, it will start showing in your eyes.

Modulating Your Voice

Modulating your voice and controlling your language are definitely ways to develop charisma. Some women love men with a deep masculine voice while others prefer a man with a thinner voice but better control over language. You also need to take care of how you speak - women hate being around a man that is too loud and vice-a-versa. You should also control the speed at which you speak. If you speak too fast, the person across you will not understand and if you speak too slowly, they will think you are insulting them. Your voice is also related to your emotion and just like you control your eye contact with your emotions, you can control your voice and your language with the emotions that are playing in your head. You may have seen this with children and with other adults too. If someone is excited about something it will automatically reflect in their voice and you need to keep this in mind when you are communicating with others.

Now let us look at the ways you can build charisma as an introvert. These points can help you develop a personality however there are a few things you should keep in mind as an introvert. These pointers will help you sound confident and build a charismatic personality along with being seductive and charming. The only hindrance for an introvert is their batteries tend to run out very quickly. Let us look at a few points to keep in mind that can help you develop your charisma.

Be Aware Of Your Limits

Introverts have a limit as far as their energy levels are concerned and you will have to be aware of what your limits are. You cannot go on a wild spree for a couple of days and then take a week to recover from it. Swapping between being an introvert and an extrovert can take a huge toll on your emotions and this can be very difficult to recover from. You should first see how long you can stay at your energetic best and build from there. Developing a charismatic personality is all about changing your emotional and physical capacity. Rather than pushing your limits on the first day, you have got to make sure that you know your limits first and then work from there.

Pushing Your Limits
Now that you know what your limits are, you will have to slowly but surely start pushing the limits. You also have to stop short before you start draining out. It is important that you start pushing your limits rather than staying comfortable in your zone. Until you start getting out of your comfort zone you will not be able to develop your charisma.

Practice Even When No One is Around
There will be times when you are not socializing and you should start practicing your charisma even in your daily life. You could start making a few comments when you go out to have a cup of coffee or even to a restaurant to grab a bite. Start flirting harmlessly with the waitress or try to get a few drinks from the bartender by complimenting him or her. When you start developing your charismatic personality you will get more confident and you will be able to employ these tactics when you socialize. If the above attempts fail, it doesn't matter. These are random people in your life that you would never meet again.

Start Planning in Advance
You will have to start filtering the events that you attend rather than attending anything and everything that is within sight. You do not have to stress about missing out on a couple of events just because your friends are attending it. Being too social can take a huge toll on your emotional health and you will end

up feeling low on energy quite often. Plan your social schedule in advance and slowly build your social momentum.

You also have to remember that building your charisma is not like waving a magic wand. Things are not going to change overnight and you will need to start putting in the right effort in order to improve your social interactions. Right from your personal life to your professional life, you have got to make sure that you display the right body language and say the right things at the right time. The tips mentioned above are just an outline to help you take a step in the right direction. Slowly start by going out with your friends and see how comfortable you are while mingling in a social environment. If you love what you feel then you will be more confident while building your charisma.

Chapter 7:
Tips for Networking and Making Friends

Making friends may seem difficult for introverts because they often shy away from people and do not open up to them as easily as an extrovert would. That doesn't mean that introverts can't make friends and while you always stay close to the people you know all your life, there's no harm in exploring a little further and getting to know new people. Although socializing is something that doesn't come naturally to an introvert, it doesn't mean that you can never learn how to make new friends. If you have shifted to a new city or a town and you are finding it difficult to adjust because there is nobody you really know, then you have to make a little effort to get to know people and start living a social life.

If you want to socialize in a new place it's important to have somebody to go with. While making that friend could be a little difficult at the start, with a little effort you will be able to make new friends and learn how to stay close. If you are wondering what you should do to make new friends and increase your circle of friends here are some things that can help you.

Think About People You Already Know
The best way to expand your social circle and get to know people a little better is to begin with acquaintances or people who you see on a regular basis. If you head to a coffee shop every morning to grab your cup of coffee and you notice

somebody is sitting there reading a newspaper or with a laptop, begin by exchanging pleasantries with them. The reason it is always better to begin with people you see on a regular basis or the people you acknowledge, is because you will start to feel more comfortable with them. Write down a list of people that could potentially be your friends and while this may sound weird; it's a great way to begin a friendship with someone who you will be able to select rather than randomly talking to somebody just because you felt like it. When you shift to a new city it is very likely that you feel left out because there is nobody to talk to. Unless you begin to look for people who you can call your friends you will always feel this way.

Whether it is at your workplace or outside of work, there will always be people who you see, and be able to socialize with regularly. These are the kind of people that could be there for you. Even when you are at work try to look for someone who lives close to your house so you get to spend more time with the person. Introverts need time to open up and for this reason, you may want to look for someone who can spend time with you at work and outside of work, if possible. The reason it is important to look for someone who lives close to you or works with you is because it is that much easier to schedule meetings with them in comparison to doing it with someone who lives out of your locality or works at a different schedule from you. Even if you find somebody who doesn't work with you, try to ensure they have a similar schedule so you will be able to socialize a lot.

You May Have to Make the First Move

You will spot a lot of people who you may believe are potential friends for you but they might not approach you. This means that you are left with no option but to go ahead and make the first move. While you are an introvert there is also a chance the person you may want to go and begin a conversation with is also an introvert and they may not have the courage to approach you to start the conversation. Whether you want to speak to somebody you want to be friends with or someone that you would like to get romantically involved with, it is important for you to understand that making the first move is not wrong and in fact it gives you the upper hand in deciding which people you want to talk to and which ones you may not want to be friends with.

Making the first move can be really difficult but it is a lot easier than you think, especially when there's no other option. You can always begin with small talk and analyze the person to decide whether or not you will manage to get along with them. While you won't have to put in too much effort to make friends with somebody, it will take you a little while to understand whether or not you can be friends with someone who approached you depending on the kind of lifestyle they lead. If they are extremely social and they love going out on a regular basis, you may not be able to keep up with them because socializing is one of your weaknesses. While you may manage to incorporate socialization for a couple of times in your routine, it may not be something you look forward to doing on a regular basis. Looking for somebody who has similar interests as you always work out well, so if you enjoy reading you may want to hang out at the library to see similar faces you can interact with.

Taking off the Mask
One of the biggest mistakes an introvert makes is to try and behave like somebody they are not. The truth is that while it may seem like a great idea at the start because it will help you make many friends, it's not an ideal solution because you will eventually get bored of portraying an image you are not. This also makes it difficult for you to live up to the expectations of your new friend.

Honesty is always the best policy and even if you like somebody but you do not share similar interests, it's better to be honest and figure out how to work out your differences rather than pretend to like what they like, just to get in their good books.

Introverts are often labeled as submissive people who give in to the needs of others; the truth, however, is very different from that. If you don't like something, you'll eventually figure out excuses to get out of the situation and that won't benefit your friendship in any way. It makes more sense for you to let people know your true personality, beliefs, likes and dislikes rather than asking them to like you by pretending to do something just because they like it.

It may take you a while to find people who get along with you, who understand your needs, and your likes and dislikes, but it doesn't make sense to make friends with someone just because you do not like being alone. One of the strong points of an introvert is that they manage to analyze people really well and this can work out in your favor when you look out for somebody to make friends with or even start a romantic relationship with.

Questions Are Good

If you want to make friends with someone, it is important for you to start questioning them. While this may sound like an unreasonable thing to do, once you begin questioning, you will realize that you get to know more about them than you ever thought possible. This will also help you to get closer to them. Whether you want to get close to somebody at your workplace or outside of your workplace the more you question them the more you learn about them. This will help you to connect more effectively with the person you are in conversation with.

There are various people you will be surrounded by and once you've narrowed down the people you think you should get close to; you should try to talk to them at every possible opportunity so you can get to know them a little better. You don't have to have a detailed conversation but simple questions about how they are doing or their personal life is something that will definitely grab their interest and you will also manage to strike conversations with them easily. Your listening skills are definitely your strength when it comes to questioning. When you ask somebody a question you always make it a point to put all your efforts into listening to what they have to say because every little detail matter to you. This not only helps you to use their information as a conversation starter later on, but it also lets them know that you are actually interested in getting to know them and this helps your friendship take another step closer.

Pay Attention to Your Feelings

Introverts often get confused with regards to whether or not they should become friends with a particular person. It may take you a while to understand your compatibility with somebody and in case you find it difficult to know your feelings at the start, take a little time to analyze the situation.

Your feelings towards the person matter a lot and whether or not you are actually happy to see the person is something you need to consider before making friends with them. When you look at someone and it makes you feel like going and approaching them to talk, this is a good sign. It means that you want to be friends with them, not just because you are lonely, but because you believe that they are good people. Take time to see how you feel when you see someone or plan to briefly interact with them before you actually have a longer interaction, because this may help you understand how effectively you will be able to bond with them. Subconsciously, introverts make an extra effort to bond with people they actually like. So, try to look for these people before you begin your friend hunt.

It's the same with somebody that you want to get romantically involved with. In case you are being set up on a date with someone, see how you feel about the date once you meet them and whether or not meeting them for a second time makes you feel happy or anxious. As an introvert, the one thing you should always pay attention to is meeting someone who is as comfortable as you are in a conversation and makes you feel happy rather than stressed out about discussing a topic. While there are a number of people who can make it very easy for an introvert to talk to them, there are some that are little difficult to get through and these are the kind of people you may want to stay away from, especially if you are approaching them alone.

The Awkwardness Eventually Goes Away

One of the biggest problems of being an introvert is the awkward feeling you have every time you walk close to someone to greet them or even to exchange pleasantries. It's funny how this feeling is extremely strong at the start but once you repeat the habit over and over again, you notice that it goes away.

It's the same with every new person you see. For the first time, you may have a little choking sensation in your throat and you may not want to talk to them or even let your eyes meet theirs, but once you start talking you will realize that it's not that bad and you are getting comfortable around them. Some people are easier to get along with and others may take a longer time, so don't give up on the first instance - just push a little harder. At the end of the day, you won't lose too much if exchanging pleasantries is all that you are stuck on. The good news is you don't have to have a full conversation with them but you can still manage to get a little comfortable when compared to what you were at the start.

There are going to be a lot of people who work around you and you can't expect to get along with all of them. You have to pick the people you hang out with. Pick the kind of people you know you will be yourself around. This may not happen instantly. Sometimes it may take weeks and even months but when you do find your clan, you will start adjusting a lot better, whether it's your workplace or a new place that you settled in.

Schedule Meetings Regularly

Everyone is busy these days and leading a hectic life has become one of the most common excuses to get away from social situations. If you keep on delaying a social interaction with people you just met, you will not manage to blossom the friendship or even a relationship that you plan on starting out.

As difficult as it sounds, you have to schedule regular interactions or meetings with them. This could be anything as simple as catching a movie where you don't really have to talk to them for a long time. Meeting them over a couple of drinks to get to know them better is also perfectly acceptable.

It is a little scary to do this but it's something that will help you come out and become more confident. The reason you should always try and interact with people as much as possible is to you learn more about them and to learn whether or not you can get closer to them as a friend or whether you just want to have them as one of those people you know. Introverts need a lot of time to open up to someone and the more you spend time with them, the easier it will get for you to do this. When you make friends, make sure that you make the most of it and try going out as often as possible to let the awkwardness out of your life completely.

Go Slow

Introverts always fear that they will get hurt if their friendship doesn't work out the way they wanted it to or a romantic relationship does not turn out to be a good relationship. All good things take time and that's the same for genuine, strong friendship or relationship. So, you have to make sure you invest that time whenever possible.

You also need to remember that just because there are a few differences between you and your friend doesn't mean you give up. Everyone has to make a little adjustment and you are not going to like everything about a person. So, give them a fair chance once you get to know them a little better and let them get to know more about you too. Once you start spending time with them you will learn a lot more about them and you never know which way it could go. If you decide after few months that you are not happy hanging out with these people, you can always look for a new friend to hang out with. But if it works out in your favor, you would have found yourself a group of people you can actually call your own and the kind of people who understand you for who you truly are.

Chapter 8:
Survival Guide for Social Events

No matter how hard you try to come out of your shell, there are certain limits for every introvert. Social gatherings are always a stressful matter and while introverts make an effort to go to social gatherings, they believe are important, they often look for ways to escape. While it is good to make excuses every now and then if you're overdoing your social interaction, you also need to make sure that you involve yourself in socializing as much as possible so that you get to know more people, moving out of your comfort zone a little every time. If you are a loner and you have never gone out for social gatherings then this social survival guide can help you get through the scariest of social gatherings without any problems. It is something that you should keep handy so you can use it to your advantage.

Find a Quiet Spot

There is no denying that introverts tend to look for the quietest spots and go park themselves in those spots for the rest of the evening. It's not easy to find a spot every time because sometimes you go to a gathering at a new place and you are not really sure about the venue. If you are hosting a party then you know exactly where the quiet spot is but you may not be able to get to the spot as conveniently as possible. This is because you have to stay the center of attraction and constantly greet guests when they walk through the door.

If you are visiting somebody's house, look for a quiet spot in one of the corners where not a lot of people are gathering around. A trick to find these corners would be to look for places that are as far away from the bar as possible because the bar is where all the extroverts and the talkative people will usually gather. Once you find your safe place you can then get comfortable and maybe look for someone to talk to. Introverts prefer to talk to one person, or probably two or three people, at a time. Try to look for these people and try to gel with them for the rest of the party. If it's an outdoor event then you may want to look for places such as the corners of the venue that are not too close to the door because people will keep coming in and leaving. If it's a house party then bedrooms, bathrooms, corridors, and the kitchen are great places to hangout. If the bedroom door is shut, you may want to stay out of it because you have absolutely no clue what's going on inside and you do not want to be the person to witness it.

If it is a restaurant where you are meeting then you can always take the corner seat at the table so you don't have to be in between a lot of people. If you want to make sure that you get the corner seat you may want to arrive at the restaurant a little earlier than the rest of the crowd.

Keep A Check on Your Energy Levels

Socializing can get your anxiety levels right to the top and it could become difficult for you to constantly interact with people by staying in a pleasant mood. The best way to keep yourself calm and composed during these interactions is to talk to people for a little while and then focus on what you are eating or maybe even pull out your phone to distract yourself from the conversation. There are going to be constant outbursts of high-energy where you feel comfortable as a part of the group and are constantly discussing things with them without realizing that you were awkward in the first place. There will also be moments where you want everyone at the table to just be quiet so you can relax for a while.

The minute you start feeling a little anxious you can always excuse yourself and go to the bathroom until you calm down your nerves. Sometimes you just feel a little overwhelmed by the conversations that are going on around you and because you don't want to be mean, you try to make an effort to talk but that does not help. This is normal for an introvert and when you start feeling this way just give yourself a little 'me time' away from the crowd so you can get back into your high energy zone.

Sometimes it can take you a little longer to get back to your original high-energy zone so you can always let people know that you are not feeling too well, which is why you aren't talking. This helps you to relax for a while and it gives you a fair chance to listen to what is happening around the table. When you know the conversations around the table, it gets easier for you to jump in whenever you feel comfortable or when the conversation starts to interest you. This is a great way to face your fears and deal with it at the same time without letting your anxiety get the better of you.

Go with Someone

If you are really nervous about attending a party alone, look for someone you can go with. The person that you plan on going with should always be somebody that you trust and you are close to so that you can plan an escape whenever possible. While introverts can make a lot of effort to attend parties and also make it a point to talk to people, they don't know that well, large gatherings make them feel uncomfortable and the only thing they want to do is head home and stay away from the crowd.

If you have made an effort to get to a party with your friend, it's a great achievement on your end and there's nothing to feel embarrassed about in case you are not feeling like staying for the rest of the evening. The reason it is always recommended to have somebody by your side is because leaving a party alone can make you feel upset and sad and it will also make you feel like you have no friends. When you have someone by your side you don't tend to feel so bad about it and you can even choose to go and head out for a dinner or even grab a couple of drinks a little later on.

Friends are the kind of people you feel comfortable with and if you do not go with someone then you will have a low energy level even after the event. However, taking somebody with you will help increase your energy as soon as you are out of an uncomfortable situation. It also ensures that you've done something productive rather than getting home and talking about not being able to participate in socializing. You need to remember that whether you are out with one person or you are out with a ton of people, it is still considered socializing so don't beat yourself up just because you had a bad day or you couldn't get along with the people at the party.

Plan Your Leaving Time
One of the worst things that an introvert contemplates is when they can leave a party the minute, they step in. Instead of doing this, have a clear plan in your head from the start and tell yourself that you are not going to leave the party any sooner than a particular time or any later than that. While staying a little

later is definitely a good sign, leaving earlier is something that you should prevent yourself from doing.

If you absolutely dread the party, you need to remind yourself that you only have a couple of hours more to stay till you can escape for the night. During this time, rather than focusing on how much time is left before you leave, try to interact with people and do something to help kill the time. This is another reason it is highly recommended to go with a friend; because you can always strike a conversation with your friend at the party and talk about the things you like. Not only will that help you to relax, it will even help you to take your mind off your agenda of leaving the party early.

You never know, you may end up finding a bunch of people who interest you, make you feel comfortable even though you just met them, and make you feel like these are the kind of people you would want to spend more time with. Just because you set a certain time to leave the party doesn't mean you have to leave it at that time. If you're having a good time, try staying for as long as you can but make sure that you are safe and you always have somebody with you that you've known for a long time.

As an introvert you should also make sure that you have a lot of independence which means you should have rideshared applications on your phone or even the number of a cab driver you trust who will be available all the time and can come and get you wherever you are.

Make Sure You Know the Guest List

This may seem irrelevant because you can't really control who attends and doesn't attend the party but the reason it is better for you to know the kind of people on the list is because you know exactly how comfortable you will be right from the start. If there are a bunch of people you usually enjoy spending time with on the list, you know that you would be able to enjoy the party but if there are a number of people on the list that you find awkward to talk to, then you can plan your escape or even consider skipping the party.

Just because you are making an effort to socialize doesn't necessarily mean you have to attend every single party you are invited to because then it will be pushing yourself to a limit that's not healthy and comfortable. You need to balance your life in a way where you attend a certain number of social events that you actually enjoy and avoid the ones you know you are going to have a bad time at. This is not going to happen instantly and you may end up attending some really bad parties and miss out on some really good ones. However, with a little trial and error you will be able to figure out which are the ones you should go to and which are the ones you should sit out. Knowing the guest list is a great way to decide which one you should attend and which one you should sit out because the kind of people that attend the party is the only thing that is important, rather than what kind of food was served or what was the venue of the party.

Listen Attentively and Talk Less

When you are an introvert at a party, listen attentively to everything the people are saying and talk as little as possible. This benefits you in a number of ways because when someone speaks to you and asks you something, you know what to say to them because you have been paying attention to the conversation.

This doesn't necessarily mean that you stop talking completely. It just means that you listen to other people a little more than you talk. You will come across a lot of self-centered people who love talking about themselves and how great they are and this may bore you completely. In such situations the best thing to do would be to move away from these people and focus on a group of people you actually think you will be able to blend in with.

You do not need to be apologetic for not liking somebody or not being able to get along with them. You have your choices to make and at the end of the day every party is for you to feel good and not embarrass you or make you feel awkward in anyway. The minute you realize you are in an uncomfortable situation you should try and move towards a situation or a group of people that make you feel more comfortable because that's when you will start liking social gatherings rather than dreading them. Instead of forcing yourself to do something you do not like, find something you like at social gatherings because that's what really matters.

Take Up A Helping Role

One of the smartest ways to be a part of a social gathering without actually involving yourself in an active conversation is by lending a helping hand to the host. This could be anything such as cutting of the cake and making it into smaller pieces that people can eat or even trying to arrange the salad on a plate.

This works really well because you start blending with people in a certain manner and this is what works in your favor. Instead of pushing your boundaries, you may want to do something you are comfortable with.

At the end of the day every introvert is different from another and you have to find your comfortable space at social gatherings to make yourself like the gathering. You cannot push yourself to do something you don't like because that would be trying to become a person you are not. Find a reason to enjoy this party rather than looking for ways to do it because that will help you a lot better.

Chapter 9:
Outsell the Extroverts

Just because you are an introvert doesn't mean you won't be able to do well in life or you will not be good at what you do. As I stated before, most introverts tend to be highly successful as long as they know how to use their strength to their advantage.

Just because you may struggle to proactively stand up and talk to somebody doesn't mean that you are not going to form healthy relationships with people. As long as you know when to say things to people, not only will you be able to achieve success but there is a chance that you will do better than an extrovert ever will. Let's look at some effective ways with regards to how you can use your strength to gain success and give yourself an equal chance to stand out in front of your peers.

Be Consistent

One of the major lessons you have got to learn in life is to maintain consistency at what you do. While you have to strive to get better every day you have to make sure that you do not step backward in the race. You should keep motivating yourself to get better and improve your skill sets so that you can deliver great results. You will not have to be a part of a lengthy discussion in order to deliver better results. However, what you should do is to make sure your work speaks for itself. There is no denying that actions do speak louder than words and this is where your actions will come into play.

You will have to communicate with people to ensure the message is clearly passed on and everybody who is part of the team understands the job correctly. However, pondering over the same discussion for a long time is not going to benefit you because that way all you will do is waste time talking rather than doing something for the organization. Communication should always be short, precise, and consistent so that your team knows exactly what sort of questions they have to ask you in order to flawlessly complete the task on time. Swift communication is definitely better and this helps you to be more consistent without complicating matters.

Focus on Your Goal
Whether you are leading a team or whether you are part of it, your main aim should be to focus on the goal and achieve it in the best possible manner rather than seeing what all the people are doing. If you are a leader you need to pay attention to what others are doing so that you can direct them in the right path but it does not mean that you hover over them and tell them how they should do their work. Everybody has their own way of working and the reason an introvert is better able to deal with the situations is because they do not like to interfere with the working style of a person and they give them their space.

At the end of the day your main goal should be delivering effective, consistent, and reliable results rather than seeing how your team works on it. When you try to correct them too many times it won't work out in your favor because you will constantly interfere with the workflow and this will de-motivate them. The reason an introvert needs to learn to push the buttons of their team members a little bit is because they sometimes tend to get overheard and nobody pays attention to what they are saying.

While you should not force your team members to work in a particular style you should always give them a path that you believe is strong. Whether or not they choose to walk on that path is completely left up to them, as long as they deliver the result in the manner you have requested. This is where your consistency, systematic and effective practice comes into play. It helps them become better and eventually not only will you be strong and goal oriented but you have a team of strong headed and goal-oriented members working with you.

Take Calculated Risks

Introverts don't like to step outside of their comfort zone and this also includes the fact that they do not like to take risks because they believe it will not work out in their favor. If you are certain that something can be done better with a little risk involved then you should consider trying out the new techniques to see where it goes.

Success and failure are all part of the plan and you cannot expect everything to go your way all the time and move ahead in life. There are going to be times when you are challenged with questions you may not be comfortable answering and decisions you may not be comfortable taking. However, it's all about how you approach the situation and what you do under the circumstances that let you know whether or not you are doing the right thing. Take your time to calculate the risks involved and see whether or not it actually pays off so that you can decide how to spruce up your game.

Another smart thing for you to decide whether or not taking risks makes sense is to observe what your competition is up to. Admiring their techniques and seeing how certain strategies worked out for them is something that can help you come up a strategic plan. It doesn't take you too long to learn new things and neither will it take your team to do so. All you have to do is understand whether or not the decision you want to take will work out in the benefit of your business or not.

Learn New Technology

Learning new technology is something that will accelerate your growth, not only professionally but also personally. It is something that can help you to learn to develop new skills and if you someday dream of becoming an entrepreneur, it is these technological advancements that can help you take that step ahead. Becoming a leader is important and in order for you to do this, embracing new technology is something that you may want to consider doing. It helps you to get a competitive edge and it helps you to learn the market in a smarter way.

You will not be able to try out new technology unless you are open to taking calculated risks which is why you need to first learn how to do that properly. While it is important for you to learn certain business strategies by working for someone, your end goal should always be to start a business of your own that you can handle from scratch and you will only be able to do this once you increase your knowledge. In order for you to increase your knowledge you have to be open to change and taking risks that you were uncomfortable taking in the past. You have to learn how to challenge yourself if you want to grow because if you do not challenge yourself to do something new, you cannot get different results by doing the same thing over and over again.

Analyze Your Business

One of the most important things that you need to do is to analyze your business so that you are able to identify every little mistake that is made and come up with solutions before other people. Introverts are always at a benefit because they spend a lot of time analyzing situations and paying attention to every little detail that is discussed. You should always use this to your advantage and make note of the important things that you listen to from time to time. This is information that you can definitely use to your benefit and make the most out of. Once you get this sort of information sorted out you will manage to invest in your own business ideas in the future.

Nothing is irrelevant and the more information you gather the stronger your business will grow which is why you should start paying attention to every little thing that you hear around you, even if it does not relate to your area of interest.

Just because you are an introvert does not mean that you cannot become a successful businessman someday. You need to start building your strong foundation from today and it all begins by taking the right decisions. Small changes in your life can make a huge impact in the future so begin making the changes today so that you become a creature of habit to do the right thing at the right time.

Once you gave laid the foundation towards learning effective tips on how you can become a successful entrepreneur you then need to put these tips into action.

It is common for an introvert to feel overwhelmed when they start something as big as their own venture but with a little practice and the right measures not only will you manage to make this a successful business but you'll also manage to grow and achieve your goal that you set out to achieve.

Introverts make amazing entrepreneurs because they are smart, self-aware and they invest a lot of time in research which is vital for the growth and success of any business. Since they do not invest a lot of their time in discussion, they have that much more time to invest in the actual business and this helps them to maximize their revenue by enhancing their skills and exploiting the talent to the fullest. There are various reasons why introverts can be successful entrepreneurs but if you are still a little worried with regards to how you should actually go about setting up your own business here are a few strategies that you could definitely apply.

Maximize Your Leadership Potential

An introvert usually spends time researching the best possible business practices that they believe will work well in their favor. However, a particular business strategy will not necessarily work as effectively for your business as it did for another business. If you want to truly become successful and grow your business the smart thing for you to do would be to spend time understanding what everyone around you has to say. Introverts are more likely to take advice from people rather than make their own decisions, so when you ask a team of employees for suggestions and ways to spruce up the business, you are more likely to come up with a foolproof business plan that will not only increase productivity amongst the employees but also help the business grow more effectively. The best part about a business growing like this is you have a team of highly motivated employees who have given inputs towards the business which make them feel proud about every achievement the business makes.

Consider Hiring an Extroverted Partner

There is no shame in admitting that there are certain skills an extrovert possesses that an introvert does not and it makes sense to have a charismatic character in the business for betterment and growth. There is a high chance that an introvert has many extrovert friends and for you to be able to comfortably include someone in the business, it always makes sense to look at someone who's been around with you for a long time.

If we look at history, then the most prominent businesses usually started off with an introvert-extrovert pairing. Once you find someone you can actually set your rhythm with, it makes sense to include them in the business because they come with their own skill sets and those skills can definitely help a business grow in leaps and bounds. When it comes to handling meetings and taking certain decisions an extrovert will always step up and prove to be a valuable asset.

Schedule One-on-One Meetings

Introverts often have a problem with large groups and when you have to talk to a room full of people you might not be able to get your message across as effectively because your anxiety levels will automatically start increasing. The smarter way for you to deal with the situation would be to have a one-on-one meeting with people you believe can work well for you. The reason this is important is because this meeting not only turns out to be more productive but you also manage to convey your side of the story to your employer and you can let them know what you are looking for. Another way to go about this is to hire a manager that can handle the handling of the team for you. You will be able to conduct one-on-one meeting with them; they can take charge on their own and make sure that they get the message passed down to the rest of the team. While one-on-one meetings are highly beneficial it can't be done when you have multiple employees because that will take up a huge amount of your time. When you have a manager to handle all of this for you, all you need to do is to get the message to your manager effectively and they can then take charge.

Self-Promote

Self-promotion can be difficult for an introvert because they don't find it easy to strike a conversation in front of people. However, considering today's technologically savvy industry, one can now share their story by simply writing it down and putting it on social media or on a blog for the world to see. This is a lot of fun and it also helps you to let people know what your business is all about and how effective it actually is. The suggestions you get on your social media page can not only help you feel more confident but it also helps you to bring about the change that is necessary to spruce up your business. Most introverts are amazing writers so you may want to give this a try.

If you are adamant about establishing your own business, the one thing you should always make sure is that you got it all covered and you take your decisions one step at a time when jumping into a completely new venture. As exciting as it may sound, introverts need to do their homework properly so that they can carry out the business operations successfully.

Chapter 10:
Crush Your Competitors

Introverts find it a little difficult to deal with competition in comparison to extroverts but that does not mean that they should give into the pressure and succumb. If you've gone as far as to establish your own business and decided to become an entrepreneur nothing will stop you from being successful as long as you learn how to beat your competition effectively. Just because someone is outgoing and charismatic, it does not take away your own charm and while they have skill sets of their own, you possess your own unique skill sets that can make you stand out and shine.

According to Forbes about 50% of the US population happens to be introverts so you are not alone out there. About half the population in your country is exactly the way you are. Although there are different levels of introversion, they are normally disregarded. They're also often passed off as submissive people who can't make decisions. The truth however is that an introvert doesn't necessarily have to be an outgoing person and while they may enjoy going out and having a good time, they just like to do it with a chosen few people because they are not comfortable with a large crowd.

Introverts can make amazing business leaders, just like extroverts, and when it comes to crushing competition they are not far behind. If anything, introverts can give extroverts a run for their money because of their intuitive behavior and listening skills. If you are wondering how an introvert can push the limits and become successful to beat competition then here are a few things you should know about yourself.

You'll Make a Great Leader

Introverts often believe that they cannot handle a business because they can't face a large crowd and this means that they can't lead a group. The truth, however, is that an introvert is just as effective as an extrovert when it comes to running a business and while they may not be able to look into the eyes of a large group of people for a meeting, they will still be able to be effective. A number of large businessmen today happen to be introverts so there is nothing that can stop you from achieving your dream as long as you have a plan in place. The reason an introvert has a strong chance of becoming successful is because they take calculated risks and they invest sufficient time in research which helps them to understand the market they are venturing into before they get into it. An introvert will not make an immediate decision but rather spend time understanding whether or not it is worth taking before they actually decide on it and this means that the risk of losing money is drastically reduced. Extroverts on the other hand end up making impulse decisions they later regret which is why the chances of them becoming successful entrepreneurs is actually lower than an introvert.

An introvert masters many skills when it comes to growing a business and these skills turn out to be the reason an introvert is also known to be great at relationships, personally and professionally.

- Reliable

- Dependable

- Adaptable

Although a number of people believe that it is difficult for an introvert to adapt to new situations the truth is, they know to do it better and with ease in comparison to an extrovert. If you want to crush your competition then here are a few things you should remember

Focus on Your Strength

It is easy for an introvert to get excited about business ideas they are passionate about, but they also get really scared once they have actually taken the step into it. Once you have decided you want to become an entrepreneur you should aim to be a successful one and this means that you need to start making the most of your strengths. Even though you may not enjoy talking so much, you will definitely enjoy researching, writing, and even mentoring so try to figure out what works best for you and put that to your advantage. The minute you start paying attention to your strengths, you will learn how to use it to better your business, which will help your business to grow leaps and bounds.

Modify Your Weakness

If you know that you are not good at something then always try to get somebody to get the task completed for you. This could be anybody from a business partner to an employee you trust. Everyone comes with their flaws and it's the same for an introvert, so there's nothing to be ashamed of when it comes to lacking in a particular area of skill or expertise. If there is something that you cannot do or you do not understand, asking questions is not a shame even if you are at the highest position.

Hiring a Business Partner

The reason it is important to try and look for an extrovert is because you will always compliment and balance the skill set perfectly. A partnership that is in the form of an extrovert-introvert partnership turns out to be the smartest and the most successful partnership because this partnership will be highly skilled. It also helps you to cover up your flaws and it works the same way for your partner as well.

Recharge Yourself

No matter how far you come with your life an introvert will always need a little more time which allows them to relax and go back to everything that happened during the course of the day. The reason this is something you should not let go of is because it helps you to reflect upon the various things you did and this helps you figure out where you went wrong, in case something did not go your way. When you let yourself relax and look back upon what you did during the course of the day, it helps you to better your actions for the following days and also make better decisions in the future.

Rejuvenate

Another important task that you should always focus on doing, no matter how busy you are, is to rejuvenate. Whatever you like to do, you should make time to do. This could include walking a nature trail or simply spending time in bed thinking about your next move. If you like visiting the salon and getting a massage alone do it because this is something that will help you feel fresh and geared up for the next hectic day at work.

When it comes to beating competition, you can't do it instantly. You need to have a strategic plan in place. Begin working on your plan from day one and continue working on it for the rest of your life. When you beat competition today, they going to try and get back at you so you should ensure you don't let them reach you once you have overtaken them. This requires a lot of work and planning.

Now that we have established that introverts can become successful entrepreneurs it's important to figure out strategies that can help introverts market their business effectively. While it is easy to handle your business with a strong team, marketing is something you might not be really good at because this is when you have to face the audience and talk to people you don't really know that well. As an introvert you will manage to handle every other aspect of your business confidently but when it comes to dealing with people that you are not familiar with, things could get a little difficult. Let's take a look at some effective strategies you can apply to your marketing strategies for your business.

Use Low Introduction Marketing Techniques

While face-to-face marketing may be something you are not confident with, you can always explore various other methods of marketing that can use your strength to your benefit. These days there are a number of marketing techniques that work out really well and this includes online marketing which does not involve any sort of interaction. The best part of online marketing is that it helps you to touch base with a ton of people without having to worry about personally interacting with them. This is one of the best ways to market your business especially when you are an introvert.

Sending out emails is also a smart technique of marketing if you are involved in a B2B (business-to-business) scenario because you will need to start a conversation with unknown businesses or people that you've never met before. Emails are a great way to break the ice and begin a conversation without any awkwardness. Design a few email templates to use for the emails you send out and you can choose between them whenever required. This can help you to build rapport with the person before you actually pick up the phone and give them a call or schedule a meeting with them. If you are still not very confident meeting somebody face-to-face then you can always send in your marketing representative to do the rest of the job.

Podcasting is another way for your business to stay at the top of its competitive edge without you having to face the crowd, literally. Everybody wants to hear from the entrepreneur at least once and this is the reason why podcasting is highly beneficial. It helps people know what you are thinking and you can confidently discuss the matter by simply recording whatever it is that you want to portray. Podcasts are a great way to make you famous without having to step up on a stage and discuss with people.

Blogging and guest posting also works just as effectively because it helps you to explain your business in your own words. Introverts are really creative and they can come up with articles to share with potential clients that can help grab attention.

Regular social media marketing and other techniques also help you to market your business without getting out there in the open. This helps you to feel confident and it ensures that your business grows without having to step outside of your comfort zone.

One of the best things about being an introvert is that you have a ton of skills. Extroverts may not possess these skills and this includes spending a lot of time in listening to what other people have to say and researching about material that you can share with others.

When you send out emails or create videos or talking to an audience, you can always address all of these problems and ensure that you get all questions answered. Introverts have amazing problem-solving skills and this makes them stand out amongst the crowd when it comes to offering advice. While you may not be great at the traditional marketing methods, this is where you'll actually shine and you will not only manage to let people know how skillful and knowledgeable you are but it will also help in establishing a strong relationship that matters. One of the best things about introverts is that they do not use marketing gimmicks to promote products and they try to be as authentic and real as possible.

Once you learn how to use your skill set to your advantage not only will you manage to crush your competition but you will manage to stay at the top for a really long time. Not only do introverts manage to grow their business fast but they also manage to establish a brand name that stays in the market for a long time thereby ensuring that their business adds value to customers.

Chapter 11:
Make Yourself Known

All said and done, one of the most difficult things for any introvert is to start executing a lot of confidence in themselves. While it is difficult to feel confident when you are not comfortable talking to strangers or a large crowd, this is something you will have to learn to do on your own - one step at a time. There are a number of decisions you need to make in order to feel confident but it will not come to you instantly. It requires a lot of hard work and effort from your end but once you do make an effort, it will eventually pay off. You need to remember that just because you can't talk to many people confidently doesn't make you a shy person or a bad person. However, if you want to improve your skills and learn how to approach a large crowd without feeling anxious then these confidence tips will help you get there.

You May Need to Pretend A Little

An introvert needs to learn how to socialize with people and there is no denying that they can't do it instantly because they are not confident enough to get it done at the first try. However, if you want to feel confident about yourself then a smart thing would be to approach the situation in a systematic and effective way. You need to start pretending that you actually enjoying socializing and talking to people even though you don't know who they are. The reason it's important for you to try and pretend is because this helps you to cover up the anxiety that you begin to feel the minute you come across a situation you are not comfortable with.

Pretending may sound fake and this is something you may want to avoid but honestly, it's the best method to practice being confident when you are actually not. It helps you to work with your head held high and it makes you feel a lot better about yourself. The reason you should try pretending to enjoy certain situations is because pretending over and over again will eventually make you actually enjoy the situation and you won't even realize when that changed. In order for you to pretend, you need to make sure that you don't push yourself too much because that's when things will get out of hand and you will eventually give up. Start with little changes and pretend to enjoy them bit by bit till you actually start liking them. Introduce these changes one step at a time.

Stay Close to People You Know
Irrespective of what you do in life or how successful you become; your close friends will always be the most important people to you. These are the kind of people you will feel comfortable with and spending time with them will help increase your confidence levels tremendously. When you start feeling confident with a small group of people, that's when you eventually start getting more comfortable with larger crowds. If you want to try out something new, it is safest to try it out with your own group of people because you know that they will never judge you and never say anything bad about your behavior. One of the biggest fears that introverts have is that someone will make fun of them and that's the reason why they stay quiet. When you start experimenting with your friends, they will be honest with you and tell you in a very nice way whether or not it works. This helps you to try out things that work in front of people you

do not know that well and when they appreciate your actions your confidence level starts to increase.

It is also important for you to be in a relationship that is not toxic and filled with negative energy. You should always try to surround yourself with people who fill your life with positivity and eliminate the negativity from your life rather than introducing it into your daily routine. If somebody keeps telling you that you cannot do something, try avoiding these people completely because they are bad for your confidence level.

Give Yourself Alone Time that Counts

It is important for every introvert to spend some time alone, without socializing, in order to reflect on what has happened in their life. However, when you do take a break from the world you need to do something positive with it, like reading a book or watching a movie that is educational and informative. The time you spend with yourself should not be reflected upon feeling bad for yourself or making decisions that will make you feel sad. Rather it should be something that can help you boost your confidence levels by relaxing. Watching a comedy is something that's really important because laughter is the best medicine for almost everything and it's a great way to feel more confident about yourself.

Once you start releasing a lot of positive energy you automatically reduce your stress levels and when this happens, you feel better about who you are. Lowering your stress levels is important and while you may not be able to do this in front of a group of people, you will manage to do this when you are by yourself and it is important that you do this regularly. Even if it means trying to get home a little early from work just so that you could spend time rejuvenating by soaking your feet in warm water and essential oils - Do it! Soothing music is also known to work wonders to relieve stress and help you feel good about yourself. If you had a hectic day at work and someone has said something to lower your morale, all you need to do is give yourself some 'me time' and do something positive with it so you can come back with a bang and be more confident than ever.

Dress Your Best

This may sound redundant right now but it is very important for you to dress well and dress in a manner that you are confident. You shouldn't be wearing something because everyone is wearing it. You should do it because you are happy when you wear it. Dressing up is an excellent way to boost your confidence and it will help you to feel good about yourself. Every month make sure to set aside a certain amount of money to invest in good clothes, accessories and shoes that you can flaunt.

Not only are clothes and accessories an amazing conversation starter but they will make you feel good. When dressing up, you have to ensure you wear clothes that are stylish and classy. Always ask yourself how you feel once you are wearing a particular outfit and make sure that that's the way you want to present yourself in front of a large crowd. When choosing the right kind of clothes try to invest in quality over quantity because good clothes speak volumes about you and make you feel a lot better about who you are. A good tailor-made outfit can also help you cover up your flaws which happens to be a downer for a number of introverts.

Stop Comparing

If you want to become a confident person the first step that you should take is to stop comparing yourself to others. Your individuality lies in who you are and not what you can compare with others. You have got to learn how to be comfortable in your own skin and appreciate your own skill sets rather than looking at what another person has done and try to copy them just because you think they are better than you. If you want to become a confident person the first thing that you have to tell yourself is that you are unique, there is no one like you, and you are the only competition you have to face.

If you want to improve as a person, then you should start competing with yourself and try to get better each day rather than seeing what others are doing. Once you start competing with yourself, your confidence level grows because you start feeling like a better person with every stepping stone and it makes you more positive in your approach as well. This confidence will continue to grow on a daily basis.

Start Getting Active

Being active is a great way to boost your confidence and this is just because it's so much fun to do. Getting active does not necessarily mean heading to the gym and lifting unnecessary weights that make your arms and back ache like crazy. Getting active is all about indulging in outdoor activities you enjoy and this could be anything from going for a swim to cycling or even playing lawn tennis at your local club. If you are in the mood for dance, you should even enroll for a dance class just to see whether or not you have two left feet. If you manage to dance amazing, it will be a talent that you'll always cherish and want to look back and laugh at. It's important for you to understand that you may not be good at everything but trying a few new things won't harm you in anyway. When it comes to getting active you may want to do something that you enjoy because it's something that you should do on a regular basis. Any sort of exercise helps to release negative energy from your body and has a lot of positive impacts in your life. Not only do you start feeling more confident but you start enjoying yourself everyday which is essential for you to stay productive.

Do What You Enjoy

Apart from the outdoor physical activities that help you stay healthy and positive; you should also make time to indulge in a hobby you enjoy. If you like cooking, make time to prepare a home cooked meal for your loved ones at least once in a week. Cooking is a great way to release a lot of your stress and it also helps you to connect with your loved ones a little more. If you're not a good cook it doesn't matter, you can still do something you enjoy such as painting, something crafty, or even collecting stamps for that matter. Repeating something over and over again is healthy because it makes you improve every time you do it and this encourages you to feel better about yourself. Once you do this, your confidence level starts to increase.

Inspire Yourself

Confidence is something that will come from within so you need to learn how to generate self-confidence by inspiring yourself on a regular basis. It's funny how one simple positive quote can change your entire day and make you feel more confident than ever before. If you tried reading a positive motivational quote and it worked in your favor you may want to consider downloading a mobile app that can send you these positive quotes on a daily basis. There are tons of videos you can watch online as well to increase your confidence level and feel good about yourself. You just need to find what works well and stick to it. While most people find positive motivational quotes highly helpful there are some that find solace by simply hearing the voice of a loved one.

How Quiet Introverts Thrive in An Extrovert World

If you are romantically involved with somebody make time to talk to them about something positive every day before you head out to work and you will realize that your days are a lot better. If someone who is not close to you picks up the phone, have a few words with them. Try to make this a regular routine. There are different things that work for different people and spirituality it is also something that plays a huge role for a few. If you realize that by saying a short prayer every day your confidence is increasing - Do it. You can choose to do anything that works to you.

The key to becoming a confident person is to constantly try something new every time. Albert Einstein once wisely said "Insanity is doing the same thing over and over again and expecting different results". If you are looking to change or you are looking be a better person then the important thing you need to do is to learn how to push yourself and try new things every once in a while. You may be surprised at the number of changes you will introduce into your life and how confident you will become.

Chapter 12:
Persuade People Even When You're Nervous

Sometimes you find yourself in situations where it is difficult for you to open up and talk to people around you. While you will be able to work your way through this problem it's not something you can deal with immediately so you have to understand how essential it is for you to take one step at a time. There are various tips and tricks that you can apply to your life. When it comes to overcoming social awkwardness, you can still be confident among people with a little effort.

The first step you have to take to believe that you will be able to persuade people in the worst of situations is to believe that you are not boring. Most introverts believe that they should not talk much because they often believe that their conversations will bore people. The truth is that none of your conversations can bore someone because every conversation you start is something that is relevant to you and you are highly interested in. Introverts do not like to indulge in unnecessary chatting. They always come up with thing things to discuss. No matter how nervous you are you should always try to begin a conversation because the chances that someone will not like what you started discussing is very slim.

Another reason why lots of introverts try to stay as quiet as possible is because they think that they are being judged. This is something you have to understand; people are not trying to judge you but rather they are trying to get to know you because they don't know you as well as they know an extrovert. Instead of letting that get to you, it's better to make an effort to try and talk to the people you believe do not know you. It is very difficult for you to begin a conversation when you feel that you are being judged but the minute you make an effort to begin talking you will realize that no one is looking at you in a negative way.

Even if someone is judging you, it is something you should not worry about because you can't control the way people think about you and it's not going to affect how well you do in life. Do not let somebody else's interference affect your success or come in the way of what you plan on getting done. You should do what you believe is right irrespective of what people around you have to say, so stop thinking about the world and begin thinking about how you will do things in the right way.

Being rejected by society is another unnecessary worry amongst introverts which prevents them from beginning a discussion or talking to the people they find interesting. You have to understand if you want to become successful, you will have to make an effort and even if somebody does not like you or rejects you it's not going to be as devastating as you think it will be. If anything, it will be a learning chapter in your life and you learn exactly how to deal with this situation in a better way the next time. Just because someone doesn't like your ideologies or ideas does not make you a bad person or make you worse than your competitors. It simply means that they do not understand your methodology and you have to try different approaches to help them to understand.

You also need to keep reminding yourself that what others think about you will not define who you are and the only person who can truly define what you represent is yourself. You have to let people know what you think and how you see society so that you will manage to perform better and more effectively. You also need to remember that nothing is really black and white. There are multiple shades of grey that come in between black and white that can also help define yourself.

People do not Always Think About You

When you are an introvert and you are going through a bad day the major thing that you constantly worry about is that people are talking about you and thinking about your actions. Let's get one thing straight - everyone has their own life to worry about and their own problems to deal with so it's really rare for somebody to spend a lot of time pondering about what mistakes you made. You have to remember that social interactions barely have any effect on a person. Once the interactions are over and the only one who will be worrying about a certain conversation that happened in the past is you. Remember that people don't have a lot of time to judge you, so you have to let it go and even if the conversation was a horrible and horrendous conversation it's not something that you should worry about because the other person isn't thinking about it right now. If it was a completely embarrassing situation and you know people will talk about it, you can still save yourself a little grace because you will just be the talk of town for a few days and then people will find something new to talk about. Whether or not people are talking about you or thinking about you, you need to understand it's not going to affect you in any way.

People are Also as Awkward as You are

If you thought that you are the most awkward person in the room you are actually mistaken. Extroverts also tend to feel awkward or socially anxious in certain situations so you are never alone. Somebody who is standing with a big smile slapped across the face could be just as nervous as you are and they could be pretending to be confident. Remember how we discussed trying to pretend to be confident? This is probably a good time for you to apply that theory and behave as though you are confident even though you are really nervous inside. Once you start doing this you will manage to put yourself in situations you are not really comfortable in. Apart from helping you feel more confident about yourself you will learn to take one step at a time. You will be comfortable to face social awkwardness with a confident approach. Do not let awkwardness get the better of you. You need to learn how to keep it in control so you can persuade people into liking you and letting them know that you're here to stay.

People Are More Tolerant Than You Think

You may end up saying something that's embarrassing and horrifying but it's ok. You may believe that people are going to judge you but the truth is that they will not. People are more tolerant than you give them credit for and they may not even remember what you said or did to make a joke about it. Everyone goes through mishaps in their life and while some of them may be extremely difficult to deal with it, you to remember that you need to let it go and move on.

The minute you learn how to accept yourself for who you are, you will stop scrutinizing and judging everything that you do and every word you say. This will help you to deal with your anxiety in a more effective way and you will stop worrying about whether or not you are socially awkward. In all probability you are not, but even if you are it doesn't really matter because the people who will get to know you will like you for who you are and will remind you of what you say. When you have a certain amount of people you trust, they accept you completely - quirks and all. So, stop holding back just because you think you are not going to be liked.

People Will Like You Even When You are not Perfect

You don't have to be the perfect person for somebody to like you or to establish relationships with, whether it's professional or personal. Imperfections are just as beautiful and they are accepted irrespective of what you think. Just because someone has seen your inabilities does not make you a small person but rather it helps you to be more beautiful and also gives you the scope to learn to grow. When you let people in on your insecurities and weaknesses there is a strong possibility, they can help you overcome them and learn a better technique to deal with it rather than try to cover it up. You should never be apologetic of who you are or try to hide your flaws from the world.

You Should Make Mistakes - It's Fine

If you keep telling yourself that you shouldn't make mistakes then you will end up making more mistakes than ever. Everyone is human and it is only human to make mistakes. So, don't be afraid if you make a few mistakes along the way - it is part of your journey. The minute you learn how to accept the mistakes you made, you realize that you are getting better at it and you are also improving on the kind of job that you do. When you think about situations with a clear head it helps you to get better at your task and this will lower the number of mistakes you make rather than increase them which is most important.

Don't Self Evaluate

The biggest mistake introverts tend to make is they self-evaluate themselves and believe that they are worthless because they can't handle certain aspects of life. Don't do this because it's not right and it will make you go through a negative phase in life which will put you down. You need to accept that everyone cannot do everything and there are certain things you will do better than the others, while there will be things that they will be better at. Make sure you take your time to understand what you can do well and focus on getting that done rather than trying to do something you may not be able to do well. There is no harm in learning new things. However, you should focus on what you are highly skilled at while learning something new in the background.

Face Your Social Fears
While you are ready train yourself to be present at social gathering it's now time to take a step ahead in these gatherings and make yourself more comfortable. Instead of standing in the corner at a party you may want to bring yourself towards the center one step at a time and meet people whom you may not have met in the past. Begin by introducing yourself and asking them questions about themselves. Follow the same techniques you would follow to break the ice with people at work. You can also begin to initiate a conversation with a few people you feel comfortable with. In case you can't start a conversation, you can always join one that you think is more approachable. Remember when you are trying to face your social fears do not put too much pressure on yourself but rather try to go with the flow. Most of the time you won't have to do a lot of work and you will realize that you have automatically taken every step that's required in order for you to be an active social member of a party.

While this may seem extremely difficult when you are nervous but with a little effort and smart approach, not only will you be able to overcome the awkwardness but you'll also start feeling more comfortable talking to a stranger under a pressure situation.

Chapter 13:
Understanding Other People's Emotions and Thrive

When you are an introvert it becomes very difficult for you to understand how to express yourself but the one thing that you will be a pro at will be to understand what other people are feeling and be more sensitive towards them. Introverts are highly elusive and they spend a lot of time analyzing people. This is why they are more sensitive and they manage to have a higher emotional intelligence in comparison to an extrovert. While emotional intelligence is something that you can achieve, the level of emotional intelligence in an introvert is already high and all they need to do is learn how to channel their energy into learning something new to use to their benefit. The more connected you are with your emotional intelligence the better it works for you and for the people around you. Once they learn how to master emotional intelligence, they manage to achieve something that adds meaning to their life, which can be used professionally and personally. Here we look at the five aspects of emotional intelligence and the elements in each of them.

Self-Awareness

One of the best things about being emotionally intelligent is that you are able to identify your weakness and your strength and you also learn how to deal with it more effectively. It also gives you the confidence to learn how to accept your flaws and forgive anybody who may make fun of you. When you learn not to get affected by what people have to say, it starts to build a lot of confidence in you and this works wonders for introverts.

#1 - Self-Knowledge

One of the best things of being emotionally intelligent is that you understand your personality, you build up your skills, and you know exactly how to act upon them when required. When you know yourself, you don't underestimate yourself and you are not over confident which helps you to make the right decisions in life.

#2 - Accurate Self-Assessment

An introvert who is emotionally intelligent manages to self-assess themselves more confidently. They also know how to handle interactions and when they get uncomfortable, they know exactly when to drift away from those conversations which helps them to deal with the situation that much better.

#3 - Self-Confidence

The more emotionally intelligent you are, the more you understand your self-worth which helps to build confidence.

#4 - Emotional Awareness

When you have strong emotional intelligence, you are aware about what's happening around you and you also know how to acknowledge your feelings which makes a lot of difference with regards to the decisions you take.

Self-Regulation

Emotional intelligence also comprises of self-regulation which is an integral part of an introvert gaining confidence. Apart from helping you to manage your emotions it also helps to keep your stress levels in control. It also works wonders to control your impulses that are usually responsible for the wrong decision that you end up making.

#1 - Emotional Self-Control
When you learn how to control your emotions, it brings self-control and this ensures that you do not make impulsive decisions that turn out the wrong way. It also ensures that you do not stay in a negative state of mind for a longer time.

#2 - Integrity
One of the most important values of being emotionally intelligent is integrity. It helps you to enhance your personal performance and learn how to trust yourself as well as others. It gives you a feeling of responsibility and makes you understand how essential it is for you to stay truthful. This ensures that you make the right decision instead of choosing to do something that is not morally right.

#3 - Adaptability
One of the best things about being emotionally intelligent is that it helps you to learn how to adapt to changing situations and this is one of the best methods for an introvert to learn how to grow.

#4 - Conscientiousness
If you want to make sure that you understand the job at hand and you get it done in an efficient and organized manner then your emotional intelligence plays a huge role in determining how you will sort it out.

Motivation

Even when you are an introvert your emotional intelligence can help you to motivate yourself and become passionate about whatever you do. It helps you to look at situations from an optimistic perspective and this works well when it comes to achieving something in your personal or in your professional life.

#1 - Achievement Drive
Emotional intelligence plays a huge role in helping you to strive to meet standards of excellence and this not only pushes you to achieve your goals better but it also ensures that you stay persistent with what you do.

#2 - Commitment
One of the best things about being emotionally intelligent is that you learn how to commit to certain situations and follow up with it. When you are an introvert you tend to learn to make yourself comfortable with the commitment and this helps you to push a little harder.

#3 - Initiative
One of the best things about being emotionally intelligent is that you are always willing to identify solutions for different opportunities and you also possess the ability to try out something new even when you are not confident about it or you are a little shy.

#4 - Optimism
The best part about being emotionally intelligent is that you have a positive attitude towards various things that you do. It is important to have a positive attitude towards any steps that he or she is taking because this is what enables them to push a little harder every time and attempt to do something, they never thought possible.

#5 - Learning Orientation

Apart from making a commitment about things that they want to complete; an introvert also learns how to focus and continuously make way for improvement when they are emotionally intelligent.

Empathy

One of the best things about being emotionally intelligent and being an introvert is that your empathy is right up there and you automatically learn to be kind to other people. Apart from being a pro at listening to the problems you also try to help them figure out solutions.

#1 - Understanding What Others Are Going Through

Being sensitive and putting yourself in another person's shoes is something that only an emotionally intelligent person can do and introverts manage to do this really well. They also put a lot of efforts into finding solutions to help deal with problems.

#2 - Service Orientation

You learn how to anticipate what the people are looking for and help them to find it in order for them to do better, not only in the workplace but also in their personal life. Contributing towards a common goal or contributing towards something that is good is common for intelligent introverts.

#3 - Appreciating Diversity

One of the best things about being emotionally intelligent and being an introvert is that you learn how to appreciate diversity which is not everybody's cup of tea. Whether it is dealing with people who belong to different economic backgrounds, nationalities, or even gender, it is always easier to do it when you are emotionally intelligent.

Social Skills

There is no denying that introverts lack social skills but when they gain emotional intelligence, they are able to spruce up their social skills a lot better and learn how to use it to their advantage.

#1 - Communication
An emotionally intelligent introvert not only spends a lot of time listening to what others have to say but they pay careful attention to every little detail which helps them to come up with solutions rather than just listening to them and not having anything to offer in return.

#2 - Developing Others
One of the best things about an emotionally intelligent introvert is that they help to develop others by contributing their knowledge towards creating a better background and skill for them. Whether it is coaching them into doing something more effective or helping them spruce up their skills emotionally intelligent introverts are always at it.

#3 - Collaboration
It is a lot easier to work with an emotionally intelligent introvert to collaborate and get the job done without having to face too many problems.

#4 - Dealing with Conflict

How Quiet Introverts Thrive in An Extrovert World

Emotionally intelligent introverts try to resolve issues rather than create more and this helps them to negotiate and deal with the conflict rather than blow it up into an unnecessary problem.

Chapter 14:
Tips for the Sensitive and Shy

An introvert is always referred to as the one who is shy and sensitive and there is no denying that most of these traits are common with a lot of introverts out there. If you are wondering how you can deal with some of your problems, here are the most common questions that introverts often have in their head.

How Do I Get Better?

It's only natural for an introvert to constantly wonder how he or she is going to get better and whether or not they are ever going to be able to be socially active without feeling awkward.

The truth is that you can get better as long as you put in a little effort and you begin by taking the very first step of doing something that you are not comfortable with. As mentioned in the book, the minute you learn how to make a list of the things that you are uncomfortable with and learn how to deal with them one step at a time, you will manage to overcome your social anxiety and fear and you will eventually get better. This may take a few days for some, while others may require weeks or even months to learn how to deal with it but you will get there.

How Do I Take the First Step Towards Overcoming My Introvert Nature?

You don't have to overcome your introverted nature. You just need to learn how to live with it and make the most of it in a way that can prove to be beneficial to you. Throughout the book there are a number of tips and tricks that you can try and see whichever one works best for you. You need to understand that when it comes to overcoming your shyness or being able to get comfortable in a room full of strangers, you have to put in certain efforts and challenge yourself to do it even though you are not confident about how it will turn out.

Is Being Introvert and Being Shy the Same Thing?

The truth is that an introvert doesn't necessarily have to be shy and a shy person doesn't necessarily have to be an introvert. An introvert is the person who may find it difficult to talk to a large crowd of people or speak in front of too many people they do not know that well. An introvert may not necessarily be shy. They may be outgoing and fun loving in front of their special few people they are comfortable with. A shy person, on the other hand, does not open up to the public and no matter how close they are to someone they will still have the traits of being shy.

How Do I Acknowledge My Fear?

This is a big step for introverts because it is difficult to acknowledge what you are scared of and then start to face it. If you are scared of being in a room full of strangers you need to understand why you are scared in the first place. What triggers your anxiety and what makes you feel like you will not be able to survive. Figure out why you are scared and you will then manage to address the fear and then learn how to deal with it. You have to understand what causes your fear if you want the fear to go away.

What If I Make Mistakes?

It's common to make a lot of mistakes along the way and there's nothing wrong with it. All you need to understand is that you have to stay accountable for the mistakes you make because it is only then that you will begin to learn how to change your attitude towards society and improve on your social interaction. While some days may be great, there may be times that you would wish you could go back home and never step back out again, but you have to understand that the good comes with the bad and it is important for you to face the bad just as efficiently as you accept the good.

What If I'm Upset?

As much as we would like to believe that an introvert is generally a calm person who does not lose their temper, the truth is introverts can also be hot tempered and in case you are upset about something, the last thing you want to do is have an outburst in front of people. Considering you don't talk much; an outburst is not acceptable so you have to learn how to stay calm and try to lighten the mood the minute you get upset. You should also try to divert your attention to things that you actually like so that you forget about why you were absent in the first place. If it is not helping, the best thing to do is think back on happy memories from your childhood and see what a difference it makes to your mindset.

How Do I Deal with Stage Fright?

Stage fright is more common than you think and as an introvert it is something that you have to learn to cope with especially if you plan on becoming a successful entrepreneur. If you are not comfortable with taking your first steps in front of a crowd and you know that you are going to freeze, you may want to start by releasing web-based versions see how people react to it. You can also ask your family members or your best friends to help you. While a mirror will help you gain confidence, you may or may not be able to face a crowd of people staring back at you. Start slow with a small group of around three or four people and move forward from them. Be prepared for honest feedback from your practice group because this will help you overcome your fright.

What If I Know the Answer but I Am Too Afraid to Speak?
This is a common problem introvert's face and in case you find it difficult to speak to people or reply to somebody even though you know the answer because you are not familiar with them, you may want to start practicing by looking in the mirror. If there have been multiple meetings where you found yourself dumbstruck just because you couldn't reply to certain questions then you need to start having a conversation with yourself in front of the mirror because believe it or not, this gives you a lot of confidence. If you are still not sure how you can build your confidence, you can even speak with your best friend and see his or her reaction. Ask them to be honest with you with their feedback.

How Do I Deal with A Loss of Energy?
Introverts tend to lose out on energy a lot faster in comparison to an extrovert because they end up using a lot of energy communicating when they were not comfortable doing so. If you realize that you are at a stage in your day where you are going to feel completely drained then you may want to take a break of silence or disconnect from people for a while till you recharge yourself. As an introvert you should constantly recharge yourself from time to time because this helps you feel energized and you will be able to deal with the day better and tackle uncomfortable situations efficiently. You can also try and do something that will help recharge you faster. This could be anything like listening to music or just picking up the phone and speaking to a loved one. It is important

that you disconnect from the rest of the elements that are causing your energy to drain out.

What If I Am Not Interested in A Conversation?

It's very common for introverts to feel bored in a conversation that doesn't include them and, in such situations, the smartest way for you to deal with it is to be honest and transparent about your opinion. If they are discussing something that is not related to your work or something you have no clue about, you can always ask to be excused by saying you have other things to do and let them know that the conversation does not interest you in any way. It is important for you to let people know what conversations interest you and what don't interest you because they will not try and make an attempt to talk about things that don't interest you in future. While others may think that you are rude, there is no point worrying about what they may think. Your time is precious and you need to make it clear to people that you would rather spend your time doing something productive.

Is Something Wrong with Me?

Introverts often feel that there is something wrong with them because they can't deal with social situations and they look at all the other extroverts out there who are blending in with the crowd as seamlessly as possible. There is nothing wrong with you and it's just who you are, so your social anxiety and fear are normal. You just need to learn how to deal with them so that it doesn't affect your personal or professional life in anyway. Do not let anyone else put you down. You need to be confident in your abilities and do not let self-doubt creep in.

How Do I Approach Uncomfortable Situations?

When you know that there is an uncomfortable situation you need to approach, it's important to prepare yourself for it in advance. You also need to try and keep a backup for the plan because this is what will help you deal with the situation in a better way and ensure that there is nothing that can go wrong. For example, if you have to head to a party that you dread, keep a backup in the form of a friend calling you up, and asking you to rush back home. You need to make sure that you think of such situations in advance so that it looks natural and the host of the party will not feel bad about you leaving abruptly.

What If I Start A Conversation and I Am Not Comfortable with It?

While this will rarely happen but if it does, all you need to do is try to end the conversation without being abrupt. When you strike a conversation with someone and you find the conversation uncomfortable there is a strong chance the person who is having the conversation with you will find it just as awkward. So, if you try to stop the conversation, they will not want to continue it and will end it from their side as well. Do not be afraid of being judged because that is not going to be the case at all. People have a lot on their plate and the last thing they would want to do is judge you when you are ending an uncomfortable conversation.

You need to keep reminding yourself that there are a number of socially awkward people around you and just because you are an introvert does not make you a different person from the rest of the crowd. You are like every other person out there with your own differences that you are learning to deal with. The minute you learn to accept who you are and understand what you need to change in order to be a better person, not only will you lead a happy life but you will also lead a more successful one.

Robin Samuel Dean

How Quiet Introverts Thrive in An Extrovert World

Emotional Intelligence Primal Leadership 2.0

Discover Why EQ Applied Matter More Than IQ Boosting Your Social, Conversation, and People Skills for Relationships, Project Managers, and Sales

Robin Samuel Dean

Introduction

Everyone has some intuitive notion of a definition of Intelligence but we usually express our understanding by reciting a list of related ideas and words. Words like Genius and Creativity come to mind but there are a lot more. We feel comfortable as laypeople in discussing Intelligence because we are not burdened with too much knowledge on the subject. We do not demand an exact definition.

People like psychologists, neuroscientists and other experts may not have our comfort level because they understand all about what it is and what it is not. However, even the experts have difficulty giving a short succinct definition for it. Maybe they know so much even they can't define it either.

Are geniuses intelligent? Yeah, probably most of the time but not on all topics. The list of people referred to as geniuses certainly includes people like Leonardo da Vinci, Wolfgang Amadeus Mozart and Albert Einstein. However, that does not mean they were geniuses at everything. They often have difficult personalities, may lack social skills and some even had very unhappy lives. For example, Mozart, regarded as a musical genius, was deeply in debt at his death because he was not intelligent about his finances. It has been reported that Albert Einstein had such a short memory he sometimes could not be trusted to find his way home. Some also have areas of weakness in topics other than that of their genius. So, how do genius and intelligence relate to each other? That depends on how you define intelligence.

Wow! Now that is another long list of words that Wikipedia recites. Still not what you might call a succinct definition. It is more of a description than a definition so we should not be upset that we can't define it either. However, you should get the general idea. Intelligence is the ability to function in our environment and our world. Some people seem to have a lot of it and others, not so much. Notice that the definition of intelligence does not speak of education. After all, people without an advanced education function fully in our environment and meet the descriptors above from Wikipedia. Having a higher education does not guarantee intelligence; in fact, we have all heard of 'educated fools,' people with lots of higher education but are unable to apply common sense.

We can be certain that the human brain is the seat of intelligence but it is extremely complicated. Neuroscientists specialize in understanding the brain. However, intelligence is a combination of the 'wet ware,' that is the actual organ along with many other components that include experiences and the ability to interpret and use the knowledge contained therein.

To understand intelligence, we need to understand how the human brain works, beginning with the physiology. The following chapters describe the human brain in simple terms that should be easy for anyone, with an advanced education or not, to understand. For most of us, this means learning some new terms and concepts, but it is not necessary for us to study neuroscience.

Chapter 1:
What is Emotional Intelligence

Nowadays, people are more aware of their emotions. We have entered an age where in a profound understanding of how we feel and how others feel is essential at home, in school, in the workplace and with the many relationships we form during the course of our lifetime. Psychologists and sociological experts agree that logical intelligence alone is not the only gauge of an individual's maturity and reliability. Employers understand that applicants with a high emotional intelligence level are more likely to succeed in their chosen careers than those who have outstanding recommendations but fail to get along with others.

This section highlights what emotional intelligence is, how much we know about it and why it is important. This chapter will prepare you for the rest of the book's contents and will introduce you to concepts as well as terms often used in the discussion of emotional intelligence.

What is Emotional Intelligence?

Emotional intelligence is the ability used by individuals to gauge, understand and control their emotions, as well as those of their peers (What Is Emotional Intelligence, Daniel Goleman, 2018). Some theorists and psychologists hold strongly to the belief that emotional intelligence – or EI – is an inborn trait, while others say that it can be trained, improved and even degraded.

Why is Emotional Intelligence Important?

Our entire lives revolve around happiness, satisfaction, despair, loss and achievement. These are just a few of the emotions that dictate how we react to certain situations. Our identity and the people we meet do not matter, we will always be in touch with how we feel, just as much as we are aware of how we think. It is easy to see the use and importance of emotional intelligence.

Individuals who have a high level of emotional intelligence can easily relate their feelings to others, inasmuch as they can understand what others are feeling. This facilitates better communication between individuals and groups and strengthens relationships — whether familial, professional or romantic. Furthermore, people who are aware of the importance of emotional intelligence have been proven to have better control of their emotions. They are less prone to engage in arguments or petty fights and are more diplomatic when it comes to handling sensitive issues such as religion or race.

A person's emotional intelligence speaks volumes about their personality and maturity. People with relatively low emotional intelligence are not only more impatient, irate and immature; they are also more prone to be depressed or anxious. On the other hand, people with high or at least average levels of emotional intelligence have the ability to arrive at well-thought decisions based on facts, and not on emotional bias. Several studies have proven that emotional intelligence is directly linked to a person's ability to be successful in his or her career, and to form lasting, meaningful relationships with others.

Overall, emotional intelligence and a high awareness of it are important because they contribute greatly to the personal development of an individual. In effect, an individual's emotions and control also affect the people in his or her social circles. You will get an overview of the benefits in the sections to follow.

History

A ballpark base for emotional intelligence came into being in 1983 when Harvard psychologist Howard Gardner presented his 'Theory of Multiple Intelligences' which laid the foundation for different types of intelligence models. It described interpersonal intelligence and intrapersonal intelligence. Interpersonal intelligence is an individual's ability to understand the motivations, needs and intentions of others. Intrapersonal intelligence, on the other hand, was defined as a person's capacity to gain an understanding of his or her own fears, emotions and motivations. This set the stage for a more widespread and universally popular psychological concept related to a person's ability to manage emotions.

The term 'emotional intelligence' was initially created by university professors and researchers Pater Salovey and John D. Mayer in 1990 (Virkus, 2009). They described it as a type of social intelligence that comprises the ability to identify your own and others' emotions to distinguish between them and leverage this information for guiding one's own thoughts and actions.

Though the researcher duo developed a couple of tests to measure an individual's emotional intelligence, they aren't widely known outside the academic community. The person more famously associated with emotional intelligence as a term and concept is Daniel Goleman, as previously mentioned.

In 1990, behavior science writer Daniel Goleman reinforced Salovey and Mayer's work in his path-breaking book, Emotional Intelligence. Goleman was a behavior science journalist specializing in mind, emotions and behavior research for Popular Psychology and later the New York Times. He studied psychology at Harvard University, working closely with David McClelland and other eminent behavior experts. McClelland was from a group of prominent university researchers who were looking out for intelligence test alternatives, owing to the view that these tests revealed little about the traits that are required to gain overall success in life.

While researching for his book on emotions and evolved emotional literacy, Goleman chanced upon the findings of Salovey and Mayer. According to an Annie Paul article, Goleman obtained permission from the behavior experts for using the 'emotional intelligence' term in his book. The permission was swiftly granted subject to the condition that Goleman would make it clear where he originally came across the term. While earlier the book was to be a discussion on 'emotional literacy,' Salovey-Mayer's research inspired Goleman to focus on emotional intelligence.

Goleman debated that it wasn't cognitive intelligence alone, which guaranteed an individual's success in life. He emphasized the importance of emotional intelligence that awarded people four characteristics – 1. Understanding your own emotions, 2. Managing your own emotions, 3. Being empathetic to other's emotions, 4. Handling others' emotions by demonstrating high social skills.

Daniel Goleman's book promoted the idea of emotional intelligence as more powerful than intelligence quotient in predicting an individual's life success. Emotional intelligence as a concept became so revolutionary and significant that the book sold a whopping 5 million copies within the initial five years itself. The world lapped up the concept of emotional intelligence with both hands. Though the book emphasized on the importance of emotional intelligence in everyday life, work and relationship success, it didn't throw much light on how to identify one's and others' emotions. There wasn't a cohesive theory on describing core human emotions. Also, the book didn't offer information about increasing one's emotional intelligence.

In 1998 Daniel Goleman published another book titled 'Working with Emotional Intelligence,' which sought to widen the emotional intelligence definition. He broadened the scope of the concept of emotional intelligence to include 25 skills, core competencies and abilities.

One of the biggest criticisms that came in the way of Goleman's theory was that emotions can be highly complex, multi-layered and often limited by any language's inability to describe them. Even languages featuring the most extensive vocabulary sometimes fall short when it comes to assigning labels to specific emotions for self-reflection or interpersonal communication. The Salovey-Mayer tests encompass a few broad emotions and feelings that are limited by the inability to articulate the exactness of some of the most complex/multi-dimensional feelings/emotions.

Though the concept of emotional quotient is widely received and extremely relevant today, the measuring of emotional intelligence scores through tests has always been under the scanner. The Salovey-Mayer emotional intelligence test team themselves stated that though they attempt to measure an individual's emotional intelligence through a series of evaluations on paper, it is hard to tell if the individual would act in a similar manner in real-life scenarios or when subjected to extreme conditions/stress. These may be the very situations in which he or she may need high emotional intelligence. So, tests measuring a person's emotional intelligence may gauge actions in regular situations and not situations of extreme duress when he or she actually needs to display developed emotional intelligence.

Goleman, Salovey and other pioneers in the behavior sciences field met to discuss the latest research and best practices at the 5th Annual Nexus EQ Conference in the Netherlands in 2005, called 'Leading with Emotional Intelligence: Tools and Wisdom for a Sustainable World.' It featured experts from 19 nations and was the most inclusive Emotional Quotient global summit. The 2013 Nexus EQ Conference hosted at Harvard University featured participation from 32 nations.

Several corporate bottom line studies have demonstrated that the ability to get the best out of people directly affects the company's profit performance. Research revealed that L'Oréal sales representatives selected on the basis of higher emotional competencies recorded an increase in annual net sales revenue by $2, 558,360.

A Brief on Emotions

With the study of emotional intelligence inevitably comes discussion and debate which focus on emotions. What are emotions? Where do they come from? How do they work? This section will explore, in brief, the basic questions people often ask about the complexity of human emotions.

What are Emotions?

Psychologically speaking, an emotion is a state that involves thoughts, actions and experiences. This broad definition of what an emotion is has, to this day, not yet been entirely resolved because of the problematic nature of emotions themselves. Usually, people relate a specific emotion as one of the results of a certain event or trigger. For example, if an individual fails an important exam, he or she may experience the emotions of anger, disappointment, depression, sadness or frustration. In fact, the individual may experience those emotions and more altogether.

Several psychologists have tried to capture the essence of emotions in a single sentence or phrase; however, there is still no one definition for emotions except that they are states where the mind enters upon an encounter or experience. The paragraphs below will briefly discuss some of the theories that aim to explain how emotions work.

The James-Lange Theory

The James-Lange theory of emotion, proposed by the 19th century scholars William James and Carl Lange, states that experiences are the basis of all human emotions (Cherry, 2018). Through their theory, James and Lange illustrated how experiences cause physiological changes such as heart rate and muscular tension. In turn, these physical reactions trigger the brain to interpret the experience or situation in a certain way. The brain's consequent interpretations of those experiences give birth to different emotions.

The Cannon-Bard Theory

Contrary to the beliefs of James and Lange, Walter Cannon and Philip Bard suggested that the physical reactions of the body to certain experiences happen immediately after, or in the same period as, the brain's interpretation of the event (Cherry, Understanding the Cannon-Bard Theory of Emotion, 2018).

The Lazarus Theory

This theory simply states that, to trigger an emotion, a recurring thought must first be interpreted and released by the brain to the other parts of the body. For example, imagine that you are a six-year-old child who has just heard horror stories from your cousins. Your parents have requested you to go to bed. The lights in your room are all off; there is no night lamp to comfort you. You hear strange sounds coming from outside your bedroom window. You start to think that a ghost or a monster, such as the ones from your cousins' stories, is out there waiting to get you.

The thought that there are ghosts or monsters just outside your bedroom window triggers physical reactions from your body. You begin to sweat and tremble. At the same time, you feel fear and apprehension. The Lazarus theory suggests that individuals cannot have emotions if there are no thoughts to act as triggers and experiences to be thought about.

The Facial-Feedback Theory

The Facial-Feedback theory states that emotions are the results of the changes in our facial muscles. Simply speaking, smiling or grinning makes us feel happy, while frowning makes us feel angry. The changes in our facial muscles serve as cues for the brain to interpret and name the emotions that we experience.

Benefits of EQ

Now that we understand what exactly emotional intelligence is and its brief history, let's discuss the benefits of this super psychological tonic in everyday life. How does having a high emotional quotient or emotional intelligence impact our everyday life? What are the benefits of possessing well-developed emotional intelligence? How can it be leveraged to make our lives more meaningful and rewarding? How can it bring us greater success at work and in business, as well as more harmonious interpersonal relationships? Some advantages of being an emotional intelligent individual include:

Positively Handling Change

Emotionally intelligent people are brilliant at responding to change. Their awareness of the situation, controlled reactions and understanding the merits/demerits of the change help them remain unperturbed and handle the change more effectively. They are aware of the fact that though one can't control one's circumstances, one can control his/her reaction to it. Emotionally intelligent people will often make the most of these changes to benefit them. Their response to changing people, circumstances and events remains positive.

Conflict Resolution

The reason emotional intelligence is such a sought-after factor in the corporate world is that it equips managers with the ability to deal with a challenging workforce and situations. Leaders must possess social skills in the form of empathy, motivation, self-awareness and awareness of other's emotions to resolve conflicts successfully. Leaders must be able to inspire loyalty and this comes by empathizing with people and understanding their inherent needs. You can resolve conflicts efficiently by displaying superior negotiation skills, empathy, positivity, assertiveness and understanding. You can emphasize on the overall good if you are empathetic yet assertive. As a leader, you also need to understand how your emotions and behavior affect the situation and direct your actions to better manage the crisis. You have to work with others to take more positive decisions for the overall good.

Boosts Self-Motivation

Self-awareness and self-regulation are the cornerstone of emotional intelligence. When we are able to understand and manage our emotions more effectively, we know how to keep ourselves motivated. Emotionally intelligent people know what drives them and hence find it easier to achieve goals they set their sights on. There is a greater commitment, initiative and readiness to take action. Such people also display greater resilience, determination and optimism when it comes to achieving their goals. They are more organized, display better time management skills, have a higher sense of priority and are more assertive when things come in the way of their goals.

More Collaboration Less Competition

Emotionally intelligent people are generally high on self-confidence and self-esteem. They know their strengths and weakness, and are able to manage them successfully. They don't suffer from insecurities or a false sense of self-importance. They don't feel the need to reinforce their abilities and superiority by competing with others or showing them down. An emotionally evolved individual incites more collaboration than competition. His or her focus is on the overall positive outcome of a situation and not individual victories. Sportspersons possessing a high emotional quotient will keep aside their personal scores and records, and play for the overall benefit of their team. Their actions will be in tandem with what's good for the team and not their individual performance or accolades. Emotional intelligence equips you with the power to collaborate more and compete less with people. It rids you of the one-upmanship syndrome to drive you to do what's beneficial for everyone involved.

Boosts Sales for an Organization

A bunch of emotionally intelligent salespersons will be able to display greater understanding of the needs, emotions, fears, challenges, driving factors and aspirations of their target audience. This will help them create more impactful and compelling sales pitches which will appeal to their potential customers. When you know the core emotions of your market, you will know how to adjust your campaigns to get people to listen to your marketing message. A study of more than 40 Fortune 500 firms concluded that sales personnel with high emotional quotient/emotional intelligence out-did those with average to low emotional intelligence by about 50%. Emotional intelligence helps you empathize with your audience before selling to them, and thus increase the organization's overall sales.

Enhances Overall Well-Being

Imagine a scenario where your manager has admonished you early in the morning for a task that wasn't performed up to the mark even when you know you've put in your best. How would you feel? How would you react? What would you think? People low on emotional intelligence will start having doubts about their abilities, will be more prone to stress over the incident throughout the day and generally display a foul mood by letting the situation get the better of them. However, people with high emotional intelligence will not take it personally. They will be more aware of their manager's stress, penchant for perfection and go-getter attitude. They will know it's not so much about their capability as the need of the other person to be the best.

Emotionally intelligent people understand others' needs and emotions enough to not blame themselves for everything and stress over the smallest of things. In this case, rather than fuming, they will try and understand what exactly the manager wants and more importantly why he/she wants it. They will then manage their emotions and reactions in response to others' emotions to arrive at the most positive outcome. This helps you manage your reactions, decreases stress, boosts positivity and improves your overall well-being.

More Conditioned for Success

People with a high emotional quotient are more conditioned to be successful in life. They are intrinsically motivated, less prone to procrastination, display higher self-confidence, are better negotiators and conflict resolvers, and are more focused on their goals. They know how to deal with their and others' emotions to build more supportive networks. Emotionally intelligent people are able to overcome setbacks more efficiently and are more perseverant while handling challenging situations. They possess a more resilient outlook and know how to control their reactions in circumstances they can't control.

A company operating in a particular region decides to terminate the services of people belonging to a certain community for vested interests. Now, if you are a person belonging to the community, you are aware it's beyond your circle of control that you were born into the community. You can't change your origins and can do little about the situation (other than fighting a legal battle). However, even when emotionally intelligent people cannot influence their circumstances, they are savvy enough to choose their reaction to these circumstances. They quickly grab the next best opportunity by channeling their actions more positively rather than mulling over things where they have little control. They rule over circumstances rather than letting circumstances get the better of them, due to which they are more slated for success.

Enhances Leadership Skills

Emotionally intelligent people have a well-developed knack for understanding others and identifying factors that motivate them. They then use this information positively to forge greater loyalty and stronger bonds. An able leader can understand the needs, emotions and aspirations of her or his people. They know how to direct this understanding to encourage better performances and people satisfaction. An emotionally savvy manager will be able to create stronger, more motivated and loyal teams by strategically using the team's emotional diversity. They will intuitively harness the strengths and weaknesses of the team for optimal overall benefit.

Individuals who are emotionally intelligent have the ability to manage their emotions better and this makes them less prone to outbursts, and more focused on assertiveness, which automatically earns them greater respect. When we master self and other people's emotions, we know exactly how to direct them to create more harmonious surroundings.

Better Relationships

Emotional intelligence helps us enjoy better relationships by being aware of our and others' feelings, thoughts, emotions and behavior. We can communicate in a more positive and constructive manner to forge stronger interpersonal bonds. Gaining an awareness of the needs, responses and emotions of our loved ones leads to more fulfilling and gratifying relationships. Emotional intelligence helps us show empathy, makes us less aggressive and helps us manage conflicts within the relationship more efficiently. We find ourselves resorting to less manipulation, aggression, submission and power games. Emotional intelligence makes us confident enough to assert our rights within a relationship without damaging the other person. It awards us the ability to balance conflicting situations to maintain a positive and harmonious environment. The ability to manage our emotions in relation to others makes us react/respond to people we care for in a more thoughtful and empathetic manner. When we are able to relate to others in a more efficient manner, we form better and more lasting relationships.

Let's consider a scenario. 'A' and 'B' are involved in a serious romantic relationship. 'A' is more gregarious, social, and has lots of friends due to an amicable and easy-going nature. 'B' is more of a thoughtful introvert who enjoys reading, meditation, and bonds with a group of selected friends. 'B' doesn't take too well to 'A's' time out with friends, social media activity and generally being accessible to everyone.

Now, if 'A' isn't emotionally intelligent, 'A' will simply label 'B' as insecure, jealous and possessive, inviting more conflict within the relationship. Let's now assume 'A' has a high emotional intelligence. 'A' will be likelier to understand where 'B' is coming from, what 'B's' insecurities are and why 'B' thinks the way 'B' does. 'A' will make a greater attempt to involve 'B' in social activities to make 'B' feel a part of it. 'A' will take time out to discuss feelings and arrive at a more positive plan of action that benefits both. There will be an attempt to put forth 'A's' view of wanting some time out with friends without hurting 'B's' feelings. Rather than blaming others, emotionally intelligent people attempt to understand them and arrive at a middle ground, which is beneficial for everyone involved.

In the above scenario, 'A' may keep aside some days exclusively for 'B,' while working out a way to go out with friends once a week so 'B' doesn't feel neglected. This way, 'A' has used knowledge of 'B's' emotions and feelings to empathize and to arrive at a solution that makes them both feel better, which allows them to share a more meaningful and fulfilling relationship.

Boosts Physical Health
This one's a no-brainer. When we are mentally happy, it reflects on our bodies. Emotionally intelligent folks are able to control their emotions and cope with stress more constructively. They don't try and control what's outside their circle of control, but are able to manage their reaction to the stressful stimuli.

This leads to better emotional health, and subsequently glowing physical health, since an individual's mental health is closely tied with their physical well-being.

Enhanced Communication Skills

Individuals with a high emotional quotient are able to articulate themselves better according to the needs and aspirations of other people. They have the ability to listen to people, which is one of the most significant aspects of communication. They understand what to say to manage pulling the heartstrings of people. Emotionally intelligent folks know what motivates people and structure their message accordingly to elicit the most positive response. They are masters at inspiring people to take actions. Teams are likelier to listen and respond to a more emotionally savvy leader, who understands their feelings rather than a technically competent leader who fails to empathize with them or make an emotional connect.

Less Prone to Addiction

Addictions are typically a result of our failure to deal with our emotions. The inability to deal with underlying emotions and feelings makes life tougher for a person, which often results in turning to substances to 'help them cope.' It is often under-developed emotional intelligence that leads people to addiction, and gets them stuck in a miserable pattern. Even sobriety on the face of it is only a temporary solution, unless the addict develops emotional intelligence. People who aim to get rid of their addictions can be more successful if they tackle the underlying emotions that lead to it by gaining more self-awareness.

Such individuals who are emotionally intelligent are aware of their strengths and weaknesses. They have a good understanding of their feelings and emotional make-up. They are aware of the emotions behind their actions. They don't struggle with their feelings and their inability to cope with it. Emotional intelligence equips you with the capacity to deal with your emotions in a more positive manner by gaining complete awareness of it. People who possess high emotional intelligence are mostly confident, happy and fulfilled. They don't feel the need to depend on anything other than themselves for their challenges and inabilities. Emotionally intelligent people are less prone to use substances as coping mechanisms because they are emotionally self-sufficient and more adaptable to change. They know how to cope with complicated situations based on their understanding of their and others' emotions. They've mastered the art of managing their emotions to adapt to and cope with changes around them to bring more positivity in their lives. When a person is mentally strong, emotionally self-sufficient and has complete awareness of their feelings, s/he is less likely to seek the recourse of external factors such as abusive relationships, drugs, alcohol and other similar addictions.

Difference Between EQ and IQ

Imagine yourself as a manager leading a team of a few competent, talented and highly qualified individuals. Your team has been assigned a rather challenging client contract that if done well, can be a huge achievement for the firm. Trouble is, it involves a lot of hard work, hours of research, staying up after work hours and working on weekends. As a leader, you're proficient enough to deliver all the technical training and expertise required to complete the task. But how can you persuade your great team to work on the project more positively and without getting them petulant about the entire project?

Your technical expertise, ability and knowledge will help you impart technical skills but it won't help you successfully motivate them to fulfill the task at hand. You may solve all their technical problems, come up with expert industry solutions and even expand their skill base. How will you get them to complete the project in a rewarding, inspired, productive and positive manner? Enter – emotional intelligence.

While your technical expertise is a result of your intelligence, quotient and ability, your ability to manage your team's behavior for the organization's benefit by gaining complete awareness of their emotions is emotional intelligence. By engaging in a deeper and better understanding of their feelings, thoughts and behavior, you can better manage their behavior to your advantage. When you know what motivates people, how they react to certain situations, why they behave the way they do, the underlying emotions behind their actions and other similar insights, you will be able to direct your behavior more productively. This is the main difference between IQ and EQ.

Though a person's IQ determines his/her competencies and unique capabilities, his/her EQ determines how s/he will interact with and treat other people. It demonstrates how an individual will deal with pressures or crisis.

Intelligence is a measure of your cognitive abilities such as logical thinking, problem solving, analytical thinking, memorizing and creativity. Emotional intelligence, on the other hand, is being aware of and managing your and others' emotions for optimal positive results. While IQ measures the mathematical, verbal and logical prowess of a person, EQ reinforces their ability to form balanced interpersonal relationships in both their personal and professional life. It encompasses empathy, stress management, integrity, intuition and flexibility. Emotional quotient tests emphasize questions related to one's emotions in different situations and other people, while IQ questions focus on our reasoning skills and logical abilities. It is often said that while IQ ensures success throughout your academic life, EQ ensures overall life success.

Let's take another example to illustrate the difference between the two concepts. You know there's a huge problem of uninspired workforce in your workplace, due to which performance is suffering. Your employees are simply not motivated enough to work. You are aware of all the facts, statistics and reasons for the poor performance. That's your intelligence quotient. When you are able to use these facts for motivating your employees to boost their performance, you display a more evolved emotional quotient. Simply being aware of facts but not displaying empathy with the employees is a demonstration of high IQ but low EQ. However, when you use the knowledge and facts for appealing to your employees' emotions, you're showing high EQ.

An individual's EQ determines how he or she interacts with people. Therefore, it has a huge bearing on their happiness and success. People who possess a higher EQ tend to know how to direct people's actions by appealing to their emotions and reasons. A major difference is that though one can't change their intelligence, they can learn to manage his/her and others' emotions to lead a more successful and rewarding life.

A fundamental difference between IQ and EQ is that while IQ is inborn (influenced largely by genetics), EQ can be developed. An individual's reasoning powers and logical abilities cannot be altered by a large degree. However, the ability to handle emotions and manage them to your advantage can be learned. This is the biggest advantage of EQ over IQ. EQ gives you greater flexibility to change situations, people and your life by optimally managing your and others' emotions. While IQ is arguably something that's primarily outside your circle of control, EQ can be cultivated to increase your career and personal relationship prospects.

People with higher EQ can successfully express, control and identify their emotions, assess other people's emotions and have a greater capacity to perceive emotions in general. People with a high intelligence quotient show a marked ability to absorb, comprehend and apply knowledge. They also possess higher logical reasoning, creativity and abstract thinking faculties.

Though we've seen how research has pointed to EQ as the single largest factor for success at work, both IQ and EQ are important in their respective ways. Sometimes, gaining an awareness of your and others' behavior for managing emotions can be futile if not backed by technical expertise. IQ is closely connected with the mind's nourishment and manifested during our academic years. EQ is more developed over a period of time based on our experiences and learned behavior. However, what makes EQ more sought after for the corporate world today is that while almost everyone qualified and trained for a job possess the same required expertise, it is EQ that helps companies distinguish the average workforce from future leaders. It is something that can be constantly developed, is more complex and encompasses a wider range of behavior pattern controllers.

People with a high EQ are generally self-confident, possess greater self-awareness, and are able to handle challenging emotional experiences more efficiently. This is why EQ has a correlation with a person's chances of workplace success and interpersonal relationships. Individuals with a more evolved EQ are better able to identify and manage their own emotions, while also recognizing other's emotional states to adjust to them accordingly.

Unlike IQ, the worth of emotional intelligence is not immediately apparent. IQ is more conspicuous in our academics, performance tests, memory skills, intelligence testing games and other cognitive activities. However, your ability to better manage emotions is not obvious or even easily measurable. How can you gauge if a person is emotionally intelligent other than subjecting them to psychological tests? The results of an emotionally intelligent decision are not as apparent as intelligent quotient driven decisions because emotions are difficult to name and measure. Since they are so complex and multi-layered, the sheer challenge of identifying them had regaled them to secondary position compared to a more easily measurable intelligence factor in the early years of psychological studies. IQ was believed to be more clear-cut and therefore easier to measure and gauge. EQ can never be precisely measured even with the most path-breaking tests. You may gain rough insights on the emotional make-up of an individual, but seldom an exact mind map of the emotional patterns of a person.

Politicians and advertisers harness the power of emotional intelligence brilliantly to influence masses to make purchases or vote in their favor. Ad agencies quite successfully manipulate emotions such as fear and aspirations to accomplish their client's objectives by using information about their target audience's emotions and how these emotions function for influencing voting or buyer behavior.

Emotional intelligence is distinct from one's intellect in the sense that it taps into the fundamental elements of human behavioral patterns. Also, there is no established connection between intelligence quotient and emotional quotient. You just can't predict an individual's EQ based on their smartness. Also, your IQ will be the same at age 15 as it will be at age 60. Emotional intelligence, on the other hand, will most likely evolve over the years according to practice and experiences. It is a more flexible set.

Some psychologists are of the opinion that regular measures of intelligence are too constricted to include a complete range of intelligence parameters. Instead, they suggest that the power to comprehend and express emotions plays an equally important if not greater role in determining the chances of an individual's success.

Your intelligence quotient is calculated with the help of standardized intelligence tests. It is measured by dividing a person's mental age by his or her chronological age and subsequently multiplying the number by 100. For instance, a 10-year-old child possessing a mental age of 16 will have an IQ of 160. Scores of many IQ tests today are measured by comparatively analyzing an individual's score with the scores of others within the same chronological age group.

Though there are many studies to calculate emotional intelligence, the Mayer Salovey Caruso Emotional Intelligence Test (MSCEIT) is known to be the most comprehensive measure of an individual's EQ. It was the result of an intelligence-testing legacy established due to a scientific awareness of human emotions with the intention of gauging an individual's emotional intelligence. The four scales that are used to evaluate emotional intelligence in the MSCEIT test include perceiving emotions, understanding emotions, facilitating thoughts and managing emotions.

Research undertaken by the Carnegie Institute of Technology demonstrated that 85% of one's financial success is due to human engineering skills, communication abilities, negotiating abilities, leadership skills and personality.

Surprisingly, a mere 15% was attributed to technical knowledge. Nobel Prize winning psychologist Daniel Kahneman discovered people are more willing to do business with people they like and can trust even if they offer lower quality products/services or products/services for a higher price.

Though IQ is recognized as a vital attribute for success, specifically for academic achievements, experts have recognized that it's not the sole determinant for a successful life. It is a single component in a huge field of complex influences including emotional intelligence and other factors.

While hiring, companies look for a person's EQ over IQ. A high IQ helps you build interpersonal skills only until a certain degree. It gives you the knowledge, technical finesse and industry expertise to perform your job optimally. EQ is more geared towards your character and emotions based in the manner through which you respond to your colleagues, reply to your e-mails, collaborate with your team, network with contemporaries, lead and instruct subordinates, and work towards fulfilling the organization's goals.

Chapter 2:
Emotional Intelligence Basics

Human characteristics that are innate are those which one is born with and from which instinctual responses are derived. A debate exists as to whether emotional intelligence is inborn and is part of a person's personality, or whether it can be acquired in adulthood even when one did not previously have it.

The term personality is used in psychology to refer to an individual's thoughts, emotions, behaviors and attitudes that are unique to that person. Emotions, especially, are a core aspect of the subject of this book. For example, some people are by nature happy, talkative and full of energy, while others can be described as having a steady, calm and reliable disposition. This is to mean that personality influences introversion and extroversion tendencies in people.

The reason why the subject of personality is of importance here is due to the fact that it is inborn or innate. Although we can improve on our personalities, the changes incurred will be very slight and will tend not to vary much from whom we innately are. Emotional intelligence on the other hand may involve the application of already present natural abilities into practical everyday situations, such as in exercising sound judgment based on clear thinking patterns.

Whereas two people may share common tendencies in reference to their personalities, the manner in which they apply themselves to real-life situations will tend to be very different. For example, of two individuals with a melancholic personality, one may possess very high levels of personal motivation and ambition while the other one may not.

If as a manager you are seeking to employ someone as a salesperson, conducting a personality test will not be sufficient although it may show that the person is talkative and friendly enough to make contacts and sales. There would be a need to know how a person would cope under the pressure that comes with deadlines, and that they will persist in the face of insurmountable challenges and work-related disappointments. A test of their emotional intelligence would equip you with that kind of information.

An employee may have a very pleasant and 'fun' personality but that does not necessarily equate to being a success at the workplace. Employees who possess high emotional intelligence levels will be able to manage and control negative impulses that stem from their personalities in such a way as to bring themselves work-related success.

Some studies claim that human beings are to a certain degree born with a measure of emotional intelligence, which they term as 'innate emotional intelligence.' They point to an infant's ability for emotional sensitivity, as well the potential they have to retain and later recall all the emotional information that they are taking in from their environments during infancy. This information later forms the core of an individual's emotional intelligence.

An infant emotionally learns over time to sense when its mother is angry because they associate some of her repetitive reactions to anger. As they grow, this stored information forms the basis from which they are able to sense other people's feelings. This so-called 'innate intelligence' can be continually developed or damaged through life experiences.

It is very possible for an infant to start life with some degree of emotional intelligence and then unlearn it by imitating unhealthy emotional tendencies from his caregivers. Unhealthy environments of abuse and neglect can also contribute to this unlearning process. Similarly, some infants may show low levels of emotional sensitivity but with the right emotional nurturing, end up scoring very high as emotionally intelligent adults.

EI/EQ Framework

Now that you know the definition, importance and history of emotional intelligence, you are ready to learn about its characteristics as stated by the American psychologist Daniel Goleman. Knowing the characteristics of EI will help you reach a better, deeper understanding of how you can manage your own emotions. This section will also give you a good idea of the current level of your EI.

The Five Elements of Emotional Intelligence

According to Daniel Goleman, people with average or high emotional intelligence levels share the following characteristics (Emotional Intelligence Theory: Highlighting and Developing Leadership Skills, 2016). Below is the framework designed by Goleman to show the five basic elements of EI:

Self-Awareness

Self-awareness, as defined in psychology, is the state in which individuals become cognizant of their physical, mental and spiritual or emotional traits. It is among the first components geared towards building an individual's self-concept. The other two components of an individual's self-concept are self-esteem and the ideal self.

Researchers have long tried to pinpoint when an individual first gains self-awareness. The psychologists Lewis and Brooks-Gun performed what is now known as the 'Rouge Test' on infants of varying ages. The test involved dabbing the infant's nose with a red dot, and then placing the infant in front of a mirror to check whether he or she would reach for his or her own nose. The individuals who reached for their noses during this test were evidence that they already had a measure of self-awareness.

Lewis and Brooks-Gun observed that there were almost no children under the age of one year who would consciously reach for their noses while looking at their reflection. Only 25% of toddlers aged 15 to 18 months reached for their noses during the test, while 75% of toddlers between the ages of 21 to 24 months touched their noses in recognition.

A person displaying a high level of emotional intelligence usually also has a high degree of self-awareness. Such individuals are capable of understanding their emotions, of putting situations into perspective, and of seeing themselves as others might view them. Because they understand their emotions better, they are less prone to bouts of low self-esteem.

Instead, individuals with a good level of self-awareness are often confident and comfortable about how they talk, look and move. This allows them to be more honest with themselves; thus, they know their respective strengths and weaknesses. Additionally, they are aware that, if they have strong points and weak points, then the people around them must also have their own set of achievements and failures.

Self-Regulation

Self-regulation refers to the consistent ability of an individual to control or manage his or her emotions. This is especially important in situations of anger, misunderstanding or rage. Self-regulation is also connected to an individual's ability to calm him or herself during particularly emotional and stressful events.

Psychologists agree that self-regulation is important in the growth of an individual. Without a certain measure of self-regulation, people would be more prone to lashing out, arguing and engaging in dangerous activities. Self-regulation should be taught and practiced during childhood. The child must learn how to evaluate what he or she is feeling, and be knowledgeable enough to discern whether his or her emotions will lead to good or bad results. With self-regulation comes the all-important ability to say 'no.'

An emotionally intelligent person has a good grasp of self-regulation. He or she is able to think effectively before acting and speaking, is thoughtful and mindful of others' feelings and is less impulsive than others. People with a high level of self-regulation often find it easy to refuse vices, bad habits and bad company.

Motivation

When it comes to motivation, none are more focused on their goals than those who are emotionally intelligent. Science has proven that people with high levels of social skills readily trade fast results for a better long-term goal. Motivated people know exactly what their goals are, what they must do to achieve those goals and how to stay focused.

Employers often look for motivated applicants because such people follow a strong cause or dream in the course of their lives. These dreams often take the form of challenges, thus making motivated people unafraid to take risks. Motivation is an important element in Goel's EI framework because it determines what kind of person an individual is and can be. Without proper motivation, people tend to give in to laziness and counter-productivity.

Empathy

It has long been known that emotionally intelligent people are not those who think too highly of themselves due to their numerous achievements, but those who are able to effectively understand even the lowliest person. Empathy is the ability to feel and think the way others do, without necessarily pitying those in a depressed state.

Empathetic people are often described as good and open-minded listeners. They are excellent at handling their relationships. Such people are able to compromise with almost anyone because they have achieved a profound knowledge of what it is like to be in another person's shoes. Empathy, not sympathy, is one of the most important elements of emotional intelligence.

Social Skills

The need to form meaningful and lasting relationships with others is a trait that is inherent in the entire human population. We are social creatures. We crave communication and interaction with different people, whether they are of the same or different sex, age, race and religion. However, not all have the talent of slipping into an easy conversation with a stranger, making small talk with an acquaintance or having a genuine fun time at a party.

An emotionally intelligent individual has developed social skills. These skills were honed through experience, as well as practice. In the workplace, individuals with high social skills are often dubbed as the team leaders, the representatives and the all-round workroom friend. They are excellent in balancing the traits of each of their team members and act as the backbone of the team without being too bossy or demanding.

Social skills are important in the growth of any individual as these help in the formation of relationships. People who are too shy often experience trouble when it comes to making new friends, not because they do not want to, but because their social skills are not strong enough to provide them with the confidence to go out and interact with others.

Chapter 3:
Signs of Low Emotional Intelligence

Now that you are familiar with the theories, concepts and importance of emotional intelligence, you most probably want to know the level of your EI, or emotional quotient (EQ) as some call it. Below is a mini checklist designed to help you have a clearer picture regarding the degree of your emotional intelligence. Though this section is not a scientific test of your EQ, it will certainly help you to know what your weak and strong points are when it comes to emotional intelligence.

The Signs of Low EQ

People with low emotional intelligence are often described as immature and irresponsible. They sometimes act as though they own the world, or they deserve everyone's rapt, undying attention. They also exhibit traits such as impatience, indecisiveness and oversensitivity (Bradberry, n.d.).

A Person with a Low EQ:

- Is incapable of explaining his or her feelings to others, whether in written or verbal form

- Is unable to express him or herself well enough to be understood by others, thus he or she feels oppressed

Robin Samuel Dean

- Is unable to reconcile him or herself with intense emotions such as despair, loss, agony and elation
- Lacks a sense of responsibility, integrity and sincerity
- Is rarely sensitive to the feelings of others
- Thinks emotions expressed through tears are irrational or degrading
- Is rigid when it comes to the beliefs of others
- Rarely shows sympathy or empathy
- Is unable to listen in a genuine manner to other people
- Thinks the worst of others
- Is incapable of trusting friends completely
- Lacks the strength to forgive and be forgiven
- Is afraid of responsibility
- Holds grudges with most of his or her peers
- Quickly criticizes or judges' others without first understanding the situation or individual
- Is often overly pessimistic
- Has a habit of voicing his or her doubts and regrets about him or herself, but is unwilling to listen to the woes of others

- Rarely thinks before acting or speaking
- Is rarely a team player as he or she most often acts for his or her own good only?
- Makes others feel inadequate and insecure
- Presents insecurity about him or herself through repeated apologies
- They are not able to make up their mind about critical social issues

On the other hand, a person with a high EQ is a joy to be around. He or she is sensitive to his or her emotions, as they stay in tune with the feelings of others. Such a person does not shy away from responsibility, but sees it as a challenge to become greater or better.

A Person with a High EQ:

- Expresses his or her emotions clearly, whether in written or verbal form
- Is comfortable talking about what he or she feels to others
- Acknowledges that emotions play a big part in self-formation
- Is open to different ideas, beliefs and opinions
- Does not let his or her emotions cloud his or her judgment
- Is sensitive to the feelings of others
- Knows when to speak, when to keep silent, when to stay and when to leave

- Appreciates the efforts of others who try to cheer, comfort or console him or her
- Is not ashamed to cry or express frustration, anger, happiness and satisfaction
- Allows his or her feelings to lead him or her to better experiences, better choices
- Acknowledges that individuals have different ways of coping with both emotions and experiences
- Is not arrested by fear or worry
- Can identify the factors or aspects that lead him or her to stress
- Can effectively rid him or herself of negative stress
- Understands that even sadness and anger play a role in mental and emotional growth
- Is not afraid of responsibility
- Does not throw the blame on others when things go wrong
- Is comfortable when talking to strangers or acquaintances
- Knows how to draw the line between being sympathetic and empathetic
- Is motivated by his or her goals
- Is patient with the mistakes of others

- Is determined to grow into a better person

Of course, there are other signs that show whether a person has a low or high emotional quotient. The web of human emotions is so complex that there are times when individuals possessing relatively high EQs may be prone to displaying the behavior of individuals with lower EQs, and vice-versa. Remember that the first step to improving and understanding your emotional intelligence is to accept that you are not perfect in emotional stability.

Chapter 4:
Boost Self-Awareness

One of the most fundamental areas of emotional intelligence is the concept of self-awareness. It is the foundation on which the entire theory of emotional intelligence rests. To be aware of and manage others' emotions you need to be aware of your emotional patterns. Self-awareness can be gained by practicing different types of meditations and mindfulness. You can enroll for a meditation course, join a mindfulness group or hire an instructor to help you practice techniques of mindfulness. These methods can increase your awareness about your body, feelings and thoughts. You learn to tune into your innermost self to understand the rhythm of your feeling and emotions. There is a greater understanding of your emotions, and behavior patterns.

Meditation will help you on the road toward getting to know yourself better, but what else can you do to become more aware of this wonderful person you are? Well, there are several self-awareness exercises that you can use to help you and this chapter deals with those.

Keep a journal – This should be your record of all the feelings that you had over the course of a day and you can also have a section in your journal where you keep quotations that deal with things of an emotional nature. There are some amazing quotations online and printing these out or writing them into the back of your journal will help you. After you write down what you feel, if you find that any of it is negative, try to counterbalance it with positive things as well. Then, at the end of the exercise, write down what made you grateful getting up this morning. Try a list of five to start off with because these helps you to fuel yourself with positive thoughts.

Get into the habit of journaling your thoughts after practicing meditation/mindfulness exercises. Recording your feelings and thoughts increases your self-awareness and allows you to gain higher insights about your emotional framework. This will boost your emotional vocabulary, and allow you to identify and assign terms to specific emotions. You will get into the habit of consciously describing a full range of emotions at various points in time to help you develop greater awareness of your emotions. Apart from identifying emotions and describing them, this practice will also help you pay close attention to the intensity of these emotions. The better you can estimate them, the higher your chances of being able to monitor and alter these emotions efficiently.

The other thing that you need to do is create a **life program.** People get a little nervous when I say this, but it's not that complex. Try to decide where you want your life to go and if you find this is a little too difficult to start off with, at least set yourself up with some small goals each day, so that you feel a sense of achievement. This helps you to know your limitations, but it also helps you to face the world with realism and overcome emotional obstacles. If you have large jobs to do, split them down into manageable chunks, because you won't achieve many pats on the back if you always set your goals too high and can never meet them. Your life program has to include the following elements:

- A set time to get up

- Time for meditation

- Breakfast, lunch and dinner (all sat down and not eaten on the go)
- Tasks for tomorrow
- Tasks for the week
- Sufficient 'me' time
- Sufficient exercise
- Sufficient sleep time

When initiating this demanding voyage, you begin to realize that if you fuel your body with all the right things, your body responds by being less emotional and more sated in every day. Spend your 'me' time undertaking things that you like doing, or at least enjoying something for your own sake. When people forget this element of their lives, they tend to find resentment sets in and that's a very negative trait that doesn't help the emotional intelligence quota. The foods you eat fuel your body, the exercise you take fuels your energy levels and sufficient sleep helps the mind to be fully restored the next day. Even if you go through emotional events in your life, these essentials need to be a priority in order to reach that level of self-sufficiency that adds to your emotional responses to life.

Let me try to explain this in plain English. If you don't eat a balanced diet, your body responds by being less capable of performing the functions it needs to perform. If you don't sleep properly, your body cannot release the hormones that sleep allows in order to mend your body and mind. If you don't take time for yourself, you begin to feel that life is a drag and that you are not important enough when nothing can be further from the truth.

The Self-Awareness Exercise

This is something I do with all the people who come to me for help. We choose to go to a location that brings out the awe in you. It may be a beach at sunset or sunrise. It may be a tropical park or somewhere that takes your breath away, but wherever it is, this is the beginning. To become emotionally intelligent, you have to be emotionally aware. Close your eyes for a moment in this place that you have chosen and then open them to the splendor of it. What this does is help you to feel very small. Why would you want to feel small? It's actually comforting to know you are just one small piece of the bigger picture. It doesn't make you less important. Imagine a beach without sand. It wouldn't be the same – so each grain of sand plays a part. Thus, this helps you to embrace humility and understand that the world will always be bigger than you are. This helps you to approach life from a humbler perspective and when you can do that, you exercise emotional intelligence at its best. You listen to people. You care about others and you don't put yourself first. That's something that you need to experience because it also helps you to experience a nearness to something you maybe cannot explain. Christians call it God. Others call it their maker. No matter the title you refer to it, it's the acceptance that you are very small and the world around you is huge and diverse.

This helps you considerably, especially if you combine it with your meditation practice. When you meditate you concentrate on the breath? You drop all of the emotions of the moment and breathe. You are in that moment in time. Similarly, when you can do that and are in the habit of doing it daily, it means that you are able to isolate moments that need more attention and recognize those that are merely unimportant events within your day, getting things in better perspective. Remember, I said that you observe thoughts without adding on emotions?

Well, meditation encourages that. It helps you to stop filling your mind with clutter that takes away clarity. When you have a clear mind, all of the emotions you feel are positive ones that help you and help the world in which you live. Then, and only then, can you say that you know what emotional intelligence is all about. It's about the silences between the words, the waves that lap up on the shore and the rhythm of your breath. That's all it is and it is forever changing. Don't cling to a moment because very soon that moment is gone. Embrace the new moment with the same enthusiasm that you had when you approached the last moment and if you found that any part of your day was negative, move away from the negativity and find positive solutions.

Self-Esteem and Uncertainties

The moment you have the feeling of lacking sufficient emotional intelligence, you have probably dealt with self-esteem issues and so it's a good idea to up your self-esteem to the extent that you are happy with who you are. Ways of doing this are easier than you may imagine. If you have suffered from other people's criticism in the past, you don't need to lean heavily upon people's approval anymore. Approve of your own actions. Be happy with what you do and if you can manage that, it helps considerably. Here are some exercises that you can do to improve your self-esteem:

Get Rid of Negativity

Be very aware that emotional negativity is not your friend. It doesn't help you and can only hold you back from being the best person you can be. Thus, when you feel negative during the course of the next day or so, write down what made you feel negative and try to come up with a reaction that is positive to take its place. For example, a work colleague said something unkind to you. Write it down. Then think about potential solutions. However, be very aware that the negativity started when your colleague said something that upset you. Thus, it didn't start with you. It started with your reaction. From this, you should learn two things:

- Things only become negative when you allow them to be.

- You should feel empathy toward people who rely upon negativity in their interactions with others.

The emotionally intelligent way to deal with a situation that makes you feel out of place or unhappy is to assess the situation and try to respond to everything that happens in your day in a positive manner. If you get feedback from someone at work that seems negative, thank the person for their feedback and then decide what you can do with the feedback. If it's true what was said, the intelligent way to deal with it is to try to improve. If it's unjust, then you can disregard the problem because your emotional response to it will be noted by the person who tried to make you negative. If it doesn't have any effect, it's likely that they will stop being negative.

Boost Your Self-Esteem

It is an easy task to undertake and one a lot of people don't think about. Give something to someone without expecting any thanks or any kind of reward. That doesn't mean a physical thing. This means some action on your part that is totally volunteered. You may bake a cake for a neighbor. You may give a friend something that you made. You may even volunteer your time to a good cause. Walking your dogs at the local shelter is one area that would be a good one because you are not about what other people think. You are all about how YOU see yourself. You should not be so egoistic as to believe you are better than everyone, but neither should you feel that others are more entitled than you are.

Volunteering helps you to find the balance but only if the volunteering is purposeful, rather than allowing people to exploit your generosity, or using you as a doormat. If you do that in your life, it diminishes your emotional intelligence because these are the kind of people who make you feel less respected or less valuable and that brings out all of the negative emotions.

Self-Management of Your Emotions

There may have been events in your life that bring emotions to the forefront. No-one can change what has happened in the past. However, if you start to manage your emotions and step into the NOW, you can make yourself a much better person. Let me show you how. Eleanor is a young woman who is very pretty. Her boyfriend dumped her and she feels ugly. Whenever she thinks of him, she gets sad and is very negative about life. She feels that the whole situation was her fault. Now, the way that an emotionally intelligent person deals with rejection of this manner is to ask what you can do to protect yourself from that kind of hurt in the future. It's a challenge when there are many negative feelings inside you, but by using mindfulness, you can control those feelings. This implies that every time you feel negative toward life or someone in particular, you drag all of your senses into this moment in time. Past events have gone. There's nothing you can do to change them, but dragging them with you into each day isn't going to help you in your life. Mindfulness is breathing in the moment and accepting what IS rather than what HAS BEEN or COULD HAVE BEEN.

Try this for a moment. Sit very still and let go of your present thoughts, replacing them with this moment in time. Observe everything around you and allow your senses to be in the moment. What is the atmosphere? What's the weather like? What's the aroma you can smell? What can you taste? You have to take control of your emotions and let them know that you are not prepared to be dragged into the retrospective point of view. That moment is gone and now you are in another moment. Make the most of that moment. Treat yourself to something you enjoy. A cup of coffee and peaceful thoughts will help you to get back on track and if you do that each day of your life, you distance yourself from the negativity that was holding your emotional intelligence back in the first place. Now give yourself some positive affirmations to say to yourself each morning, so that you can read them in your journal and start the day on a positive note.

Chapter 5:
The Need to Manage Emotions

Mastering Your Emotions

Emotional intelligence is all about understanding your emotions and the emotions of others and turning them to beneficial use, like enhancing your thoughts. Therefore, in order to have more emotional intelligence, you need to develop ways of mastering your emotions. If you can master your emotions effectively, the journey to emotional intelligence will be easy.

Controlling your emotions doesn't mean repressing or ignoring them. On the contrary, mastering and controlling your emotions means learning to process them and respond to them in a helpful and healthy way. Let's analyze 10 universal emotions that most of us tend to experience throughout our lives. We will be investigating how we can master these emotions.

Discomfort

This uncomfortable emotion usually leads to impatience, boredom, and embarrassment. Discomfort comes when you interpret a set of circumstances or situation in a specific way. Therefore, if you get to change and transform your interpretations of the situation, you will gain control over your emotional experience.

If you want to master this emotion, start by determining what you are doing. Secondly, determine how you are interpreting your experience of the reality. Try taking a different approach if you are not satisfied with the results of what you are doing. For instance, if you are bored by what you are doing, try to do something else with your time. Let your approach employ some flexibility in order to master this emotion.

Fear

This debilitating emotion can leave you anxious, worried, and indecisive. Fear results from an emotional response of what might occur in the future, especially if you take specific action or make a specific decision. Fear can stop you from achieving your objectives and goals. The first step to overcome fear is to separate the 'real' from the 'imagined.' Most fear is based on imagined things that may occur in future.

Our fear mostly comes from lack of knowledge and lack of adequate preparation. Therefore, if you want to manage your fear more effectively, you must first clarify what you really want. Secondly, you must prepare thoroughly for actions you ought to take to achieve your desired outcomes.

Hurt

Hurt makes you feel powerless and leaves you with a sense of loss and jealousy. You may feel hurt due to failure of communicating your needs to others effectively. Therefore, start communicating what you want from your relationships today in a clear and non-threatening manner. If this doesn't work for you, you can evaluate your expectations. Maybe your expectations are not reasonable, have changed over time or they are simply no longer applicable in your current relationship.

Anger

This can spin you out of control emotionally and lead to resentfulness. Anger can actually serve you if you get to understand its underlying meaning. It is important if you get to know that anger often arises when others have violated our rules. We end up feeling angry because we no longer feel in control of our situation. You can actually let go of your anger quite quickly, by evaluating your rules. Maybe, they are out of date, unreasonable or too mean to other people.

Guilt

This emotion leaves you deflated and it can lead to regret. You experience guilt because of your interpretation of what you failed to do, and your view of the exact impact it had on other people. The actual impact your actions could have been quite different than what you guessed them to be.

You can change this by interpreting circumstances and events in your life in a new and unique way to make peace with yourself. If you manage to do so, your guilt will turn into something that can motivate you and empower you to take positive actions.

Frustration

Frustrations occur when you are trying to do something, but you are not getting the desired results. It looks like being held back by some inside force that you cannot control. You can take charge of this feeling by thinking of new possibilities, ideas and other possible solutions to your situation. Look for new information that will provide you with new insight on what you are trying to accomplish.

Try changing your approach or take a look at the issue you're facing from a different angle. Determination, curiosity and a flexible approach will get you there.

Inadequacy

Inadequacy makes you feel unworthy, miserable and incompetent. You are probably experiencing this because you don't have the necessary knowledge, experience and skills to live up to your own high expectations. You may decide to either change the expectations you have for yourself or go out and gain the necessary skills and knowledge to meet your expectations.

You may also experience inadequacy because you undermine your own capabilities. You can ask your friends about their perspective concerning your abilities. You might be surprised at what you hear.

Improving your level of confidence is another way to control this emotion. Self-confidence will help greatly when trying to control any emotion.

Overwhelm

This emotion makes you feel out-of-control and unable to respond to what you're experiencing in a logical and rational manner. What you need is to get back the control, but trying to do it all at once is not a very realistic approach.

You will need to take back the control in small chunks. Take part of your life and divide it into small manageable chunks that you can successfully work with. Let go of any unnecessary commitments and obligations that are weighing you down and take it one chunk at a time.

Disappointment

Disappointment is the emotion that leaves you with a sense of defeat; you didn't achieve the desired result you were working towards.

Handle disappointment by learning from that experience, so that you can better yourself in the future. Look for opportunities that may arise from your disappointment. Change the way you view the experience into a positive one. Instead of thinking you failed because you didn't meet your expectations, think that you just found a way it didn't work and try again.

You can also avoid disappointment by lowering your expectations which will increase the likelihood of them being met. Additionally, evaluate and adjust your goals in order to make them attainable.

Chapter 6:
Self-Motivation to Thrive

It is not enough to just recognize your various emotional states and the implicit role that they play in your life. People who are emotionally intelligent must be able to take control of their emotions and regulate them. Motivation is another critical part of emotional intelligence that must be honed, as your own self-talk and your beliefs about yourself have a direct impact on your motivation and the things that you achieve in life.

Self-Regulation
Self-regulation is about understanding the connection between your thoughts, emotions, and actions and how to hijack this process to help you stay in control. Experiencing emotion as you go through your day is not only natural but a major element of the human experience. By learning to regulate these emotions, however, you can stay in control during strong emotional periods.

Taking Control of Your Emotions
Earlier, we talked about how the subconscious mind perceives the world around us as well as the internal state of our body and mind, that triggers an emotional state. After an emotion is triggered, thoughts and actions follow. By understanding this process, you can take control of your own emotions at critical steps in the process.

You have little control over the emotions that you are experiencing, especially since most result from our previous experiences through the interaction with our surrounding. Instead of trying to control emotions, it is easier to hijack the process between thoughts and actions. You can take control of your thoughts by consciously sending the information that you want to communicate with your mind. Then, these conscious thoughts can change your behaviors.

For example, someone who is going through a break-up after several years may be devastated the first week or so, feeling so distraught that it becomes difficult to focus on work and carry out basic day-to-day tasks like cooking food or taking a shower. The overwhelming sadness is a natural response, but being upset is not a productive emotion. In this scenario, this person might take back control of their emotions by consciously thinking the following:

Feeling sad is a natural response, but it does not contribute to me reaching my goals. I am going to take the energy I would have used on crying and apply it to making positive change in my life. Instead of crying over the relationship, I will accept that it is over and focus on myself. I will use this time to excel at work and cultivate deeper relationships with my friends and family.

By taking over your conscious thoughts, you give yourself the opportunity to control your experience. You have validated your emotions but made the conscious decision to set these emotions aside and continue looking toward the future.

Make Weighted Decisions

Another part of self-regulation is using emotion appropriately during the decision-making process. Weighing your decisions involves being aware of the emotional and logical aspects and how each effect the situation. When you have to make a major decision, create a list of pros and cons. As you list each factor that must be considered, think about the weight that it has on the overall decision.

For example, imagine that you are a surgeon considering a position at one of the most prestigious hospitals — but you have to move to a different country to do it. If you are married or are in a long-term relationship, you may have to consider your partner's wishes if you want to preserve the relationship. If you have only been seeing someone casually for a few months, breaking off the relationship may seem the obvious choice. They do not have as much of an impact on your decision as someone you have a long-term relationship with.

You can practice this skill by visualizing different scenarios in your head where you have to make two decisions. Consider the pros and cons, and then identify which aspects of the decision have the most weight. You can also do this for fictional scenarios with fictional characters — this will give you some insight into the way that other people may make decisions as well.

Plan to Stay in Control
Instead of waiting until you feel a particularly strong emotion to try and exercise control over it, take the time to learn about your triggers. Your emotion journal can help you with identifying the strongest emotions that you experience. Think about some times that you have felt this emotion and what caused it. For example, you might be a level-headed person that becomes angry when you feel that people are ignoring you or when injustice is happening and people are turning a blind eye. Even though being angry about injustice is a natural response, the energy that you feel is better spent trying to fight against injustice or spread awareness.

As you identify situations where your emotions were triggered, write down what caused them. Then, write down what you can do next time instead. For example, imagine that you have seen some news that has made you upset. This might be the death of children in a foreign country or starvation. When you are angered by injustice, a good plan might be, "Take a deep breath. Is there anything I can do at this moment to change it? If not then I should make a mental note of the issue and revisit it later." Some good options for fighting injustice involve making donations to organizations that help or spreading information to people who may not know what is going on.

By having a written plan, you have a clear idea of what to do next time you are upset by injustice. This allows you to respond in a positive way instead of reacting with anger and taking it out on the people that you interact with throughout the day.

Practice Stress Management
Stress management is a major issue for some people especially when they allow situations to take an emotional toll on them. By learning to manage stress, you reduce health problems and increase your longevity. A major part of stress management is having emotional intelligence because your EI gives your insight into what is wrong and how to fix it. Through solving conflict and your ability to identify the source of your stress, you can come up with a creative solution that reduces levels of stress.

In addition to addressing specific causes of stress, it can be useful to promote a bodily environment where it is easier to improve your emotional intelligence. Some of the following habits can ensure that your mind is in the best possible state to use your EQ skills to improve the stress levels in your life:

- Getting 7-8 hours of sleep each night

- Finding time to exercise

- Having fun outside of work

- Spending time alone to recharge

- Choosing foods and drinks that nourish you

- Practice meditation or breathing exercises regularly

- Laugh more often

- Find a good balance between home, work, and a social life

Motivation

One of the biggest problems that people face when they want to achieve something in life is finding the motivation to do it. It is easy to continue putting your goals off until 'later.' Have you ever tried to quit smoking or go on a diet? It is all too easy to say that you will quit after 'just one more' cigarette or start your diet 'in the morning.' Without the motivation to actually do these things, however, they continue to be postponed.

As you increase your emotional intelligence, you will find yourself with a greater sense of motivation and purpose than you might have not experienced previously. Emotional intelligence gives you the confidence that you need to maintain motivation when you are facing obstacles.

A good way to help yourself develop motivation is to look toward the future. Make goals for yourself and get into the habit of doing at least one thing each day that sets you a step closer to your goal, even if it is something small. For example, someone who hates their job might start assembling their resume or do research on different careers they might be interested in. Someone who has the goal of starting a family one day might compile a list of traits that they want in the perfect partner or bring up the subject with their existing partner.

Motivation is a habit that can be slid into as easily as procrastination. By continuing to work toward your goals, you are instilling a sense of confidence in yourself that will help you overcome obstacles to your success. Additionally, you will give yourself that critical forward motion that is necessary if you want to achieve great things in life.

You understand your character more than anyone else does, but you would be wise to ask a good friend what that friend feels you lack emotionally. Tell them that you are trying to become more emotionally intelligent and that you want their help to pinpoint your own weaknesses. The reason I say this is because people who are close to you observe your reactions more than you do. They see you worry and fret over things and they will be able to pinpoint your weaknesses such as:

- Do I worry too much about what people say to me?

- Do I avoid doing things because I am emotionally afraid of failure?

- Do you see me as someone who lets their emotions get in the way of making decisions?

- Do I listen to others enough?

- Am I emotionally ruled by others?

- Am I easy to manipulate?

- Do I ask for people's approval all the time?

Asking your friend these questions, note down the areas where they feel you lack skills and don't take it personally. A good friend wants the best for you and will be able to pinpoint where you could use a little help. It's good to have another individual observe your reactions to others and good friends can really help in this regard.

There are several explanations to why you may react negatively to certain discipline, or why you fight all the time within your mind, rather than accept who you are and what your position in life is. Perhaps you have experienced the busy mind and sometimes ask people to repeat what they said because your mind is too filled up with emotional jumble.

The first exercise that I want you to do is to use something that is used in Buddhism. It's an extremely useful tool and helps to calm the mind, but also helps to change the way that you view life and your interactions with others. It helps you to become calmer by nature and be aware of people around you, which will, in turn, improve your emotional intelligence.

Breathing

I want you to sit somewhere where you are comfortable and where your back is straight. Now, I want you to start to breathe in the manner explained so that you become calmer.

- Breathe in via your nose as you count to eight.

- Breathe out to the count of ten.

While you are doing this, I want you to try and clear all thoughts from your head. Of course, it won't happen straight away because your mind is filled with stuff and it's natural that this should take a little time to tackle. However, breathe in, breathe out and concentrate all your attention on your breathing. This is all there is to basic meditation, but you need to do it for 20 minutes in the morning before you go to work and before your breakfast. What you are doing is giving your mind a little space so that you can see situations with more clarity. When a thought comes to your mind, do not judge it. Imagine it as a picture that you see and then it is gone. The whole point of the exercise is that you learn to be neutral in your approach to your thoughts. Instead of judging things, you simply see it and then it's gone. If you don't distort life by letting your emotions take over each thought that you have, you instantly free up your subconscious mind to finding more intelligent solutions to your problems.

You won't find that this will happen straight away, so keep at it and make this meditative breathing part of your daily routine. It will slow down your heartbeat and your blood pressure and can be made use of during the day if you feel that the world is getting too chaotic for you to deal with. It helps you to build energy within yourself and your posture is also important because you are feeding the inner energy points of your body at the same time.

Keep this practice up and what you will find is that you are not quite so quick to retort to life in a negative fashion. You change your perception and start seeing the bigger picture and are able to control your emotions when it comes to dealing with people. That's a huge boost to your morale because it means that you are more in control of your life and thus more likely to gain promotion and be able to deal with people in a more mature manner. That's what bosses are looking for when they go to promote people and emotional intelligence is important to your welfare too as it stops you from feeling stressed out. Instead of stressing, breathe. Give yourself space to resolve problems rather than letting automatic retort kick in.

Chapter 7:
Learn to Understand Others and Develop Empathy

Empathy is a trait anyone can easily learn and to some extent we all practice empathy in varying degrees as we interact with each other. But showing empathy and being an empath are actually not identical.

Here's how to process the difference between the two.

Imagine you are sitting down at Starbucks with two of your friends that you very much adore. Both are strong in character and while different in personalities, you know they both have big hearts.

Suddenly a couple sitting next to you causes a scene. The guy bangs the table in anger, spilling a perfectly wonderful Frappuccino all over and yells a few words before stomping out. The woman left behind feels utterly crushed and embarrassed. Tears stream down her red cheeks and she hangs her head as low as possible as she quickly tries to clean up the mess created. For a moment, all eyes are on her and you could literally feel everything that she felt.

One of your friends turns to you and asks, "Should we go over there and see if we can help?" As you look over to your friend you notice her cheeks are flushed and her eyes are just as teary as yours. It's almost as if you're both experiencing what the couple experienced. Before you can even respond, your other friend jumps in and says, "Na, she'll be fine. Look she's already stopped crying. Let it go."

What just happened in that scenario?

One of your friends did show some empathy and recognized the discomfort of the woman but that's as far as it went. She was glad to just get on with her day as if nothing happened. The other friend, however, seemed to have had a completely different experience. Her entire body chemistry changed and you felt it too, didn't you?

This is the subtle difference between showing empathy and being an empath.

Empathy is the ability to understand and share the feelings of another. With a little conscious effort, every human being has the ability to demonstrate empathy when the situation calls for it.

When one is an empath, however, it's an entirely different experience. It's more like having an elevated gift and an ability to step into another person's shoes. An empath has the power to step outside his or her own experience and understand what another person is saying, thinking, and feeling. It's more than just being a highly sensitive person and it goes beyond sensing emotions.

According to science, empaths are highly sensitive and can process emotions faster and more intimately. The common acronym for this is HSP meaning a Highly Sensitive Person. A highly sensitive person isn't to be confused with an attention seeker or overly sensitive people who enjoy unpleasant tantrum infused behaviors. It means you are high in sensory processing sensitivity. A true

HSP is usually very aware of the feelings of others and very reluctant to cause a scene.

So, from the example I shared of your two friends, one of them does demonstrate empathy, which is great. But the other friend is more likely to be considered an empath.

A true empath goes beyond being an HSP; he or she also has empathic abilities which, when mastered, result in a very powerful being, capable of various things such as healing others.

The natural question that follows is: how does one know whether they possess empathic abilities or not?

I mean, do you actually know if you're an empath? How about we finally shed some light on that.

Here's the Most Important Thing to Always Remember:

When you realize there's a pattern in your life where certain people, situations or triggers result in physical discomfort that cannot be medically diagnosed, know that you're not imagining things or going crazy. You are simply a highly sensitive person with a gift that must be developed, nurtured and successfully managed.

The whole purpose of learning to embrace your empathic abilities and becoming a true empath is so that you can stop being at the mercy of other people's pain, stresses, and conflicts.

Highly sensitive people absorb anything and everything and often they have no control over it. A true empath has mastered his or her abilities and doesn't automatically get overwhelmed by the emotions of another. This is how I've personally redefined for myself what it means to be an empath. How are you going to redefine it for yourself?

If you are truly ready to gain mastery over your special abilities, then it's time to equip yourself with simple living strategies that will empower and help you center yourself so you can finally stop absorbing other people's dysfunctions.

1. Use the Power of Your Breath

First, you need to realize the power contained in your breathing. Whenever you suspect you're picking up someone else's symptoms, bring all your focused attention to your breath for a few minutes. Surrender to this simple act of breathing deeply in and out. Use it to ground yourself and connect to your power.

2. Name It to Tame It

Next, ask yourself, "what is this emotional or physical distress I am feeling?" Whenever we put a label on something, we decrease the momentum of the impact, which gives us ample time to constructively handle the issue.

3. Evaluate it 'in the moment'

Once you've brought it to the forefront of your mind, evaluate this emotion. Don't let this slide and take over your mind and body. Deal with it immediately before it grows into a monster.

Is the distress really yours or have you picked it up from something or someone? Sometimes the answer is both. If for example you're feeling deep fear and it's yours, gently confront what's causing it. You can do this either on your own or by getting professional help. If, however, you realize it isn't yours, pinpoint the obvious generator and work on releasing it.

4. Take a Step Back

This can be physically moving away so you can get into a mindful space to handle the situation or it can be a mental movement. Either way, you want to be able to create some movement that allows you to start reaching for that sense of relief that's absolutely essential in releasing unwanted energies.

5. Become More Aware of Your Mind-Body Connection

Keep breathing deeply. Seek to find where in your body you feel most vulnerable. Chances are if you can find that spot where the alarm is going off you can quickly turn things around and step back into your power. The more you practice this exercise, the better you'll know how your body works.

For example, in my case, my solar plexus is where I go first because I know my tummy is always the first place my alarm hits. By the time I start feeling it on my left shoulder I know it's reached stage two which means the issue is more serious and I need to do something fast.

The physical sensations may not be identical but the same rule will be true for you. Our bodies are such wonderful communicators. Get to understand the signals they send.

So, let's suppose for you it's a migraine headache or a sore throat, the moment you become aware of these symptoms, sit in silence, relax your entire mind and body. Practice your deep breathing. Set your palm on the area and practice soothing yourself, giving yourself self-healing. Keep doing it and speaking with yourself until the discomfort dissipates.

Emotional Intelligence Primal Leadership 2.0

If you've been battling with depression, panic attacks or chronic pain for a long time, this simple method when done daily with intention will strengthen and comfort you. It's a great way to reconnect your mind and body and imbue yourself with that feeling of safety that we all need. You are the only one who can heal yourself better. Learn to trust that.

Chapter 8:
Handling Relationships for Success

The people around you may be strangers. They may be people with emotional problems or they may be perfectly happy people. How they feel isn't part of the issue here. What I want you to do today is to learn to be an active listener and stop yourself from voicing your opinion too quickly. Active listening helps you to be empathetic. That means you can put yourself into the shoes of others and imagine what is driving them. When you are able to do that, your interactions with others will be a lot more positive.

Start the day by greeting people in a positive way. Even a smile to a stranger on the street can make a whole heap of difference to the way you approach your day. If you feel negative about sitting in traffic too long, use the time to do something you enjoy. Perhaps you can listen to an audiobook that you don't have time to read. Make the event an enjoyable one. Use music or indulge in learning while you make your way to work. What this does is improve your state of mind, but it also helps you because learning something is positive. You are heading toward an achievement so that's got to be a lot more positive than honking your horn and making everyone around you feel as miserable as you do.

Active Listening

When people speak, they generally talk about themselves. It's not that they think themselves important enough to be the topic of conversation. It's merely because it's what they know about. Thus, you may get involved in all kinds of conversations during the course of the day. You may be fed up with listening to a colleague telling you about her dogs. You may not really want to listen to someone telling you about their love life, but stop for a moment. Why are these people talking to you about things like that? The fact is that a relationship is made up of trust. These people feel that they can trust you enough to discuss their feelings. That's a huge compliment. Thus, instead of nodding and not really listening, learn to be a little more empathetic. If you don't like the subject of dogs, turn the conversation around, but listen to the conversation because to that person, the dog may be the only form of comfort that she has. Active listening means letting others have their say without butting in. It means understanding people's need to get their feelings out in the open. It doesn't mean that you have to take on the world's problems, but it helps you to pass a congenial moment with someone and give them the same amount of attention that you expect to get when you talk to people.

This carefulness also teaches you a lot about your level of empathy because emotionally intelligent people have a high level of empathy. They know how to steer a conversation. They understand the secrets of making other people feel better than they do at this moment and when you start to do that, the reactions you get from others will be more positive.

What You Say to Others

Remember that what you say to others says a lot about you. The emotions to avoid when you are talking to people are the following:

- Anger

- Indignation

- Jealousy

- Greed

- Selfishness

If you happen to be doing any of the above, put a stop to it. Jennifer was jealous of her sister Jane. Jane got all of the attention of their parents. Jennifer grew up with this bias against her sister, but her sister had done nothing to deserve it. It was their parents who had lavished more attention on Jane than on Jennifer so if anyone was to blame, it would have been the parents. When you carry baggage with you that is negative, it spoils every chance you have at happiness. In the case of Jennifer, she wasted a potential 20 years of friendship with her sister on a mistaken belief that it was her sister's fault that the parents preferred her. When they eventually did make friends, Jennifer saw things from her sister's perspective. It was hard growing up trying to be this person that her parents were making her out to be. She wasn't allowed to make mistakes. She couldn't have fun in her life because her parents' expectations never allowed it. There are always other perspectives. Emotionally intelligent people will see beyond the veneer and know why others are feeling negative. They will also be able to contribute something that makes negative people feel better about themselves.

You cannot go through your life ignoring negative things. These are in your life for a purpose and when you learn to decipher them correctly, you increase your own emotional intelligence. When a negative thing happens, stand back from it and observe it, learning why it happened and then working out what can be done to make the situation more positive for all concerned. That's what emotionally intelligent people do. It takes a bit of learning, but start today.

Emotionally intelligent people are never afraid to admit that they are wrong and they are also unafraid of saying sorry or of forgiving people. You see, the more you insist on holding onto negative emotions, the more they can distort who you are. Forgiveness is a wonderful tool because when you employ it, you empower yourself. The problem is gone. There are no bad feelings left so try to work out who you should forgive in your life because it will take a whole heap of weight from your shoulders.

To share power, men need to be emotionally available and respect their other half, i.e., Emotionally Intelligent (Brittle, 2015).

Yet only 35% of men ARE Emotionally Intelligent.

It's a conundrum, isn't it?

There have been bona fide studies proving the importance of Emotional Intelligence on interpersonal relationships. In one study, for instance, the participants rated their marital satisfaction higher if they also rated their marital partner higher for Emotional Intelligence. Another study demonstrated anticipated greater satisfaction in relationships with a partner of Emotional Intelligence.

A meta-analysis of six studies with more than 600 participants found a *'significant association'* between EQ and romantic relationship satisfaction and it works both ways. The higher your own Emotional Intelligence, the more satisfied you will be in a romantic relationship, PLUS the higher your partner's EQ, the happier you will also be.

Isn't its worth beefing up your Emotional Intelligence for the pair of you, whether it's for your present or future Mr. or Mrs.?

The good news is that happy couples aren't necessarily better, luckier, richer or more intelligent than the rest of us; they are just in touch with their emotionally intelligent side.

As Dr. John Gottman himself, possibly the world's lead researcher on marriage, says: *"Happily married couples aren't smarter, richer, or more psychologically astute than others. But in their day-to-day lives, they have hit upon a dynamic that keeps their negative thoughts and feelings about each other (which all couples have) from overwhelming their positive ones. They have what I call an emotionally intelligent marriage."* (John Gottman and Nan Silver, 2018)

How does this manifest itself? According to Dr. Gottman, an emotionally intelligent marriage includes two partners who are committed to awareness of themselves and the other, and the ability to manage their own emotional state and its impact on the other partner. So, a classic trait of Emotional Intelligence.

To specify further, he adds: *"In the strongest marriages, husband and wife share a deep sense of meaning. They don't just 'get along' — they also support each other's hopes and aspirations and build a sense of purpose into their lives together."*

If marriage is a journey, you both know why you're in the car together and appreciate where you're going.

It's all the easier to live up to those marriage promises – to love, honor, respect and understand each other – if you are an emotionally intelligent couple. Not only can it help you avoid divorce or relationship breakdown, but as happily married people lead longer and healthier lives, it's great for your health too.

Emotional Intelligence isn't just crucial to love relationships. It's valuable for family and friends too, helping to sustain ongoing positive relationships.

But if you're terrible at EQ, how *can* you improve? How sure can you be that you are providing your significant other, friends and family the support they need?

Most of the time, in close personal relationships, your actions will be natural, and you may not even be aware that you're using your EQ skills. If you're naturally low in Emotional Intelligence, however, it may take more purposeful thought and effort, but remember that EQ skills can be learned.

The truth is that you're more likely to be aware of your EQ skills (or lack thereof) if you don't have them.

Relationships: Does the next section sound like anyone you know, someone close to home perhaps? If you can't recognize them in yourself, has your partner or family complained about you suffering from any of the following? It's probably time to deal with it.

Out of Control Feelings: We all know by now that Emotionally Intelligent people can regulate their emotions. If your EQ needs work, you may be prone to lashing out in anger or giddy happiness for no real reason, or any other OTT emotional reaction.

Poor Friendships: How many close friendships do you have? Most people low in EQ struggle to maintain good relationships with co-workers and friends.

Can't Read Emotion: Do you often find yourself clueless about your partner's emotions, or blindsided by a reaction? You may be unable to read non-verbal cues, such as facial expressions or body language, or struggle to interpret tone of voice. So much of our communication is not said verbally. If you can't interpret that, you will struggle to make an emotional connection because you never quite understand the thoughts of the other person. The good news is that we have a section on non-verbal communication coming up just for you.

Poker Face: Can your partner tell what you're thinking and feeling, or do you have a poker face, unable to express your own emotion?

Are you Emotionally Inappropriate? Do you get angry over nothing, or fail to realize you are angering someone else? Perhaps you are inappropriate, such as telling jokes or laughing at a funeral. These can be signs that you struggle with the social side of emotional expression.

Can't Handle Sadness: Do you prefer to walk away from negative emotions or sadness, struggling to show empathy or support? A lack of empathy signals poor Emotional Intelligence. Do you find emotional movies leave you cold, for instance? Don't be fooled into thinking it's a male versus female thing; it's not. It's very possibly a sign that you have low EQ.

Overplay Logic: Logic has its place in relationships, but if you over-stress logic and cognition over emotions (and typically downplay the latter), it's a sign that you are subconsciously aware of your low EQ and trying to pretend it doesn't matter. Little tip: it does, for all the reasons I mentioned above.

Odd Interpretation of Emotions/Conflicts: Have you been accused of over-reacting or having an odd reaction to conflict or emotions? Perhaps you acted hostile and defensive when there was no need. Often the root cause of this is confusion as opposed to malice, very possibly because of the above. Of course, when people don't understand that, you tend to withdraw even more.

Assuming you freely recognize your lack of Emotional Intelligence and appreciate the negative impact it is having on your personal life, what can you do about it? How can you go about developing your EQ in relationships in particular?

How to Develop your EQ in Relationships

I've already shared a lot of tips for improving your EQ in general earlier in the book. A lot of what I suggested there will help your EQ across the board, including with friends, family and significant other.

Now though I'm going to suggest a couple of further tips specific to romantic relationships. It's worth following even if you haven't found that special someone yet... who knows, perhaps becoming more in tune with your emotional side will help you land them!

Learn to Describe your Emotions

Yes, I know I've mentioned this a couple of times before, but it really is worth developing a strong emotional vocabulary in the context of relationships. Think of how you describe your emotions – happy, sad, angry... anything deeper? If you're sad, for instance, would you ever think of yourself as melancholy, depressed, grief-stricken, ill or nostalgic?

As we know by now, developing a wider emotional vocabulary allows you to go deeper and to correctly label your emotions, which in turn helps you to react accordingly. Having a wider emotional vocabulary encourages you to move past your first initial emotion, say anger, to determine exactly what lies beneath. Often our first instinctive emotional response seems like the most powerful, but it's not always the true story.

Say you have an argument with your wife. You feel and recognize your first emotion, anger. Would you ordinarily stop there? Now that you're seeking a stronger Emotional Intelligence, you should push past the anger to find what you're really feeling – could it be hurt, jealous, anxious, worried, embarrassed, ashamed?

Being hurt, for instance, feels very different from being angry, doesn't it? Or perhaps you're ashamed because you couldn't give your wife what she needed from you? Each emotion carries a different weight and influences how you relate to your partner, helping to make your relationship more genuine. Imagine if you'd just stopped at anger? You would understand a lot less.

Don't forget. While your first emotional reaction may seem the most powerful, it may also be the least honest.

Work on Relationship Awareness

The key to Emotional Intelligence is to be aware of, and in control of, our own emotions, while also recognizing emotions in others. Every single one of us needs something from our significant other, whether it's love, trust, support, affirmation.

Of course, what we need from the other changes as we age, our relationship grows, our circumstances alter etc.

What does your wife or husband need from you? What *'emotional nutrients'* do they need that would feed your relationship? *(If the word 'nutrients' is confusing to you, consider emotional needs instead. What emotional needs does your wife need you to address?)*

Just go ahead and ask. Ask your partner to write down the three most important emotional needs or *'nutrients'* that they have and want from your relationship. Write your own list independently. Swap and discuss how you can make sure the relationship or marriage can meet both lists.

How to Understand Body Language

There's a formula that's often bandied around when we start to talk about body language and non-verbal communication – the 55/38/7 rule (Belludi, 2008). It's a percentage formula that demonstrates how much is communicated when you're NOT speaking. Yes, that's right. People communicate even when they're *not* talking.

The 7% of the formula represents how much of communication is spoken. Your words, no matter how carefully you choose them, only account for 7% of all communication. Both liberating and daunting, isn't it?

In total, so the formula goes:

- 55% of all communication comes from body language

- 38% from tone of voice
- 7% are actual words spoken.

Of course, there has been some dispute with the exact figures and it's fair to point out that such a simple theory can't possibly apply to every situation. But, experts agree, it's a pretty good ballpark and it really does emphasize the importance of body language.

Understanding someone's body language can tell you so much about a person, but what if you just weren't born knowing the cues? What if it all simply passes you by, and you fail to notice your wife is angry despite saying she's not, or your son is lying to you when he promises not to have a party this weekend? Can you learn how to recognize body language?

Let me tell you a little story. I was sat minding my own business in a local coffee shop recently *(meaning I was people watching, fascinated by their interactions)*. A young couple walked in and sat next to me, arguing all the while. I politely tried to ignore them *(okay, not really)* but they made it hard. The argument seemed to stem from the fact that the boyfriend had communicated with an ex-girlfriend, a fact he was trying hard to pretend didn't mean anything. Of course, his body language gave him away.

He tried so hard to convince his girlfriend with logic but was oblivious to what his body language and tone of voice – defensive, mock offended, *'caught like a rabbit in headlights'* – really revealed. Of course, we don't see our own body language so it's often hard to be sure if it's failing our intentions.

His girlfriend, of course, a woman of obvious Emotional Intelligence, saw straight through him, but for some reason either decided to accept his protestations or was saving them up to use against him later. Finally, she calmed down and her hapless and low EQ boyfriend thought that was the end of it. They sat in silence – communicating volumes to anyone who cared to look – and he thought he'd got away with it.

When they left, he tried to seal the deal with a hug. He was happy that she acquiesced, but her body language – stiff as a plank of wood, refusing to make eye contact – should have told him that he really shouldn't touch her.

I tell you; he was so busted. The next time I saw her in the same café, she was alone. I never did ask what happened to the boyfriend, but I can guess.

You see, if you're so blind to body language, you miss out on so much.

What is Body Language?

It's everything from eye contact *(or lack of)*, gestures, facial expressions, posture, space *(do they invade yours?)*, and touch *(a weak handshake versus a bear hug, for example)*.

Did You Know: Facial expressions are universal. They are the same across cultures for happiness, sadness, fear, shock and disgust etc. The same is *NOT* true of other forms of non-verbal communication, such as gestures and body language, so be careful!

Uses of Body Language

According to The Importance of Effective Communication by Edward G. Wertheim, body language can be used to underline or complement a verbal message *(think of a pat on the back when congratulating someone)*, or to repeat what they say wholeheartedly. When it matches the spoken words, it increases trust and rapport between people.

Body language can, and often is, used instead of words – eye contact can communicate much more than words alone, don't you think? It can also contradict what someone is trying to convey with words.

The kicker about that last point – research studies show that if your body language contradicts your spoken word, people are much more likely to believe the former. Not to mention distrust you. If you can read body language well, it's a built-in lie detector.

Body language can't really be faked. Unless you're a master manipulator and 'on' all the time, your true intentions will slip out, whether it's thanks to a gesture, a touch, an eye-roll or some other little clue.

How to Recognize Body Language

There are far more clues to body language than we can possibly talk about in one chapter – entire books have been written on it, after all. However, there are a few steps that you can take to make yourself more open and effective at interpreting non-verbal communication. They include:

Managing Stress

When you're stressed, you are much more likely to miss the non-verbal signs that other people are putting out there. You'll be prone to misreading events and handling personal conversations poorly. Managing stress is important for effective communication. If you're stressed by a discussion, take a time-out.

Regain your emotional equilibrium before you say or do something you'll regret. Remember your emotions are contagious, as we talked about above.

Work on Recognizing Your Emotions

Being aware of your and other people's emotions and how they influence you is a fundamental part of Emotional Intelligence and the purpose of this book. It's also a key component of recognizing body language, so there's a bonus!

Look for Inconsistencies

Possibly one of the best tips for reading body language that I can give you is to look for inconsistencies between what someone says and what their non-verbal communication suggests. Ideally it should reinforce their words. If someone is saying yes while shaking their head no, that's something to be wary of, for instance. A word of advice, however – don't try to evaluate every single non-verbal signal that you receive; it will make your head explode. People naturally consider all the clues given during a conversation to gain an overall impression of whether their words, tone of voice and body language are consistent or inconsistent with what is being said.

Pay Attention to Your Instincts

Gut feeling is important, don't dismiss it. If you suspect someone isn't being truthful, you may be subconsciously picking up on a conflict between verbal and nonverbal clues.

If in doubt, ask

If someone's body language seems to contradict their spoken word – and it's not a potentially dangerous situation – feel free to ask for clarification. Don't get frustrated. Say something like, *"You said X and Y, but your body language suggests you think differently. Can you help me to understand?"* Just be careful not to do it aggressively or in an adversarial manner.

Well done on wanting to improve your EQ and your knowledge of body language to strengthen your relationships with your nearest and dearest.

Program Yourself to Become Successful

We all are looking for that mental edge when it comes to achieving what we want. Most often your mind is your worst enemy when it comes to succeeding in life. You should realize that instead of fighting with your mind you can program it to work in your endeavor to reach.

Success is a powerful word, which we all realize is hard to achieve. It takes something extraordinary to reach your goals, but it is still very possible. Alongside a little dedication, programming the human mind to succeed is all it takes. How do you program the mind to succeed in life?

Rid Yourself of Self-Doubt

Success becomes elusive when we give up even before we try. We always keep telling ourselves what we are not. We drive in hard our weaknesses that demotivate us and prevent us from making effective efforts. A simple way to overcome this roadblock to success is by creating an 'I-Am' list.

Note down all the good qualities that you think you possess on one side of the paper and everything that you want to be on the other side. It keeps you updated with your goals and missions in life at all times. It also boosts your confidence and reminds you of all the great qualities that you possess and would maintain once you succeed in your quest. These outlines are necessary because it is from here that you would draw strength and inspiration to work harder and perform better in life.

Positive Thinking

Positive thinking is a must for you to succeed. Emotionally Intelligent people never see the glass as half empty. They see the glass as half full and do not hesitate one bit to drink it all up when they are thirsty. Positive thinking makes one confident and surer of oneself, promoting ideas that lead you to success. Hence never feel dejected or disenchanted. Rather look for the sunny side up in matters of life. When you want to achieve something in life, it becomes important that you promote that idea in both your thoughts and speech. When you keep thinking just about the hurdles in your way, they appear much bigger. Tell your mind that no matter what it takes, you are unafraid to sweat it out to achieve what is in your mind. Take the course of action required as a means to an end with the end signifying your success.

Meditate to Gain Clarity

It is very common that people lose interest midway through their efforts and their dreams and ambitions never materialize in their lives. Meditation and self-introspection are the ways that prevent individuals from getting disenchanted in their mission. Take out a small amount of time from your busy schedule to ruminate about your actions, thoughts, motivations, desires, and plans. Think about what is preventing you from succeeding and how that hurdle can be overcome. Ponder on your strengths and how you can gain from them in your endeavor to achieve. Mentally prepare yourself for the hard work because there is no skipping that. Meditation helps clear your mind and makes you remain focused and energized while you make efforts to succeed. Our thoughts hold the power that can make us fail or succeed in life. Taking control over your mind is essential for you to succeed and to have once familiarized yourself with your mind there is no stopping you from succeeding in life.

The principle of goal-setting in the management of emotions - before deciding what to do with this or that emotion, one must answer the question, "what do we want as a result?"

'Reframing' is a tool for replacing negative emotions with positive ones.

Rapid methods of neutralizing emotions that impede effectiveness (for example, breathing practices, movement, diet).

Chapter 9:
Leading with Emotional Intelligence in Social Settings

We need to explore how your emotional intelligence can change your life through your social skills. Let's examine how having a strong Emotional Intelligence can change the way you socialize with the people around you. The practices in this section will help you further advance your emotional intelligence in a way that influences you to have more positive interactions with others.

These skills will develop you both inside and outside. This is because it supports you in getting to know yourself even more, which is one of the very foundational parts of being emotionally intelligent. It is also because it will change the way you interact with others and therefore your social circle may change drastically. At the very least, the way you engage with your social circle will change.

Here are the skills you need to begin practicing to empower and enhance your social skills through emotional intelligence.

Be Approachable and Open
Increasing your emotional intelligence is partly about putting down your guard, and letting yourself be approached by other people. When you are emotionally intelligent, you no longer fear being hurt by others because you are capable of recognizing the reality of this hurt and you trust that you can move through it effectively. As such, you are more open.

Practice how to be more open to others. Be willing to let other people approach you, keep your body language open and welcoming, and be kind to those you meet. When you are open and approachable, it becomes easier for you to increase your ability to connect with others. These connections and the relationships you may gain from them can teach you an incredible amount about yourself, who you are, and why you are that way. Relationships and connections with other humans are a great opportunity to learn more about ourselves and to develop ourselves beyond where we have already grown.

Gain Perspective

If you have ever heard the phrase "put yourself in their shoes", then you likely know the importance of being able to see things from someone else's perspective. A great way to develop your emotional intelligence and create stronger relationships is to set the intention to gain perspective. Instead of delaying until an issue arises or having someone else need to point this out for you, gain perspective simply because you are curious. Seek to learn more about how other people view the world around them.

When you intentionally learn more about other people's perspective, and you are willing to see things from their angle without having to be asked, you increase your empathetic abilities. It becomes easier for you to relate to other people, understand their opinions and interpretations of the world around them, and create stronger connections with them. It also helps inspire you to challenge your own beliefs and deepen your understanding of the world around you.

Be Curious About Others

Many individuals struggle to create connections because they do not know how to be curious about other people. As humans, especially when we are on a journey to understanding ourselves, we can find ourselves in a state of self-absorption. We may struggle to connect with others because we seem to lack interest in them. This can lead to us excessively talk about ourselves. This is not only ineffective in creating relationships, but it also stunts your growth.

Being curious about others and asking questions to learn more about them, is a way to deepen our connections, but also a way to create a stronger understanding of ourselves. When we are curious about others, it also turns into a curiosity about ourselves. We begin to learn more about life, ourselves, and others through the relationships we build with other people.

This does not mean that you should only talk about the other person. It merely means that you should consider developing a more even playing field. Ask as much as you share, and be curious as often as you reflect. Focus on creating a communication style that allows you to create a mutual relationship between yourself and others- one where you learn as much as they do and you are both engaged in the connection.

Do Not Be Afraid to Be First

If you are having difficulty being open in relationships, chances are, you have difficulty being the first one to spark a conversation or create a connection as well. If you genuinely want to practice developing your emotional intelligence in a personal setting, take some time to practice being the first person to open conversations and start-up relationships. The world is filled with people who are uncertain about how to approach other people. Social media and the internet brought changes to the way our social skills are developed, which can deeply inhibit our emotional intelligence.

Spending some time learning to open conversations, being open and friendly, and developing relationships with other people are important. This will teach you how to be more charismatic and friendly, but it will also teach you a lot about yourself. You will begin to learn how to approach certain people, which types of engagement are appropriate for each unique setting, and how you can break the ice with different personality types. These practices are a great way to understand yourself deeper and will help you discover what kinds of personalities you get along with the most.

Reduce Time on Social Media

The amount of time that the average person spends on social media is incredibly high. This time may seem harmless to you, but the reality is that it can inhibit your social skills. The way that we communicate online is extremely different from how we communicate in person. If your connections are predominantly online, it can create a challenge for you in learning how to start conversations, carry conversations in the real world, read people in person, and gauge situations. Emotions are not communicated by the internet as easily as they are in person. The internet can be completely void of emotion or can include highlighted feelings or outright lies.

Learning to move your communications to a more face-to-face approach will support you in being able to read other people easier. You will be able to identify what various body languages mean, the 'vibe' of the situation, and additional information that can support you in understanding everything you are interpreting from the other person. Being able to understand and process this information will have a powerful impact on your ability to interpret, experience, and reflect emotions in personal settings.

Practice Your Emotional Intelligence

Like any other skill you may desire to develop in your life, nothing is as powerful as practice. Taking the time to practice your emotional intelligence skills by applying the practices you have learned in this book will significantly increase your emotional intelligence overall. While consuming content and information, learning through intellect is valuable in supporting your growth, it will only get you so far. The real way to develop emotional intelligence is to apply the practices into your life.

The best way to practice enforcing emotional intelligence in your life and relationships is through choosing a few practices and mastering those before moving on to new ones. Attempting to master too many emotional intelligence practices all at once, will likely result in you feeling confused and overwhelmed. You may struggle to apply anything, increase your stress levels, and reduce your chances of success. Instead, take your time, be patient with yourself, and set realistic goals. Discover which areas you could use the most practice in and focus on starting in these areas. Then, you can begin to expand out to new practices.

Consider developing your emotional intelligence to be a process. This is something you can practice and refine for the rest of your life. The more you take your time and invest in each step, the more you stand to gain from it all. Be realistic and gentle with yourself. Make use of this move to strengthen a personal relationship with the real you.

Network Often

Networking is a great way to develop relationships with other people. When you regularly attend networking events or opportunities, you open yourself up to the opportunity to practice opening up new conversations, connecting with many different personality types, and learning new perspectives. Networking is truly beneficial on so many levels.

The best way to begin practicing networking is to look up local networking events in your area. There are networking events for virtually everything. You can join a networking event about crafting or dogs, one that is related to your career or a specific interest or hobby you have. Starting at events that are relevant to the information you know about or are interested in is a great way to get started. This way, you already know at least one thing you share in common with the other people at the event. Breaking the ice becomes easier, meaning developing your social skills and increasing your emotional intelligence through socializing becomes easier as well.

Pay Attention to Your Tone

Your voice tone when communicating, as well as the way you present yourself in communication, can say a lot. These two levels of communication can result in us sending the right message or the wrong message to the person we are communicating with. When people lack emotional intelligence, their words may be engaged as interested, but their tone of voice and body language may come across as sarcastic, rude, or uninterested. If your words are contradicted by your tone of voice and body language, you are going to struggle to have strong communications with other people.

When you are communicating, practice using a tone of voice that accurately reflects what you are saying. Furthermore, make sure that this tone of voice is natural and does not sound forced. Attempting to manipulate a tone of voice that is not coming out naturally can actually make you seem less approachable and even contradictory. Instead, focus on projecting your true emotions into your voice. This is a wonderful way to infuse your tone of voice naturally with the emotions you are genuinely experiencing; it will help you come across more open and friendly.

In a situation where you are upset or where you disagree with the other person, refrain from projecting too much anger in your voice. This can quickly come off as aggressive and hostile. Focus on keeping your voice even and fair, and use your words to communicate your feelings at this point.

When it comes to body language, you may benefit from reading a book specifically about body language, or otherwise engaging in learning specifically about body language. Body language is a vast form of communication that every human use. It can have a great impact on how you are received by others, whether or not they are consciously aware of these receptions. Furthermore, it can support you in reading others as well. Remember, our bodies say a lot about our emotions. Learning to read others' body language, and to use your body language as a tool for communication, can increase your emotional intelligence and magnify your social skills with others.

Intimacy

When it comes to personal relationships, your feelings and emotions come first. Any idea or feeling when not expressed does not have any value.

Role of EQ in Intimacy

EQ is an ability to understand and act upon others' and one's own feelings or emotions. What has it to do with intimacy? Let us consider a situation; you come home after a long stressful day, and you expect a calm and peaceful night. Your husband or wife is in a terrible mood and needs a person to talk with. He/she is continually trying to talk about the topic you want to avoid. The normal output would be shouting or yelling that you are in a bad mood or cut short the conversation by saying that you are not ready to talk about it now. A person with high EQ would try to shift the topic to a related or less stressful topic. The person may either ask to take a break by taking him or her out for a talk, along with dinner. This would ease off both.

EQ would help to be aware of the emotions at the moment and manage it, in the right way. It also helps to understand other people's emotions and work accordingly. If things don't turn out well, he should be able to be resilient within a very short period, without holding grudges or an ego. He should be able to communicate effectively.

How to express intimacy?

There is no one line answer stating that by doing so, anyone from any part of the world can show intimacy with another person. The ways of expressing intimacy differ from one person to the other. One of my friends touches his partner's nose and wiggles with his nose. However, if I do so, my partner would think that there is something wrong with his nose. For another friend, sitting on the deck with a cup of coffee and talking about all that happened during the day is called intimacy.

In short, intimacy is the way to express that you like them and you are comfortable being with them. This can be expressed in words but, not completely. You should be able to manage your emotions. You should be able to control your anger, force out a real smile or act surprised when she gives you a small gift, to increase intimacy.

Emotions and Intimacy

A friend of mine and his partner went to a club. The club was very crowded as it was New Year's Eve. He was constantly holding her hand and frequently looking into her eyes. This indicates that he is there for her and the staring made her feel comfortable.

There are a lot of differences between a tight hug and a little hug kind of action. The tight hug would mean that you missed her or you do not want to move away from her. A hug like action would say that you have hugged her for the sake of doing so.

Watching his eyes while talking or holding her shoulder while she talks about her rough childhood or smiling to assure that you are there for him/her would all increase the intimacy. Moreover, when it comes to intimacy, managing bad emotions are more essential than expressing positive emotions. For instance, you are angry at him, for a certain reason. You can either spit it out or wait till the moment passes and talk when the air is clear.

What to do When You Were Wrong

The best way is not to blame or to find fault with your partner. For instance, if she is angry that you are not organized, it is not right to pinpoint the things she is not good at. You can;

- Apologize for the time-being even if you are wrongly accused and then talk about it later.

- Let her spill out everything and then ask her ways to help you rectify it.

- If you have a valid point, wait till she completes. Reply in a soft voice. Yelling loud will not prove you are innocent.

- If your partner is deeply hurt, try to cool her off with small gifts or apologetic letters or anything that would make her smile a little.

- Make sure you admit that it's your fault.

What to Do When Your Partner Does Something Wrong?

Remember not to take advantage of the situation just because your partner has committed a mistake. When your partner is wrong;

- Talk to him/her and explain what's bothering you. Explain what can be done and how much you are willing to adjust.

- If your partner is not ready to listen, wait till the moment has passed and talk about it another time when you are both in a good mood.

Even if after continuous explanation your partner is not ready to rectify, there are two options: one is to live with it and the second is to explain how much you are affected by it and what would happen if the process continues.

Fighting and name calling will not solve any problem without causing a lot more to deal with. Remember people make mistakes and they tend to make the same mistake more than once. Just because they committed the same mistake after you explained all the points, does not mean that they ignore you. When they are afraid or sorry for making the mistake, it indicates that they care about you and do not want you to get hurt by any means.

Chapter 10:
How to Handle Conflicts the Right Way

Another aspect of strong social skills is the ability to manage conflict, both at home and in the workplace. Conflict can often seem to come out of thin air can't it, and if you're one of those people who prefers to ignore it, well, stop! Let's face it most conflict doesn't miraculously go away. It festers and grows until something breaks, often relationships.

A good conflict manager will bring the disagreement out into the open, encourage the sharing of emotions and open discussion, reduce any hidden issues, aid both parties in recognizing each other's feelings and encourage them to recognize logical positions. They will try to seek win-win solutions, where both parties feel they have earned something from the exchange.

Tips for Handling Conflict
Probably the easiest model for handling conflict is the straightforward model below:

Describe the Situation, Express Your Feelings, Ask for What You Would Like Done
A couple of quick pointers:

If you're an active participant in the disagreement, take the time to cool down before tackling the problem. Vent if you need to, rant too, talk to a friend, but identify and deal with your emotions first. If someone around you is heated, take the time to calm them down first. Do this before your email your boss back or remind your significant other that you care for them before complaining about something.

Address the problem when you are both calm. The first thing you should do is to identify what the conflict is and make sure you and the other person (or the interested parties, if you're the mediator) agree on what the problem is. This is where describing the situation in our model above comes in. You'd be amazed how many times two people in a conflict can disagree on the cause or the problems arising from it.

Ideally, propose solutions that are mutually beneficial (the win-win I talked about earlier) and be sympathetic if the other person is unwilling to concede certain things (though stand firm on your own issues too).

Try to end on a co-operative note, even if you can't agree on all points. Demonstrate to your boss or co-worker, for instance, that you want to work towards the same goal even if you disagree on how to get there. Let your wife, husband or significant other know that you will try to work on the issues he or she has raised even if you can't agree to them all. Relationships, whether at home or in business, work best when the people involved believe they are on the same page, with the aim of achieving the same goals.

I followed the model above with two of my team when conflicts arose at work. Both seemed to get on okay while I was in the office, but when I left – and my second-in-command deputized for me – communication and teamwork broke down. Both complained about the other, yet I knew that both were at the top of their game, so what happened when I was out of the office?

The first time it occurred I dealt with it independently, speaking to the two of them separately, but it happened again. Soon both started sniping at each other, and I knew I couldn't allow it to go on any further. I worked off-site at our second site a lot and relied on Mark to keep the team productive in my absence.

I called a meeting with the pair of them, warning them ahead of time that we were going to deal with the conflict professionally and calmly, with no raised voices.

I set out the game plan from the start. Victoria, the most junior, would go first as she was the one who effectively had the complaint, which was the way she was treated by my deputy when I wasn't in the room. She would have the opportunity to explain the situation and the conflict as she saw it and express her feelings, plus to say what she would like to see done differently. I made the point again that no-one would be attacked, and we would deal with the disagreement calmly.

I also made sure to tell Mark, my deputy, in front of Victoria, that he should listen to Victoria, consider if he agreed with the situation as she laid it out, and if not, to express his own view of the problem calmly and again without attacking. I stressed that he should apologize only if he felt he had done something wrong, but that he shouldn't be defensive and should be open to co-operation.

Victoria described the situation as she saw it. Effectively, it came down to Mark being overzealous with his deputy role, 'bossing' the team about unnecessarily, but also in part doing the job that he was hired to do. (The team were about to move to a different position in the media empire we worked in, and Mark had been employed to get them ready for a faster-more paced pressured role).

Mark listened to Victoria's complaints and was genuinely stunned by some of the examples that she gave of his behavior. Giving Mark props, he admitted he hadn't realized that some of his actions could be construed in the way that they had and he apologized for making Victoria feel that she couldn't be trusted with her work. That had never been his intention.

As per my instructions, however, he refused to apologize for being 'tough' on the team and pushing them to do better, pointing out that was why he was brought in. To do the hard job when I couldn't be in the office. As a mediator, I explained his role to Victoria more fully.

Victoria listened and appreciated the distinction but did point out that Mark was like two different people – when he was deputizing and when he wasn't. The conflict confused the team, and they never knew 'which' Mark they were getting. The jovial Mark who liked to joke and be one of the team, or the buttoned-up 'boss' Mark who micromanaged and never felt like anything was good enough.

Mark, of course, hadn't realized he acted any differently during those moments in charge and I hadn't been around to see them. Faced with specific examples from Victoria, however, he accepted the point was well made and pledged to find a happier, common ground. He was open to change but assertive enough to point out that he was still in charge when deputizing and wouldn't apologize for pushing the team when he felt it was needed.

Victoria respected that, and indeed I could see her respect for Mark grow from that day on. She left the meeting happy that she had been listened to.

Subsequently, Mark and I worked on his issues, specifically his confusion over his role when I was and wasn't in the office. When I was there to lead the team, for instance, where did he stand? We helped him to find a position of authority that didn't ebb and flow according to the situation each day.

Mark and Victoria never had any issues after that; in fact, they became close friends. That meeting, while challenging as a mediator and even more daunting as a participant, was the best conflict management tool we could have used.

The idea in any conflict management situation is to be assertive without being aggressive. Indeed, assertiveness is probably the most important skill in conflict management. Active listening is also crucial to ensure you understand the positions of those involved in the conflict, whether you are the mediator or an active participant.

You will need the ability to recognize emotions in others (and ideally be able to point out to others when the emotions are okay to express or when they are inappropriate. Empathy is also an extremely beneficial skill.

Be aware of the way you solve a conflict in your personal life and at work. When conflict resolution seems like a tedious, hostile, or unpleasant situation, it shows that the techniques being used are ineffective. The best thing that you can do if you are struggling with conflict resolution is to set aside time to practice. Below, you'll find some techniques that you can use to help solve conflicts in a positive way.

Solve Imaginary Conflicts
Think of scenarios, either real-life or made-up and try to come up with a solution. Write down the problem, as well as the needs of all the parties involved. Then, try to come up with a solution that fulfills the needs of all parties involved. Practice explaining this situation as you would when speaking to someone who

is potentially upset. Explain your point and emphasize that you have taken their needs into clarification. If they are dissatisfied, re-evaluate the solution or ask more about the other person's specific needs so you can reach a solution that appeases all parties. As you continue to practice and become more aware of the emotions of yourself and the people around you, conflict resolution and problem-solving will become significantly easier.

As you solve conflicts in your personal relationships, you will find that healthy, constructive relationships bring you closer to the other person instead of pushing you away. By positively resolving conflict, it shows that you trust the other party enough to let them be an active part of the conflict resolution process. When solutions are reached without either party being punished, threatened, manipulated, or neglected in some way, it brings about a sense of safety and creativity. In a work environment, you will be seen as someone who prioritizes finding a solution and people may turn to you for advice, as you are capable of rationally viewing all sides of the situation before coming up with a solution.

Describe Problems and Conflicts Using 'I' Statements

'I' statements are designed to help other people understand how you are feeling. They are designed to be non-threatening and open up the channels of communication. Rather than assigning blame, using 'I' statements allow you to describe your personal impact as a result of the problem. It is a way to communicate what you are feeling without assuming the other person has intentionally hurt you.

The basic template that you can use to form an 'I' statement is '"I feel... when you... because..." This identifies the problem clearly, as well as the reason that you are impacted by it. Imagine that your spouse is a bartender and it upsets you. Instead of continuing to feel negative emotions like insecurity and anger each time that they go to work, a better approach is to address the issue. You might say, "I feel upset when you flirt with people at work because it makes me feel like you are not committed to our relationship." This formula assigns blame where it belongs—on their position as a bartender and your insecurity in the relationship. Instead of feeling like you are accusing them or blaming them, they may reassure you of their commitment or explain their reasoning for flirting. This opens up both sides of the discussion and allows both of you to share, which is a wonderful place to begin at when you are trying to reach a compromise.

Solving Conflict in the Workplace

Part of using emotional intelligence in the workplace is exhibiting your leadership skills and your ability to resolve conflicts. Many of the skills addressed earlier can also benefit the way you interact with people in the workplace. By learning to read the emotions of people around you, you can effectively manage people in a work environment. You can also learn how to communicate your needs more effectively in a way that encourages people to do what you want.

Even when people work well together, the work environment can bring about competitiveness as people want to stand out. When working in groups, this desire to shine and the difficulty in admitting flaws can make group work difficult. As a rational thinker, you have better insight to lead the group to a collaborative solution. For example, you might have everyone write their ideas down. Then, each of them can be presented and discussed in turn. At the end of the discussion, the best idea can be chosen and altered to fit the group's needs, or a few different ideas can be combined.

Be Clear When Communicating Your Needs

One of the biggest obstacles to a seamlessly flowing workplace is miscommunication. When managers and employees are not clear about the things that they need, it leads to disappointing results that reduce morale. Instead of leaving things to chance, be clear about the things that you need. You might find that it is better to use e-mail for communication than spoken word since it serves as a record of what is required. You can also encourage people to question you when they do not understand. Not only does this invite collaboration and help employees get the task done right the first time, but it also clarifies areas of communication where you may still be struggling.

Find the Right Attitudes about Conflict

People who avoid conflict may have bad experiences with disagreements in the past or they might worry about maintaining a healthy relationship after conflict. However, conflict is inevitable — no two people will have the same needs, desires, and goals at every moment of their life. Having the right attitude toward conflict means having a confident mindset when it comes to finding a solution. As you develop your emotional intelligence skills, you will find that you also increase your abilities to solve conflicts confidently.

Ridding Your Mind of Irrational Bias

Bias is something that clouds judgment. It may cloud judgment positively or negatively, affecting the way that you evaluate others and the efforts that you put forth in your relationship with them. By using the following strategies, you can become aware of possible bias in the way you view others.

Jumping into conclusions is very easy, especially since our subconscious mind is trained to look for patterns that it recognizes from other life experiences and relay that information back to your brain. For example, someone who has been cheated on in a previous relationship may have a hard time trusting. When their current partner distances themselves for the week before their birthday, they may assume the worst. Likewise, someone who is friends with their boss may become worried when their boss does not greet them as they customarily do in the mornings. In these two scenarios, this can cause them to assume their partner is cheating or that they did something that disappointed or angered their boss. However, the reality may be that their partner is busy working extra hours or planning a surprise for their upcoming birthday or that their boss just received bad news and is not feeling social that day.

When you assume things, you give yourself a limited window to see things. This can apply to certain scenarios like those addressed above, as well as general assumptions that you make about someone's personality. For example, a woman in the business field might come across as cold, which discourages employees from approaching her to ask for help. However, she may be trying to come across as strong. The coldness that she puts off may not be her personality at all — but a way of appearing strong in a male-dominated world of business. By assuming this woman is cold, employees may not ask questions, so they may not benefit from the knowledge she has to offer. It can also cause problems with communication in the business world.

Even though emotional intelligence makes it more likely that you will make accurate assumptions about people based on their language, body language, and non-verbal communication, it is still possible to find yourself biased because of the subconscious mind. Instead of jumping to conclusions within the first few minutes of meeting somebody, take the time to look for additional clues that help indicate someone's personality.

Push Those around You to Do Better

True leaders understand that their success is a reflection of the people that work for them. When all the employees in an organization are collaborating together, it uplifts the entire organization. The best companies to work for are those that take an interest in their employees. Countless studies have proven that employee happiness and productivity contribute to company success. As a leader in the workplace, you should help motivate the people around you to do better.

As an emotionally intelligent person, you should feel confident in your position in the workplace. The employees that work under you are not trying to take your job — they are simply trying to be the best that they can. The first step to encouraging employees to be better is identifying their strengths and weaknesses. Pay close attention to the way that they work with people around them and what their body language says about their relationship. Notice when they communicate well and areas where employees could improve. Then, encourage the employees to do tasks that challenge their weaknesses. For example, have two people who do not collaborate well work with a member of management on a project to practice those skills. As they learn to collaborate, their usefulness to the work environment also increases.

Evaluate Your Ability to Solve Problems

To evaluate your problem-solving capabilities, think back to the last time you disagreed with someone. What was the end result? Were you satisfied at the end of the conflict? Did you have your own needs met? Did you take the time to understand the other person's needs and find a solution that left everyone satisfied?

By analyzing the way that you solve conflicts, both at home and in the workplace, you can get a clearer picture of your strengths and faults when it comes to problem-solving. Some common problems that people face are not being able to come up with a creative solution that makes everyone happy, having difficulty communicating their own needs or having trouble understanding the needs of the person they are having a conflict with.

Chapter 11:
Learn to Forgive

How to Forgive Yourself and Forgive Others

We've all made mistakes. There is nobody who can go through life claiming they have never made a mistake since the day they were born. You should embrace the art of forgiving yourself first before you can begin forgiving others. Accept your imperfections because you know those can always be improved.

Holding onto your past and repeatedly beating yourself up over it isn't going to change a thing because it has already happened. You're only human, and if you can accept other people for their flaws, you can certainly start accepting yourself too. Forgiving yourself is the simple part of the process; forgiving others is harder to wrap your head around. When someone has hurt us, especially if the hurt runs deep, it can be hard just to let go and let things go back to the way they were. Sometimes even the thought of the incident that happened is enough to bring all those feelings of hurt flooding right back into your mind, even if it is something that happened years ago.

Steps of forgiving those who hurt you in the past may include:

- **By Moving On** – We know this is easier said than done, but it is the only way to begin learning to forgive. Realize that holding onto the past is only hurting you, not them. You are the one that is affected by it. Your emotions are the ones being tormented over the thought of it. However, much you place your thoughts on it, it is never going to change what happened. No amount of dwelling on the past ever will. The best thing for you is just to learn to let go, leave the past behind where it belongs and focus on looking ahead, the way emotionally intelligent people do.

- **Never Go to Bed Angry** – This is one exercise you should start adopting every night from now on. Make it a habit to never go to bed again with negative emotion. It is simply not worth it. If there is nothing you can do to change it, then let it be. Why torture your emotions anymore over something that is never going to change? It's an unhealthy habit. Do, watch or read something that lifts your spirits and puts you in a happy mood before going to bed every night. Remind yourself of all the things you have to be grateful for.

- **Accepting Responsibility** – When confrontations and conflicts occur, it takes two people to rock the boat. While the other person may have had a bigger part to play in the falling out, you were also partially responsible on some level. Being someone with high EQ means that you need to use self-awareness to assess the situation objectively, to be able to see what mistakes you made and how you could have handled that better. From there, accept responsibility for the part that you played, and realize that both people involved were at fault to a certain degree.

- **Choose to Be Kind Instead** – Do you have the desire to be right all the time? Even if it means jeopardizing a relationship because you stubbornly refuse to let go of the need to be right? Such could be the reason why you're finding it hard to forgive. Instead of choosing to be right all the time, choose the emotionally intelligent way. Choose to be kind. Being a kind person is much better than being someone who is 'right'" all the time.

Forgive in Order to Move Forward

There is a saying that says, "Screw me once and it is on me but screw me twice then it is on you." There exists another saying that states "choose your battles wisely." Both are sayings emotionally intelligent people have learned and have become aware of.

Forgiveness involves letting go of everything that happened, regardless of whether it is strike one or strike two.

Forgiving is necessary in order to move on; however, it in no way means that you are giving the other person another chance or the opportunity to chalk up another strike against you. Emotionally intelligent people recognize when it is necessary to 'get along' and move past another's mistake. However, EQ's also recognize when it is also necessary to keep the wrongdoers at 'arm's length' to control the potential harm that the wrongdoer is ever capable of repeating.

Emotionally intelligent people have learned that by not forgiving a perpetual wrongdoer, breeds unchecked and unnecessary emotions that can create unnecessary battles. Digging your heels in to fight a losing battle is counter-productive and can result in irreparable and avoidable harm. Knowing your emotions allows you to choose your battles wisely and enables you to stand your ground just as wisely.

Emotionally intelligent people also realize the counter-productiveness with hanging out with negative people; including those that choose to complain about things rather than advancing past those things.

Emotionally intelligent people care about people including those that complain. EQ's also know when to 'draw the line' by asking the complainer what their plans are for implementing chosen solutions.

Emotionally intelligent people will be the first to forgive others because they know that circumstances differ for everyone and there may have been reasons why someone did what they did. The world at large is much bigger than what goes on in your head and emotionally intelligent people know this. The reason I suggested meditation as the first step toward emotional intelligence is that it helps you to see things in perspective, slows down your anger and negative feelings and helps you to be able to assess each individual situation using something people don't seem to use much anymore – intuition. When you unlock your intuition, you can trust it because it is there to safeguard you and it helps you to be able to see beyond the obvious.

People who have a high level of emotional intelligence will be calm people who are not quick to judge others, who can forgive easily and who understand that their own actions actually dictate the outcome of a situation. They tend not to blame others but instead look into themselves to see what could be done to improve any given situation. That's the difference between them and ordinary people whose level of emotional intelligence is low.

Chapter 12:
Emotional Intelligence in Leaders

I'm going to discuss the role of Emotional Intelligence on leadership and professional work later in the chapter in more depth, but it's worth mentioning it here in brief now.

As Daniel Goleman said, *"People do not leave the company, people leave bad bosses."*

Strong Emotional Intelligence enables people to understand what motivates our staff and positively, helping to improve the bond. It's a misnomer that people are motivated by only money or recognition; motivation is much more complicated than that, driven from both the external and the internal. If, as a boss you can recognize a person's individual motivations, you can appeal to them in the most effective way.

An effective leader with strong EQ skills can also identify the needs of his people and address them in a way that boosts performance and workplace satisfaction. Recognizing people's emotions can also help a talented leader build a strong team taking advantage of the emotional range of the people around him.

Our Children

It's fair to say that we learn a great deal of our Emotional Intelligence in childhood because of interaction with our parents. It can start early in our formative years where consoling a crying child, for instance, teaches them they can trust you and the world around them and helps to ease their anxiety.

The tone your family sets around emotions can influence a child and follow them into adulthood. If emotions are something to be denied or shameful, it becomes extremely difficult for a child to learn how to identify and manage their own emotions, or how to respond to others'. They are much more likely to try to hide or dampen down their emotions, meaning they can grow up ending into adults who possess poor Emotional Intelligence.

According to child clinical psychologist, Dr. Tail Shenfield, the best way to help your child to learn strong Emotional Intelligence skills is to accept and acknowledge their emotions, both positive and negative, and to empathize with them. Talking about their feelings, as opposed to trying to distract or deny them, teaches them that emotions are okay. Giving them time to process and manage their emotions and giving them the means to do so (such as giving them the words they need to express themselves) will help them to develop a strong Emotional Intelligence.

A strong EQ will help your son or daughter in childhood as well as later in adulthood.

Relationship guru *Dr. Jeffrey Bernstein* says EQ is a key predictor of a child's ability to forge peer relationships, to bond with his or her family, to reach academic potential at school and to develop a well-balanced outlook.

A child who scores high on EQ usually has an even nature and an accurate outlook of themselves. As they grow older, they can work through age-related challenges and recover from setbacks, either alone or with help. In short, they will become much happier and healthier individuals; what more could we want for our children?

Of course, it's hard to do all the above without strong Emotional Intelligence skills of your own and you may be worrying whether yours are good enough. We all worry at times about failing our children but as I have said before and will keep repeating, the good news is that Emotional Intelligence can be learned.

Why are some individuals more successful than the rest? What is it that makes them leaders who stand out in the crowd? Their work ethic and personality could be contributing factors, but that is only part of the story. The other is the *emotional intelligence* that they possess. In simpler terms, think of EQ as being *street smart*. This is the quality that enables you to navigate through life effectively, and this is the exact quality that you need to develop if you want to find yourself in a leadership position one day.

A successful leader and manager are one that can bring out the best in everyone that they work with. When you have emotional intelligence, it shows. You're more confident, determined, passionate, hardworking, and flexible to the point that you can readily adapt when the situation calls for it. You think on your feet, recover quickly from stress, and remain calm even in the most challenging situations. Being a leader is not an enviable position. There's a huge responsibility that comes with it, and when something goes wrong, you are the one that people turn to for answers and solutions.

The Characteristics of Someone with High EQ

No firm succeeds without the right kind of leadership at the helm. Being a leader and being an effective and successful leader are two different things;

one is going to be the head of a company that will just be mediocre, but the other will head a company that is destined for success.

A leader with high emotional intelligence displays the following qualities:

- **They Love Meeting New People** – They have cultivated their curiosity to the point that they never shy away from meeting new people. In fact, they have come to love it. They ask many questions, make a person feel at ease and welcomed, exhibit empathy, and are attuned to the feelings of the other person – even if they may be strangers. This is what someone with high EQ looks like.

- **They Are Attentive** – High EQ individuals are not easily distracted. They are focused, and they can see the bigger picture. They rarely settle for instant gratification. They are attentive and present to their current situation, themselves, and the people that surround them. This is self-awareness in play. They can focus and concentrate on what they are supposed to do, and they do not stop until the goal has been accomplished – no matter the obstacle.

- **They Know Their Strengths** – High EQ enables the ability to be honest with yourself. Exceptional leaders know their strengths and weaknesses, and they embrace both of these with open arms. They don't make excuses for their weakness; they find ways to work on improving them. Not only can they identify their own strengths and weaknesses, but they can also do the same for others that they work with. In a team setting, they know how to identify each team member's area of strength and use that to benefit the team.

- **They Know Why They're Upset** – Leaders always know exactly what the emotional problem is. Not just in themselves, but in others too. This is because they have fine-tuned their self-awareness ability to recognize their emotions so well that they can always recognize *why* they may be upset. They have developed the ability to recognize these emotions as they come up and identify them accurately. Moreover, because they are emotionally intelligent, they can take a step back and make an objective reflection about how the emotion is affecting them.

- **When They Fall, They Rise Again** – A leader never gives up. It is the way that they deal with mistakes which says a lot about what high EQ can do for a person. They know that giving up is never an option, and they know what it takes to get back on the horse and keep marching forward. They are resilient, determined, and never entertain negative emotions because they know it is only a distraction. They never let their motivation dwindle, thanks to high EQ.

- **They Create a Safe Space** – Leaders understand that everyone needs to feel comfortable enough to voice their opinions and concerns. If they are having difficulty working with someone else, they need to feel comfortable enough to approach you – the leader – and bring up those concerns without worrying that there are going to be repercussions for themselves. As a leader, you need to establish yourself as a trustworthy figure and encourage an open-door policy among the people you are managing – encouraging them and making them feel safe whenever they approach you with a problem of their own (knowing that you won't use such information against them at any given moment).

How to Use Emotional Intelligence to Lead Effectively

A leader of a successful company is one that can effectively manage their team and bring out the best in everyone that is under their guidance. A successful leader and manager are one that can bring out the best in everyone that they work with. A good leader is one that knows how to spearhead the journey to success.

Use emotional intelligence to become an effective leader by:

- **Displaying Mutual Respect** – Respect is one of the major principles that absolutely must be present within a team and an organization. Respect among managers and co-workers is the glue that keeps the company successful, and without it, things can unravel really quickly. Use empathy, self-awareness and social skills to help you foster mutual respect. The best type of leaders are ones that provide a work environment where employees help each other and value the contributions that each individual makes. Effective leaders constantly encourage their peers to bring their A-game to work every day and help them overcome the challenges faced in the workplace without belittling them.

- **Welcoming Diversity** – If you want to be an effective leader that solves problems for good, you need to tailor your solutions depending on the person you are dealing with. Self- awareness, empathy and social skills again come into play here. Use this high EQ trait to treat the individuals in your team just as they are – individuals.

- **Effectively Managing Conflict** – If there is one thing that nobody wants to deal with, it is conflict, especially conflict in the workplace because it really brings down morale and leads to miserable staff if not dealt with accordingly. Nobody wants to deal with conflict, but as a leader, you are going to have to. A leader with high EQ is going to depend on empathy, self-regulation, self-awareness, and social skills to help them with this. An effective leader will never turn a blind eye to conflict and will do everything in their power to address the conflict as soon as it rears its ugly head and resolve it in the most amicable way possible.

- **Engaging with People** – When you engage with your team members, as a leader, you need to go the extra mile and make a connection with each member of your team. This helps build a relationship that is meaningful and shows your team members you genuinely care about them and their welfare – not just because it is part of your job to do so. Rely on social skills, empathy, and self-awareness for this category.

- **Recognize Each Person for What They Are** – In a work environment especially, sometimes a leader can be so focused on expecting employees to be more like them that they forget to appreciate what makes that employee unique. There is nothing that de-motivates a team quicker than feeling like they are not appreciated. When they start to feel de-motivated, they begin to lose the passion and the drive to really strive to perform. An effective leader will use their emotional intelligence skills (social and empathy) to recognize each employee's contribution and work with them on developing their individual strengths. They recognize each employee for what they are, and they never expect them to be something that they are not.

- **Making Trust a Priority** – Without trust, there is no possibility of working together well. For a leader to be considered successful, they must cultivate an environment of trust at all times. You are leading others who have placed their faith in you, and you should return that faith by being as transparent, honest and open as possible. Use social skills and empathy as your guiding points, learn how to read the emotions of others well, and you will have no problems making trust a priority.

- **Being Empathic Always** – A successful leader is one who can practice empathy and compassion with sincerity. High EQ skills will enable you to do this. People are more acute at spotting insincerity than you think, no matter how good of an actor you think you are. Part of being a transparent leader means being honest not just verbally, but also with your feelings too.

- **Listening Actively** – A successful leader is one that has learned to listen intently, and not just to what the person has to say, but beyond that. For example, when having a one-on-one conversation, listen to the voice inflections, the tone of the person's voice, which words they emphasize on, and how they sound when they are expressing what they feel. This is where empathy is going to play a huge role because it is a valuable high EQ skill which is going to help you really connect with the person you're speaking to. Be emphatic towards them, compassionate, understanding and nurturing appropriately. Don't just listen to what they are saying, but listen to what they are trying to tell you and tune in to them in a way many leaders fail to do today.

How Emotional Intelligence Can Increase Your Chances of Success

To improve the quality of your life, you need to have emotional intelligence on your side. This is the key trait of making a difference. No shortcuts. No secret weapons. No magic formulas. Just developing high levels of EQ.

To achieve success in general, here is how EQ is going to play a huge role in helping you achieve that. How often have you set goals, raised the bar, and had big dreams only to have life getting in the way? Your emotions get worked up through stress, and all your initial desire to succeed just comes crashing to a halt. When someone lacks EQ, they tend to become more reactive than proactive. They are unable to adapt to the situations as they come. The experiences affect them more than they should, and they become far too overwhelmed by the wave of emotions that crash around them. This is precisely why you need EQ.

EQ trains you to manage your emotions in healthy ways. It enables you to reign in impulsive behaviors, manage your expectations and adapt to the unexpected that happens. This is how you succeed. The ability to understand your emotions is half the EQ battle, and if you can achieve this portion, you've already won (almost). The other half is, of course, learning how to understand and manage the emotions of other people. Obstacles are the biggest reason many fail to reach the goals they have set, because the challenges, the setbacks, disappointments, and failure can often strip you of the will you need to keep going – especially if you don't know how to regulate your emotions.

Here are other ways emotional intelligence can increase your chances of success:

- **It Helps You Predict Performance** – EQ has a significant impact on success because it helps you focus on results which matter. When you focus on the results, your performance is instantly given a boost, and thanks to self-awareness, you will be able to predict your actions and reactions to the situations you may be facing.

- **It Leaves No Room for Negativity –** When you've got high EQ, there is no room for any element that threatens success. Negativity becomes a thing of the past.

- **It Makes You Hungry for Success –** As we have already established, high EQ individuals never lose sight of their motivation, and they use their self-awareness and self-regulation to manage their emotions when they are faced with difficult circumstances. This ensures that the desire to quit is never stronger than the desire for success.

- **It Helps You Be Mindful –** It helps one to become aware of their thoughts and be in control.

- **It Helps You Minimize Stress –** With so much internal burden to carry around, how would you focus on achieving success? This is why high EQ makes a difference – because of how it helps you regulate your emotions and manage them properly. Minimizing your stress means you will now have the mental clarity that is needed to start thinking about the next step you need to take.

- **It Improves Your Self-Esteem –** Something that so many of us struggle with. It is impossible to succeed with low self-esteem because you simply do not believe in yourself enough. Possibly one of the best benefits of improving your EQ is how much it is going to improve your self-esteem in the long run. When you begin to continually pursue betterment in your life, you'll find more things to be happy about, which leads to higher levels of satisfaction – improving the way you feel about yourself and thereby enhancing your self-esteem. The constant pursuit of betterment is an example of you succeeding in life in general.

- **It Makes It Easier to Spot Opportunities** – Being self-aware has so many benefits, and not just because it helps you manage your emotions better. When you are more attuned to your surroundings, yourself and the people around you, it becomes easier to notice the opportunities that you may not otherwise have spotted. Negativity and a lack of EQ often cloud our judgment and perception, which is why successful people strive to develop emotional intelligence skills for themselves, so their eyes will be opened to start noticing solutions rather than problems.

- **It Empowers You** – As you learn to manage your emotions better, you start regaining confidence in yourself once more. As your confidence and self-esteem improve, with each challenge you successfully overcome with self-awareness and self-regulation, empathy, motivation, and social skills, you'll find yourself becoming more empowered, stronger, and capable of absolutely anything you set your heart and mind to. You feel like there is nothing that will hold you back, as you see each goal you set materialize before you when you smash through them, and this will serve as your fuel when your build momentum towards transforming your life.

- **It Makes You a Better Version of Yourself** – When you've adopted all the core principles that make high EQ such a desirable trait, without even realizing you're going to put in the effort to become better than what you are right now. You'll start focusing on having a passion and a purpose, and you take the necessary steps that you need to improve the things that you don't want in your life. This is what it means to be successful, to become the best version of yourself that you can possibly be.

- **It Helps You Stay Committed to the End** – Giving up is no longer an option because you've learned how to regulate your responses whenever that feeling arises. When you set a goal with high EQ, you're not only creating a goal; you're committing to seeing it through. This commitment is exactly what helps you stay productive because you're able to regulate your emotions to control your reactions and your outcome. Success would not be possible without the desire to be committed to the end.

Chapter 13:
Myths Debunked

The False Ideas You Need to Shed About Being an Empath

There are so many myths and false concepts that have circulated over the years around being an empath and I feel many of these ideas actually make it hard for us to live empowered lives. Let's start debunking a few of these and see if any of them hit a nerve for you.

False Idea #1: Is being an empath a totally spiritual thing?

This is definitely a basic misconception that segregates empaths. While the lines do sometimes cross over between science and spirituality, you absolutely don't need to be spiritual, religious or a spiritual healer to be an empath.

My Truth:

Scientific research has proven the existence of empaths. To be fair, this is a very new study in the world of science and we barely understand the neurology behind empathy in general. But new research is surfacing supporting the existence of empaths. Though we still have a long way to go, findings are showing between one and two percent of the population does report experiencing conditions associated with being empathic.

And the fact still holds true. My brain will demonstrate empathic abilities whether I'm spiritually inclined or not. Therefore, understanding empaths isn't supposed to be some esoteric wishy-washy impractical thing.

False Idea #2: Are empathic abilities a disorder or mental illness?
While it is true that we often get hit with overwhelming situations and scenarios that leave us feeling physically sick, it is certainly not true that empaths suffer from mental disorders or anything of that kind.

My Truth:
The emotions and physical sensations you have are nothing to be ashamed of. There is nothing wrong with you! You are not sick or crazy.

Let me say that again...

Don't be put to shame or feel less than because you possess abilities to perceive far greater things than the general public. The human population has become so desensitized it's easier to label and categorize those groups of people that don't fit into the model view of the status quo such as empath who possess powers of higher perception.

False Idea #3: Does being an empath mean you're weak and playing the victim?
Emotions are for wimps and overly sensitive people. I bet you've heard that all your life. This false belief has been pervading human consciousness for centuries. Showing your emotions is often seen as a sign of weakness. A lot of people assume that empaths are weak, powerless and co-dependent on others. Many believe empaths live in a state of victimhood always fearful of the world around them.

Revealing to people your truth and what you can sense in them is so scary for people that are disconnected from their own emotions, they often call you a freak. Perhaps this is why most empaths become recluse.

My Truth:
All these misconceptions are generalized biases and nothing close to the truth. The fact that we can quickly process emotions and sensations that the majority of the population does not understand doesn't mean we are weaker. If anything, we pay more attention to the feelings of others and pay a lot of attention to how we treat others. There's no need for you ever to justify or get offended when someone rejects who you are. Just remember for most people, your way of being is incomprehensible and illogical to their mind.

When it comes to taking responsibility, bouncing back from challenges and working hard to make a difference, empaths perform just as well as any other human being. An empath can be just as strong, responsible and successful in the world as anyone else, so don't let other people's limitations or fears cause you to settle for anything less than what your heart desires.

False Idea #4: Are all empaths introverts?
It appears to be that most empaths happen to be introverts but this is certainly not true across the board.

My Truth:
Individuals bearing all kinds of characteristics will possess empathic abilities. Don't feel like you have to 'fit' into a particular category of anything in order to exercise your empathic gifts. You can be an extrovert, introvert, ambivert or none of the above and still be an empath.

The idea of introversion as a pre-requisite for being termed an empath is simply not true.

Now that you've shed some of the false notions that may have played a role in constricting you, take a moment to see if any other myths come up. I encourage you to write them down on a piece of paper and right next to them write your truth. Convert all the active false beliefs in your mind about what it means to be an empath into constructive ideas that will nourish a healthy mindset.

Conclusion

Emotional intelligence is something that can be cultivated simply by stopping and thinking as you go about your life. Be more aware of your own emotions and the emotions of the people around you. When you are stressed or experience conflict, learn to pinpoint the root cause of the problem and then work to find a solution.

As you hone your emotional intelligence skills, you will find that the quality of your relationships and your role at work starts to change. As you identify the things that you need, as well as the things that the people around you need, you will find a better sense of balance in life.

With conscious effort, your emotional intelligence will rise naturally. Even confirmatory tests, you will notice the difference in the way that you think and feel. You will also notice a difference in your relationships with your coworkers, friends, and family members.

Best of luck on your journey to higher emotional intelligence and self-improvement!

The Social Anxiety and Shyness Solution

Learn How to Be Yourself and Talk to Anyone by Improving Your People & Conversation Skills to Influence & Win Friends (It's OK Not to Be Nice)

Chapter 1:
Eliminate Social Anxiety in Less Than 60 Seconds

Lots of individuals recognize social anxiety disorder as social phobia. One of the core features that define it is the fear of rejection in performance or a social scenario, being evaluated negatively, or being judged.

Individuals who are dealing with a social anxiety disorder may worry about seeming noticeably anxious or being categorized as boring, silly, or strange. Due to this concern, these individuals often stay away from performance or social situations. However, when they are unable to avoid a situation, they deal with intense distress and nervousness.

Lots of individuals suffering from social anxiety disorder also deal with physical symptoms. These could range from sweating and nausea to an elevated heart rate. They may also deal with these symptoms when dealing with a situation they fear.

Although these individuals understand that the fear, they are experiencing is not reasonable, they usually feel helpless against their anxiety.

Social anxiety disorder tends first to present itself in adolescence. Even though people diagnosed with this condition frequently report that they dealt with excessive shyness during their childhood, it is crucial to understand that this disorder is not just intense childhood shyness that has not been appropriately treated.

Mastering Your Mind

To overcome social anxiety and shyness, the first thing you need to do is to become the master of your mind. There are various ways to become the master of your mind. Here are some easy steps to take:

Listen to What Your Mind Has to Say

Listening is the first step to becoming the boss in any scenario. To be a good boss to your employees, you must listen to them. The same also applies when establishing yourself as the master of your mind.

As you listen, you also begin to acknowledge the things that the mind has been doing for you. Show a sign of gratitude for all its efforts in the past.

Come to Terms with Your Mind

The same way you cannot build a business without the help of others; you cannot survive without your mind. As a result, you need to accept the fact that you both need one another and are going to be together for life.

This step will allow you to accept the negative thoughts that you experience, so you do not waste willpower and energy trying to deny it.

Take Time to Study Your Mind

Using the art of mindfulness, you will be able to follow your mind as it moves from one thought to the other and learn how to focus the mind on a task.

What Can Social Anxiety Disorder Cause?

Social anxiety disorder can result in damage to the lives of those experiencing it. For instance, a person may not accept an enticing job opening that would require him/her to interact with new people frequently. It may also result in individuals staying home, as opposed to heading out with friends, due to worry that while drinking or eating, they would be unable to stop their hands from shaking.

Symptoms can be so drastic that they could hamper an individual's daily life and can cause significant interference with social life, performance at work, or their daily routine. This would make it difficult to complete an interview, participate in school, or get a well-paying job. In some cases, it equally prevents people from having romantic relationships and friendships.

Individuals who are dealing with this condition also have more danger of attaining serious alcohol abuse and depressive disorders. Even with the range of effective treatments available, a minimal number of individuals with this condition seek treatment yearly.

Triggers of Social Anxiety Disorder

Social Anxiety Disorder is a psychological condition that can be triggered by various situations. It could be triggered when attention is centered on you, when you are to give a speech, or when people make fun of you. Basically, you are not entirely comfortable with making new friends.

People who suffer from social anxiety experience different kinds of triggers. When this happens, they prefer to be anywhere but in that place. "Illness of lost opportunities" - this is how psychologists define social anxiety disorder. This is because opportunities may present themselves in situations that you find strenuous, and as a result, these opportunities are never explored.

What Are the Symptoms of Social Anxiety Disorder?

Social anxiety can be experienced in various stages. Different individuals experience these stages differently. For some people, it is experienced right before social scenarios, and it could be the fear of meeting people, the fear of speaking, or the anxiousness of being in the same room with strangers.

Sometimes this anxiety presents itself during the event, where the person suffering from social anxiety is experiencing nervousness, an anxiety-attack, or discomfort. They desire to be anywhere but where they find themselves. For others, it is after the event. They generally worry retroactively about their performance and how people saw them, what happened, and how they messed up. They try to avoid reliving similar scenes, and as such, stay indoors or avoid experiencing situations they consider nerve-racking.

The first step to take is to narrow down your social anxiety behavioral pattern. You must be able to identify what is peculiar to you and what ticks you off so you can eliminate it. There are ways an individual who suffers from social anxiety have learned to cope with it. For some, they become rigid in their movement. For others, they indulge in bad habits like drugs or excessive alcohol use to stop feeling the way they do. Others make sure no one ever sees them in the front row, and they hide from the crowd. These adapted behaviors mostly do more harm than good. It offers a mirage of a solution that does not address the core problem.

The secret is to stop the pattern and try something different. At first, it might not be comfortable, but it is helpful. You will feel more in control when you use positive solutions to address your anxiety. The disadvantage of adapted behaviors is the control they have over you - and the belief that without them, you cannot overcome your anxiety. These behaviors are more negative than positive.

Getting Over Shyness and Social Anxiety

People with social anxiety seldom have a social life. The development of irrational anxiety over a social interaction is known as social anxiety. It is a mental health condition that often leads to a lonely environment for such individuals. They often worry, and are very nervous about, how people see them; therefore, they have a strong desire to stay by themselves away from any social gatherings.

Some of the effects are depression and lack of self-esteem. To deal with this condition, they resort to excessive alcohol consumption and are often under the influence of drugs.

People dealing with social anxiety are mostly seen as irrational. A person with a healthy mental mind cannot understand why it is difficult to interact with another person, so they often give advice such as, "You've got to let go," or, "You need to face your demons." Social anxiety patients might be quite aware of the irrationality in their behavior, but this doesn't help since they cannot do anything about it on their own.

Curing social anxiety is not something that is done overnight. It takes time, but with diligence, it can be contained, reduced, or overcome. There are people around us who live with this condition, and it could even be our family members or friends. If their situation is chronic, it is advisable to visit a physiologist or a therapist. A great benefit of this eBook is the inclusion of different methods one can try out to approach social anxiety:

Engage in Self-Love and Show Kindness to Yourself

The first step to consider when dealing with social anxiety is to have regard for your well-being and happiness. Put yourself first, and you must start mentally. There are times when you hear an inner voice that is always negative. It tells you how you are not good enough and how you do not deserve happiness.

You must understand that the power to change this narrative is in your hands. How do you do this? You talk back to that voice because all you hear are your fears and not the truth of your person.

So, here's a secret, when the negative inner voice talks to you, respond to it with exactly what it told you, but in a positive narrative. If your negative thoughts are about failures, respond with a situation when your failure gave you an insight into solving a problem.

You should also exercise self-love thrice a day, hug yourself, look at the mirror, and smile.

It sounds crazy, but it works! You must see through the negative voice that desires to diminish your uniqueness and embrace who you truly are.

There are times when you will be very nervous and shaky; it is normal, so do not quit on yourself. Take a deep breath, acknowledge the feeling, admit it, and move forward. It could be something else, but whatever you feel, realize this feeling. If you can accept it, it holds no power over you.

The Power of Positive Planning

Most times, social anxiety starts before the social gathering itself. How? The person is thinking and trying so hard to figure out how to fit in with the crowd, how to react to people, and how to respond during conversations. Just imagine the headache from having to figure all of that out even before the event.

The one true way to overcome, manage, or reduce social anxiety is by being an optimist and planning positively. If you are to plan the future social interactions with others at the event, think and act positively. If you must plan on what to say, believe that it will turn out well.

Sometimes, it makes it easier if you can own up to your feelings during a conversation. Simply telling the other person that you are a very shy person is another way of embracing your true self.

Your Small Successes Call for A Celebration

It is very easy to forget that you have made progress, such as when you successfully stay until the close of an event without running home or throwing up (yeah, it could be that serious). To make progress, it is important you take note of your little wins.

So, you should always celebrate whatever worked for you at a social gathering. It could be your ability to not spill a drink or that you were able to hold a conversation for 5 minutes or less. Whatever it may be, make sure you take note of them and celebrate them. Sensing you are making progress encourages you to want to try more.

Become Inquisitive

The genesis of social anxiety starts with this thought, "What will they think of me?" It then makes everything about you. How you interact with people, how well you perform in public and every other experience that follows.

The second step is to remove the focus from you! It shouldn't always be about you. It should be about the next person. Be curious about them. What are their areas of interest? What do they do? Do they like singing or watching movies?

When you successfully focus on the other person, you will enjoy having conversations with others. You can just listen to what they have to say, and you don't have to do the talking.

Step by step you will begin to enjoy the company of other people without the anxiety of trying to function in a socially acceptable way. Do not compare yourself to others. At the same time, do not judge others, as this will only make you anxious. Enjoy the uniqueness in our personalities and be entertained by it.

Build Confidence

Confidence has been said to mean, "the belief that anything is possible by taking action and by believing in oneself." Having confidence does not come easily to a person with social anxiety; therefore, it must be grown through practice.

You can build your confidence using various methods; it could be the way you dress, walk, or talk. If you are unsure of how to start, look out for people you admire and consider to be confident, then try to model after them.

Walk tall, talk naturally, and dress well. This will give you the needed boost to stand and interact with others. As I mentioned earlier, never compare yourself with another person, as you will lose confidence in yourself. Simply identifying areas where you know you have shortcomings and then following the steps of someone you admire can help.

So firstly, be natural, practice how to look confident in front of your mirror until you have a hang of it. As it is popularly said, fake it until you make it.

Simplest Tips to Eliminate Shyness In 60 Seconds
The tips below are applicable anytime you start to feel anxious or during a social situation.

Overcoming the Voice in Your Head
One of the reasons why a shy person will often have difficulties communicating in public is due to a shy voice in their head. If you are shy and you want to master your mind, then you need to overcome this shy voice. There are a few steps you can take which are discussed below:

Letting the Voice Know That You Are Up to The Task
One of the things that the shy voice in your head tries to do is to make you think you are not up to the task. If you fall for this trick, you begin to accept that you are not good enough. It may also bring up comparisons between you and close friends or family members.

If you keep waiting for external interference to tell you that you are capable of so much more, you may end up a failure. It is important you let the voice in your head know that you believe in your skills.

Overcome the Voice Through Failure and Growth
The only way to experience growth as a human is through failure. When you fail, you get feedback. The feedback helps you to understand the areas where you went wrong so you can make changes. By letting the shy voice realize that failure is part of the process, it becomes difficult to stop you from taking actions.

You will also gain more insight into the best ways to tackle future challenges.

The Importance of Saying Thank You

Appreciating someone is the best way to minimize their negativity towards you. The same also applies to the voice in your head. Since it is talking to you with negativity, saying thank you is a positive response to show you are not trying to fight the voice.

Identifying the positive intent of the voice is the first step. The voice may be telling you to avoid riding a bicycle because of the injury you sustained the last time. You can reply by saying "thank you for trying to keep me safe, but I have overcome my fear."

To apply this tip, create a list of the

As the voice slowly fades away, you will get the opportunity to take charge.

Show That You Can Step Out of Your Comfort Zone

The only way the voice in your head will win this battle is if you decide to stay in your comfort zone. Your ability to accept uncertainty and discomfort is one of the best ways to quiet the voice in your head.

It may merely be trying to prevent you from embarrassing yourself, but this will limit your chances of evolving.

Give Clear Details of Your Achievements

Why does this voice want you to believe you are not good enough?

It is merely because it believes that you have not made any positive progress. In truth, there are plenty of cases where you have been faced with adversity and come out on top. Let the voice know about all these cases.

Give Yourself A Period During Which You Don't Get to Do Anything

The main problem with social anxiety and shyness are the various thoughts running through your head. Your body will also be tempted to do something, anything at that moment, other than remain in the current situation.

To eliminate social anxiety quickly, the first step is to give yourself a brief period where you don't do anything either during a conversation or presentation. It is you falling into a worst-case scenario. It can be your worst-case scenario since it can be embarrassing when it seems like you don't have anything to say.

Once you can experience the worst-case scenario, you can eliminate the fear of failure.

When you are not doing anything, you don't talk or move. Just exist in a free form.

Preparation
Preparing beforehand can provide the boost you need to overcome any situation you find yourself in. It is an essential tool you have at your disposal as a person with social anxiety disorder.

The first thing you want to do is to commit yourself to the situation. Understand that you are unable to change what will happen. Accepting a situation will also help promote authenticity. You should also remind yourself of the reason for the interaction.

Other excellent ways to prepare yourself for whatever is going to happen is to read and write. Reading provides the inspiration you need while writing is a simple skill that can help unlock the real you. You can read on different topics such as history, cooking, or geography. As a result, you can improve your knowledge and vocabulary.

There are various things you may decide to write, and it may include different questions you expect to answer.

You should also find a way to calm the mind either by meditating or listening to music. You can also improve your energy levels by deciding to treat yourself when it is all over.

Chapter 2: Make A Kickass First Impression

It is called a first impression because you only have one chance to get it right. It also takes just a few seconds to fully assess a person you are meeting for the first time.

A first impression covers both the verbal and nonverbal aspects of an individual. By assessing these two aspects, an individual can decide if they like you or not.

Nonverbal Cues

Smile

Positivity is something you want people to link with your brand as well as yourself. There are various expressions that you can associate with positivity. The most common manifestation is a smile.

There are lots of features that are easy to notice when meeting a person for the first time. One of the features that leave a lasting impression is a great smile.

Smiling has excellent benefits. It has a positive influence on your health, as it minimizes stress hormones. It also creates more comfort when you are around others.

Just because you need to smile doesn't mean you should force it. You may be trying to hide your nervousness with a broad smile. A grin is also very inauthentic. A grin usually has one side of the mouth open to reveal the teeth at one corner. It can often be interpreted as a sign of arrogance.

A genuine smile which is also known as the "Duchenne" smile is appropriate. The Duchenne smile activates the zygomatic major muscle and the orbicularis oculi muscle that expand the cheek and form wrinkles around the eyes respectively.

A fake smile only activates the zygomatic major muscle since it is the only one that we can control voluntarily. It is the reason why it is possible to tell a fake smile by covering the mouth of an individual. There is no sign of the smile beyond the mouth area.

Your Handshake

When meeting someone for the first time, a handshake is a significant gesture. Through a handshake, you can exude confidence and appear to be a polite individual.

Getting the handshake right is also very important. Your handshake can create a lasting first impression on anyone you meet.

To give a proper handshake, there are things you should do and others you need to avoid.

The first thing you want to do is to ensure that your hand is in a straight position all through the process. Another good tip is to make direct eye contact with the other individual. This usually implies that you want to establish a connection.

The next and most crucial part of the handshake is the grip. Your grip should not be too firm, and it shouldn't be weak. It is also vital that you don't shake with sweaty palms. This will disgust the other individual. Two easy ways to deal with sweaty palms is to make use of antiperspirant lotion and to have an alcohol-based hand wipe within reach.

The last step is to determine how long the handshake should last. This is often very difficult to determine. In an ideal situation, a handshake should have three pumps. If you are in a rush, then a single pump will do.

There are certain aspects of the handshake that can be difficult to perfect on your own, such as the grip. For more positive progress, call some of your brutally honest friends to help you out. Give them a handshake and let them compare it to others they have experienced over the years.

Body Language

Body language is a critical aspect of a first impression. Depending on how you use your body language, you can make a memorable first impression.

When interacting with someone, we often copy the body language of the other person. It is the same way in which you instinctively smile when your friend starts to smile.

If you can mirror the body language of someone you are meeting for the first time, you will make them feel like you both share some similar qualities.

The nonverbal cues that you observe during the conversation are the things your body automatically picks to display. Since it will also prompt the same emotions, there will be a form of trust that you will develop.

Make the Most of The First Ten Seconds

How you use the first ten seconds of meeting a new person is very important. Your introduction should be your focus in these ten seconds.

There are different phrases you can use when introducing yourself to someone new.

If you are introducing yourself professionally, you can say "My name is John, and I'm a freelance writer. I create high-quality content that clients can post on their blogs and websites."

It is always essential that you ask the name of the other individual if you are going first.

Some things that help when introducing yourself include the following:

- Preparing short answers for basic questions about yourself
- Focus on the things you share
- Understand the context. Is it social or professional?
- Avoid saying too much

A verbal introduction is a very productive process you can also use in remembering names with ease. You can start by repeating the name immediately and make a comment on it if possible. You can also repeat the name during your introduction.

A mental association of the name with an event also helps.

It Is Rude to Have Your Focus Elsewhere

Distractions are quite common in our daily life. Technology in the form of our computers and smartphones make it very easy to fall for your distractions.

If you are meeting with someone for the first time, the biggest mistake you can make is to shift your focus to something else.

A great first impression is all about establishing a meaningful connection. There is no way to develop this connection if your attention is on your smartphone or the YouTube video playing on your computer screen. You can't use the pause button on things happening around you.

People will want to be around you more if they are sure that you usually pay attention to them. Attention is not easy to get from everyone. Therefore, people will always remember anyone that offers it with ease.

Be Confident When You Speak
When making a first impression, you want to be noticed. If you are unable to convey your message, it becomes easy to achieve the opposite effect.

It doesn't matter the number of ideas you have or the great advice you can give; no one will listen if you are not confident. Be calm when speaking. This is an excellent tip to make you sound more confident.

You don't show confidence by being the loudest in the room. Don't become a nuisance to others.

Don't Avoid Eye Contact
Interest and confidence are essential traits you need in developing a great first impression. Having direct eye contact with the person you are meeting can help express these traits.

Everything must be done with a touch of professionalism. People will assume you are just staring if you don't take your eyes off a bit. There should be short intervals when making direct eye contact, during which you shift your gaze to the side. Avoid looking downwards so you don't appear timid.

If it seems like you are spending more time looking in another direction, it is easy to assume that there is something else more important than the conversation. Making direct eye contact is a sign of respect in some countries, such as the United States.

Verbal Cues

Listen More and Ask A Few Questions

Listening to people when they speak is an excellent way to make a great first impression. When you listen, you are showing that you care about others. If you try to be the one talking for most of the conversation, it is a clear sign that you like to be the focus of every conversation.

In a conversation, the best time to speak is when you are asked a question, or you have something of importance that will be beneficial to the other person. If a topic or advice applies to you, it may not have an impact on the other person.

While listening during a conversation is necessary, it is vital you don't seem like a boring person. No one enjoys a one-sided conversation. While listening, you should also ask some significant questions. These questions should relate closely to the topic of the discussion.

Asking questions is a sign that you have an interest in the other individual. It is also a sign that you are not just nodding your head, but also gaining insight into the topic.

Give A Compliment on The Little Things

Getting a compliment is one of the things that makes everyone feel good. A compliment may be based on something as simple as punctuality. It is a great feeling to know that someone appreciates the effort you put into arriving on time.

Although a compliment may seem quite simple, it is impossible to get enough compliments.

To start a conversation, complimenting people on minor details can go a long way. In addition to improving their mood, it is also proof that your attention is on them.

A good compliment is also an easy way to reinforce positive behavior in an individual you are interacting with. For example, you can say thank you to a person for their punctuality.

Let Others Know How Important They Are

The main point of a conversation is often to learn new information. It can be personal information or a different perspective on a topic.

It is critical you understand that you won't be able to learn anything new if you are the only one talking during the conversation. Your perspective and opinions will not change if you don't give yourself the opportunity to listen to others.

There are a lot of people that know things that you don't. The only way to acquire knowledge is by learning new things. Anyone you are conversing with will have a unique lesson for you, and this makes them very important to you.

Don't Expect Anything in Return for Giving

When trying to make a good first impression, go in without any expectations. Meaning, you should not expect anyone to offer anything in return for whatever you have to offer.

You may be offering free tips, excellent advice, or work-related assistance. The only way to make a great first impression is to do all these without thinking of what the other person can do for you in return. You will come off as being self-centered if your focus is only on what you can gain.

If you want to form relationships and create a real connection with others, you should only focus on giving to others.

Carefully Select the Words You Use in A Conversation

Consider these two phrases; "I get to go to the movies with Lisa tonight," and, "I have to go to the movies with Lisa tonight."

Both phrases convey the same message but in entirely different manners. In both sentences, the message is merely going to the movies with Lisa tonight. The use of "get" and "have" quickly changes the impact of each message.

In the first statement, there is a feeling of joy that the word "get" elicits. On the other hand, the word "has" defines the outing as a compulsion.

This is how your use of words can affect the feelings of others towards you. The words you use in your sentences should make people feel good about themselves.

Is Gossip Necessary?

Gossip can be challenging to understand. As much as everyone likes to listen in on a bit of gossip, do you think there is love for those spreading the gossip?

Good gossip is often a negative view of another individual. It gives an opportunity to share a good laugh at the expense of others.

How do you think people feel about others that share gossip?

If you share gossip with people, they are going to wonder if you do the same about them. Will he also laugh at me in my absence?

Gossip often makes people lose their respect for you as an individual. Imagine the impact it would have when trying to build a good first impression.

How Do You Deal with Your Shortcomings?

Humility will carry you a long distance when creating a lasting first impression. It takes humility to admit when you make a mistake. Be open to sharing cases where you have made huge blunders with others. It makes you more relatable with whoever you are conversing with.

Let people use your experience as a guide to avoid making the same mistake. If you are willing to laugh at your mistake, others will be inclined to laugh with you. This is a lot different from going behind your back to laughing at you.

If you have a good sense of humor when discussing your mistakes, people tend to gravitate towards you more.

Remember Their Name and Use It Often

You must have had a situation where you came across someone you met earlier but can't seem to remember their name. This can make a massive dent on the impression they have of you.

If you are meeting someone for the first time, exchanging names is usually part of the opening ritual. As the conversation progresses, ensure you make use of the name often.

There are two benefits of using their name during the conversation. Firstly, it implies that you were listening while they were talking. Secondly, it shows you like the person enough to remember their name.

With the kind of link, we have with our names, hearing someone use it often naturally makes it easy to remember the person. You should also be careful about how you use the name. You don't want to sound condescend.

If you avoid using a person's name, it can sometimes imply that you do not acknowledge them as an equal.

Things That Ruin A First Impression

Invading Their Personal Space

In simpler terms, you can define this as close talking. No one wants to smell your breath. It doesn't matter how fresh it is now.

A suitable method of measuring the appropriate distance is to use an arm's length. At this distance, you can hear the other person clearly. You will appear to show a lack of interest if you are standing too far away while standing too close may be a sign of aggression.

Choosing the Wrong Topic for A Discussion

If you are meeting someone for the first time, there are many topics you need to avoid. Personal finance, religion, relationships, and politics are some of the topics you should avoid at all costs. These topics can bring out an emotion that will ruin a conversation.

When talking about politics or religion, there are usually two extremities. If you are passionate about one extreme and the person you are conversing with has a passion for the other extreme, then it may be difficult to create a positive impression.

Also, avoid gossip and health issues. No one wants to listen to you go on and on about your exercise routine or diet.

Some good topics of discussion include travel, arts, sports, and entertainment.

Poor Body Language

When do you think you begin making your first impression on someone? Is it as soon as you start speaking to them? Is it as soon as you walk into the room?

Your first impression starts the moment you walk into a room. Therefore, you need a good body language. Body language speaks volumes about the type of person you are.

Your walking posture is crucial. If you are walking with slumped shoulders and your head facing down, then you don't project confidence. You want to walk with great posture. Let people feel they can rely on you.

A great posture implies that you carry your body in the right way. It refers to how you sleep, sit, stand, and walk. Steps to take to improve your posture include maintaining a healthy weight and being active. There are other steps to take in improving your posture in specific areas.

People can be watching you at any time. always Form a habit of using an excellent walking posture. It is better to be on the safe side.

Attaching No Importance to Names

Saying you are terrible with names is not an acceptable excuse by any standard. You are just being plain rude. It can also signify a lack of interest.

The same also applies to using the wrong name. Ask anyone that has made the mistake of using the name of their ex to refer to someone they just met.

Paying attention to minor details is very important in a conversation.

Avoiding Eye Contact

If you unable to make eye contact during a first meeting with someone, you are creating a terrible first impression. There are different messages you can pass across when you avoid eye contact.

Some people may interpret it as you are lacking interest in the conversation. People may also think you are lying or hiding something when you avoid eye contact.

When trying to make a good first impression, maintaining eye contact will show confidence, interest, and intelligence.

Phrases That Make Your First Impression Forgetful

"It Is Great to Make Your Acquaintance. And, What Is Your Name Again?"

You arranged a meeting with someone, and you even wrote it down in your schedule planner. The day of the meeting arrives, you are there on time, but if you use the phrase above as your opening line, it is not ideal.

This is because it says a lot about you as a person, as the other party thinks you do not value people and did not place much significance on the meeting in the first place.

You can understandably be the nervous type of which is why you forget names during a first-time meeting. Try to memorize the name of the person hours before the meeting to avoid embarrassment.

"I Can…", "I Am…", and More Self-Absorbed Phrases

Continuously using 'I' in a conversation implies that you are a self-absorbed individual. No one will have an interest in a conversation where all you do is boast about your achievements. You are making the entire conversation about you.

To make a killer first impression, don't become the focus of the conversation. If you have the opportunity, be the one to ask a question about the other person. Steer the conversation in such a manner that in the end, you will have learned a lot about the other person and have also said a lot about yourself.

"How Much Is Your Pay?" And Other Phrases Relating to Income

This is a particularly rude question to ask of someone you have just met. It is also an unwelcome intrusion into the personal space of that person. You do not have reason to ask such a question as it is none of your business at the time.

"Congratulations! Is It A Boy or A Girl?"

There is nothing worse than assuming that a lady is pregnant and then being wrong. It is a line you must never cross. Before you congratulate any woman on her pregnancy, be sure to get your facts right.

It is best you avoid this topic entirely when meeting someone for the first time. If you make this mistake, you may never get a chance to apologize.

"It Cannot Be Done," Or, "It Is Impossible"

Why would you want to portray yourself as a person with a negative attitude? That is precisely what you are saying to the other person, even if you do not say it outright. No one wants to be around people with negative energy, so saying this at the first meeting with someone is not a great idea. It shows you are not looking to see positives in situations that seem dire, which is a big turn off. People do business with people who give off positive vibes.

"Mum"

This word is mainly a filler in a conversation that tells the other person you lack confidence. It also makes the person you are conversing with easily lose focus on what you are saying. It is easy to distract people when you use "Mum" at the start of your sentences. In situations where you cannot answer a question on the spot, take a few seconds to think before giving your answer.

"Your Appearance Is Not What I Expected"

Wow! So, are you saying you are disappointed? Are you trying to say my body is not appealing?

Well, this is a phrase that can be interpreted in a lot of negative ways. Don't make the mistake of using it. You may be uncomfortable with their dressing, but who are you to judge?

In most cases, the conversation may go on smoothly, but your snide remark will not go unpunished.

"I Did Not Like Working with My Previous Boss."

You do not start a conversation with someone you are just meeting for the first time by having a rant about your former employer; it is a big turn off. The person you are sharing this with could be affiliated with your previous employers in some way or may think you could also complain about him to others.

From another perspective, it may also give an impression that working with you will be difficult.

If it happens to be a job interview, you can be sure you are not going to be considered for the vacant position.

Conversations such as this should only be held with people who are very close to you.

"Are You A Believer?"

There are specific topics you should not bring up during the first meeting with someone or even in certain situations, like your workplace. Religion is a topic you would not want to start with, as many people nowadays find it too sensitive to discuss, or feel it is a personal matter. A conversation of this kind can take place after you have known the person for some time, but not in the initial meeting.

Using Pet Names

Calling someone you are just meeting for the first time by a pet name is wholly unprofessional. If you are in the habit of doing such, you might want to limit the use of such words. Some people find it irritating.

Imagine you go for a formal meeting and address the people you are meeting with by pet names. You are making a terrible first impression. Using a nickname also falls into this category.

To avoid falling into the pet name trap, address people the way they state their name during the introduction.

"Who Is Getting Your Vote in The Coming Election?"

Political views are somewhat like the case of religion. Everyone has a personal political ideology that they passionately stand for. Broaching this topic on your first day at a new workplace is not ideal, as you could be speaking with someone who is on the opposite side of what you believe.

This could have the effect of you being at loggerheads with the said individual, resulting in low cooperation and productivity in the workplace.

"Hope You Don't Mind That I Am Late."

This is an annoying line to say on a first meeting. Why would you hope your own time has not been wasted but would gladly waste the time of the person you are meeting with?

The person most likely created time out of a busy schedule to meet up with you and you have kept the person waiting for hours on end. In cases of unforeseen circumstances preventing you from being on time to the meeting, you need to give the person a call or send a message explaining the situation.

To make a better first impression, you could suggest to the person to pick a date and time for rescheduling the meeting.

"Let Me Be Honest."

This phrase is so damning as it causes people to think that you have not been honest or telling the truth from the onset. You do not have to say this phrase before you can get people to believe what you are saying. If you have something truthful to say, be blunt and say it outright.

"I Don't Like This Weather."

If you live in the tropics where rain is a regular occurrence or dusty and hot in the dry season, you should not start a conversation with complaints about the weather.

The person you are having a meeting with experiences it as well. This opening line lets the person see how unprepared you are and that you are most likely a complainer.

"I Do Not Like Monday Mornings."

We have all had a case of the blues on a Monday morning when we would rather sleep in than get up. You should then try to motivate yourself into a working attitude instead of making a lot of noise complaining about how you do not like Mondays. It is a turn off for people who do love the hustle and bustle of Monday mornings.

Robin Samuel Dean

Why not find a permanent solution to your Monday blues instead of using it as an excuse for low productivity? For example, you could become a consultant in your field, thereby self-managing your workload, and working on days you feel most productive.

Chapter 3:
Start A Conversation with Anyone

Learning how to start and hold a conversation is an important social skill that you need to develop as an individual. It will come in handy if you are trying to build a relationship with someone new and when you are trying to interact with a prospective customer as an entrepreneur.

There are various tips to help you develop your ability to hold a conversation. Learning to implement these tips in a conversation will help you become an expert in the art.

Small Talk
One crucial skill that is very important in holding a conversation is small talk. People that learn to use small talk have an advantage when it comes to initiating a conversation and preventing awkward silences.

What Is Small Talk?
Small talk is a form of social communication that is informal and covers unimportant topics. It is a technique that assists in starting a conversation with an individual you are meeting for the first time. Mastering the art of small talk requires a bit of practice on your part.

Although there are lots of topics you can use in small talk, different topics apply to different individuals. To make small talk effective in creating relationships, you must determine the topics that work for you. Some small talk topics include career, sports, entertainment, and family.

What Are the Benefits of Small Talk?

Meeting new people is unavoidable in life. Forming a good relationship can also be quite tricky. To lay the foundation for building a great friendship, small talk can be your best option.

People with social anxiety can use small talk to make meeting new people easier, as specific topics tend to come up frequently. You can prepare for some of these topics ahead of time, thus entering an initial meeting with more confidence. There are other significant benefits of small talk which will be discussed below:

It Is Applicable in All Areas of Life

There is something about small talk that makes it very important. It is something that you can apply wherever you find yourself in life.

Do you want to close in on a major contract? Are you looking for a great place to start a new career? Are you having a gathering of friends? Do you want to interact with your colleagues at work?

In all the situations mentioned above, engaging in small talk is all it takes to make a person more comfortable around you.

You See Things from A Different Perspective

One of the significant benefits of small talk is the opportunity to gain a new perspective on specific topics. As a social communication technique, it is a great way to interact with people. Interaction with other individuals usually gives you a look at things from a different angle.

In some cases, you may also get smarter as you develop new ideas to solve a problem through these interactions.

Easy Source of Information
We often tend to leave our homes without having time to watch the news, especially if we are running late. Will your smartphone be able to give you all the information you need?

Although smartphones offer access to the internet, it is possible to miss relevant information if you don't type it into your search bar. Small talk gives the opportunity for people to share new knowledge with each other.

People with high intelligence often offer great information when they are engaged in small talk.

There Is Spontaneity in Discussions
A unique feature of small talk is the inability to determine where the interaction will end up. Sometimes, you may have the opportunity to learn about a new idea that can be beneficial to you. It may be information on a great job opening or an excellent investment opportunity.

If your discussions with other people only focus on work-related issues, you may never get the opportunity to learn about new things in life.

You Become More Likable
There is nothing more important than engaging with others. There are also lots of people that love engaging in small talk.

Engaging with people, in this case, doesn't mean you are requesting a file related to a job. The engagement, in this case, is often to find out about the well-being of others and to share information about some fundamental life issues.

People will appreciate you more if you take the time to talk about their favorite sport or ask about their family. It is also an easy way to earn respect.

Why Do You Need Small Talk?
In creating a relationship with someone new, or managing your relationship with your friends, small talk is crucial. It is a technique through which you can assess the things that help keep friends, colleagues, and family members in a positive mood.

During a conversation, there are different purposes of small talk. The way you use this technique can have a considerable impact on the outcome of any conversation. Here are some of the purposes of small talk when conversing with others:

It Helps to Initiate the Conversation
An excellent way to determine the best course to take during a conversation is through small talk. If you are meeting up with friends, small talk helps in assessing moods and determining the purpose of the meeting.

Small talk when meeting with someone new is how each person understands the intention of the other. It quickly becomes apparent if the conversation will have a positive outcome or if your interests do not align.

It Eliminates Awkward Silence During the Conversation

A lot of people find it very uncomfortable to have silence during a conversation. When having a serious conversation, there will be a time during which there will be no vital topic. Engaging in small talk can serve as a filler discussion until a more critical topic arises.

Thinking of a new topic in silence can sometimes be inconvenient to everyone in the conversation.

A Great Way to End A Conversation
How you end a conversation can often have a huge influence when creating a first impression. Bringing a conversation to an abrupt end can often imply that you do not want the relationship to grow further. It can also mean that you are not delighted with the outcome of the conversation.

Once you are done discussing essential issues, engaging in small talk is an excellent way to end the conversation. It is a great way to part on a positive note.

How to Engage in Small Talk
Learning about the benefits of small talk and why you need it doesn't make you an expert at making small talk. In truth, everyone will have a unique approach to making small talk. Nonetheless, there are specific steps you can take to improve your ability to create effective small talk.

Here are some essential tips you should apply to make excellent small talk:

Show Confidence
It is not easy to start a conversation with someone you are meeting for the first time. In most cases, anxiety usually destroys the opportunity for a great relationship.

If you decide to engage in small talk, then you need to be confident. Being confident in yourself and your abilities will eliminate the fear that comes with meeting a new person. You should start with confidence, end with confidence, and maintain your confidence throughout the conversation.

You can show confidence by giving a firm handshake, maintaining a good walking posture, and keeping your hands out of your pocket during a conversation.

Your Body Language Is Important

To put people at ease, your body language is essential. There are different ways your body language can influence small talk.

The first thing is to ensure you are giving appropriate distance. It means you should avoid close-talking. A lot of people don't like it.

Crossing your arms during a conversation may be very convenient, but it is inappropriate. You should also ensure your shoulders are facing the person, and you are maintaining direct eye contact. These show a sign of interest.

Don't Jump into Conversations

We often meet new people during a three-way conversation with someone you know. Both of you may have a mutual friend. If you find a friend of yours in a conversation with someone you don't know, be careful how you enter the conversation.

Assess the situation to determine if the conversation is open to other parties. You may need to subtly get into the conversation by looking for an opening. During specific conversations, a question may be thrown to anyone around. It may be a good time to make a positive first impression.

Pay Attention to The Environment

Preparation doesn't mean you have everything covered. It is merely a way to cover most of the crucial parts. During small talk, you may end up using up all your tricks reasonably quickly. At this moment, you need to use your surroundings effectively.

Taking note of minor details about the other person will be of help. For example, giving a compliment can be helpful. Things in the environment can also serve as excellent topics. You can start a conversation about seasonal changes if you notice leaves on the ground.

Use of Your Phone Is Not Allowed

Why should you try to talk to me if you are going to be on your phone throughout the conversation?

If you are conversing with anyone, you want their attention to be on you throughout the conversation. It is also what the other person expects. Using your phone during a conversation will show a lack of interest.

What Is Something Interesting About You?

Small talk is your primary tool to get to know others. There is no way you will get to know one another if there is no room for an introduction.

Since you are including your introduction in the small talk, your introduction should give an insight into who you are. It should also be something very fascinating.

Come Up with A Topic That Interests Both of You

A great way to connect with someone is to discuss a topic that you are both passionate about. Determining this topic may be quite tricky, but you can try to take hints throughout the conversation.

Finding a common topic is excellent, but it can also be a huge issue if you are not well informed. Just because you love a sport doesn't mean all your facts are right. You will be exposing yourself to ridicule if you keep giving wrong information.

Since identifying a common topic can be very difficult in some cases, then opting for a topic that you know is very interesting to most listeners is an alternative.

Listening Is Equally Important

Like a regular conversation, it is important you remember that small talk also involves two parties. It means that both parties need to talk as well as listen for the small talk to be successful.

Since you have a lot of information and new ideas to share, you should also be ready to let the other person talk. Listening is paramount. This is how you get to understand the perspective, experiences, and knowledge that is available from others.

How to Keep A Conversation Going?

Certain tricks can help prolong a conversation. These are also helpful to ensure that the conversation remains lively with lots of things to talk about. The longer the conversation, the more information you will be able to get when meeting someone for the first time. You can implement the tricks below:

Open-Ended Questions Are Important

A conversation where one person is asking a question and receiving one-word replies won't get very far. It is possible you are also giving room for these one-word replies.

To keep a conversation going for as long as possible, you need open-ended questions. Such questions prompt people to give a response that is longer and more informative.

If you want to keep a conversation going, you can ask a question such as, "What do you think about the premier league?" The response you will get from that question will be much longer than the response you would get if you asked, "Do you like premier league football?"

Learning how to use open-ended questions effectively will help to improve the quality and length of the conversation.

Open-ended questions may also be about personal life if you are not forceful. Also, avoid generic questions. For example, "are you fine?" and similar questions.

Use the Silence to Your Advantage

The same way silence during a conversation will make you uncomfortable; it also has the same effect on the other person. However, you can make the most of the silence.

If you have been doing most of the talking during a conversation, running out of topics to discuss may not be your fault. Anytime such a situation arises, then it is time to let the other person come up with a suitable topic for discussion.

Most people will often come up with small talk as a filler until they can raise an original topic.

This is a sure tactic that works in most cases unless you are at a gathering where the person can leave to get drinks. Don't overthink everything.

Coming up with a great conversation topic may be quite easy for you. The main problem may be overanalyzing every possible outcome. As a result, you begin to hesitate.

Sometimes it may be a genuine fear that the topic may not be as attractive to the other person as it is to you. The same applies to opinions or facts you may have about an issue.

If you stop thinking, you can develop another technique which you can refer to as blurting. It is a technique that enables you to say whatever comes to your mind now. Once you can overcome the mental restriction you have set, you notice that you can hold a conversation for much longer.

Having a filter is still important, nonetheless. Not all words may be suitable for a conversation topic in a different situation.

Don't Stay in Your Comfort Zone
A lot of people have difficulties holding a conversation because they only do it when it is necessary. If you prefer to spend more time playing games than talking to others, you may become a better gamer, but you will have difficulties holding a conversation.

If you make it a habit to meet just one new person every week, it becomes easy to hold long conversations later. It is the same way you must practice your shots to become a better shooter on the basketball court.

Comfort is excellent, but it won't always provide the results you desire.

A Simple Phrase to Use

The more a person talks, the longer the conversation. There is an easy way to get a person to talk more. Simply use the phrase:

"That's interesting. Can I know more?"

There are various parts of this phrase that make it effective. It is polite, and it shows you have an interest in what they are saying. The fact that you have expressed interest will light a spark in them. Being polite is just the topping.

You should combine it with various other positive reactions to show that you are listening.

Use Special Events to Your Advantage

There are numerous special events you can discuss in a conversation. An upcoming football event like the World Cup or Champions League is excellent topic. It may be an upcoming event or one that has recently occurred. There are lots of benefits to using an event in a conversation.

The first is that most people know about these events. Opinions on these events will also vary depending on everyone. If you are in luck, you may even learn new facts and information on the event.

Talk About Something You Know A Lot About

This will be a topic you are passionate about. If you are passionate about a topic, you should have the upper hand regarding the volume of information you have to offer in a conversation. It's time to make the most of this knowledge.

The good thing is that you don't have to limit it to just one topic. You may be a game freak and a music enthusiast. It is also very fascinating to find someone who is knowledgeable in multiple areas.

Anytime a conversation gets quiet, you can try one of these topics as a filler. Don't appear to be aggressive about these topics and avoid forcing a conversation towards any of these topics.

Simplicity is also essential. Also, make it fun. Your fun gaming sessions may bore the next person.

Things That Kill A Conversation

As much as you want to keep a conversation going, it is essential you understand that there are certain lines you do not cross. Knowing the things that make a conversation come to a quick end and consciously avoiding them will help you develop into a better conversationalist.

Talking Too Much

As much as you want the other person to talk, you won't like it if the person is talking too much. People will get bored if you keep going on and on during a conversation. The occasional nod is just a way to make you think they are listening.

Everyone in a conversation should be an active participant. A conversation is supposed to be two-way communication. Don't be the type that decides to do the talking for both parties.

Sometimes, you may not be to blame for the situation. In a situation where the other person is not talking, you can easily switch to open-ended questions. If the person is a shy type, an open-ended question will always get them talking.

It is easy to notice the glint in a person's eye when they get the opportunity to let out ideas.

Not Trying

Now, I am putting you in the other position. What if you are not making enough contribution to the conversation? Putting in 10% while the other person must come up with 90% is not a good practice.

Try to achieve a balance where you are giving 50%, and the other person is also giving 50% in a conversation. If there is a question for you, avoid one-word replies. Elaborating on your responses can positively extend the conversation.

Making the Conversation Unsettling

You may meet someone who can hold a great conversation, but your actions may have a negative influence. Different actions can make a conversation unsettling.

If you have bad breath or halitosis, you may have to keep your distance. The distance will usually have to be a bit large, which can make hearing difficult.

If you are getting too close, it may also be a problem. Close-talking is not welcome. Just because you have fresh breath, doesn't mean anyone will be comfortable with close talking.

Talking too fast can make it seem like you are mumbling. You should be able to speak clearly so everyone can understand you. Speak at a moderate pace and avoid shouting or whispering.

Making direct eye contact is essential, but it is not the same as staring. If you continue to stare during a conversation, the other person will become uncomfortable. It may lead to a brief conversation.

Avoid motions that can be distracting. If you are tapping your feet, fiddling with loose change in your pocket, or rocking a chair, you are introducing distractions into the conversation.

Don't Be an Apathetic Conversationalist

Being apathetic means, you lack interest, concern, and enthusiasm. If you are apathetic, how do you expect anyone to converse with you?

There are different ways through which you can show signs of being apathetic. If you generally have your hands on your phone, or you keep scanning the entire room from time to time, then these may be clear signs.

There are various ways to avoid being apathetic. You need to make a conscious effort if you want to change. You can start by showing a sign of interest in the conversation. If you have any experience that is relevant to the discussion, share it, and ask questions.

You also need to avoid distractions during a conversation. Don't scan the room for anything more interesting than your current conversation.

It is also possible to be in a conversation with someone else that is an apathetic conversationalist. In this case, you can make brief pauses to get their attention anytime they shift their focus.

If your topic is interesting, then you won't have to worry about your partner losing focus.

Chapter 4:
Building Massive Confidence

Building confidence is critical if you want to relate to more people without being nervous. There are various reasons why it can be challenging to grow your self-confidence. Some people have difficulties with low self-esteem, while others suffer from personal trauma. If a child is judged using very high standards from a young age, they may grow up thinking they are not good enough.

There are some ways you can build your self-confidence. These take time and require consistency.

If you are ready, you can use the tips discussed below:

Desist from Thinking About What People Feel or Think About You
The moment you start thinking of what other people feel or think about you, there is a possibility of getting discouraged. You then refuse to do anything so as not to be judged. You prefer to remain idle over to avoid the risk of being criticized.

Worrying yourself about what certain individuals think or feel about you will continue to weigh you down and may hinder you from achieving your desired goals.

It is possible you have set goals for your future, which is a necessity. If you're an ardent reader of Tiny Buddha, it makes you understand that at a stage, you do away with people's thought about you. If you don't, the self-doubt will become a part of your routine.

Don't Compare Your Achievements to Your Friends or Colleagues

If you start using your present situation as a comparison to others, you will begin to have doubts about yourself. Also, comparing your achievements to your mates will always have an impact on your mood. You may also fail to realize that the achievements of your mates are not an accurate yardstick in measuring your personal progress.

There is one thing that you need to be conscious of, especially when you find yourself in this kind of situation. Understand that everyone will have a different pace when it comes to progress.

You will discover that you are able to make significant progress in your career and daily activities as soon as you decide to do things at your own pace. It becomes possible to pick tasks that you are passionate about rather than those that you see your friends engaging in.

What Makes You Doubt Yourself?

All you must do is to invest more time in performing in-depth thinking to determine the source of your doubts. The source of your self-doubt may be an activity that you find to be positive. Taking the perfectionist route may seem like a positive step to you but may also be promoting self-doubt. Avoiding these sources can eliminate the chances of health issues.

Locating the source of your self-doubt will provide a way to eradicate it from the mind.

Healthy Sleep

Due to the present-day lifestyle, having healthy sleep is another activity that individuals find difficult to achieve.

Individuals in the modern world rarely sleep. The amount of rest they get is also too little to provide the confidence boost they need when they are awake.

Your inability to get enough sleep can result in frustration due to impatience, anger, sadness, and depression. You may also become very sensitive to little things such as an employee that doesn't reply to your message quickly. These are closely linked to low self-esteem.

Adhering to a strict 7-8 hours of sleep per night is ideal for healthy sleep.

Sleep can be described as a situation in which the body refreshes and fixes itself, as well as creates hormones such as testosterone.

Some things you can do to improve your sleep include:

- Eradicating noises from external sources
- Sleeping early to wake up early
- Switching off lights when sleeping

Other advantages of healthy sleep include positive productivity and mental balance. Mental balance is a healthy state of mind that involves the elimination of negative tendencies and accepting the potential of the mind to be creative. It includes cognitive balance, attentional balance, emotional balance, and conative balance. Your productivity is your ability to create positive results using the various resources at your disposal.

How to Get Enough Sleep?
Getting enough sleep will undoubtedly increase levels of testosterone.

Go to sleep early or stay longer in bed to attain the maximum time needed for enough rest. At least for your general wellbeing, you need to ensure you spend the minimum seven hours required in bed.

Having adequate sleep is imperative. Make sure your phone is off, avoid consuming caffeine at night, and make sure you have a warm shower before going to bed.

Believe Your Instincts
Another method of overcoming self-doubt is to believe in one's voice and vision. People tend to believe you more if you believe in yourself and what you are saying. Express your thoughts as they come to you rather than in a manner which you think is expected of you. Expressing your own thoughts and ideas helps in developing your self-confidence.

Reduce and Cope with Your Stress
Stress disruptors include meditation, yoga, listening to your favorite music, or laughing with friends.

When you are under intense stress, the body will react by creating the stress hormone, cortisol. Increased cortisol levels mean testosterone will be difficult to establish. Therefore, it is imperative to make sure you properly reduce stress in order to maintain your levels of testosterone.

Don't take drugs that mess with your hormones. Make sure you don't take substances that are like estrogen in any part of your body, such as xenoestrogens, which can drastically reduce levels of testosterone.

To do away with these substances:

- Don't preserve food using any form of synthetic preservatives
- Avoid pesticides
- Consume vegetables, meats, and natural fruits
- Adopt the use of organic skincare products

Proper Nutrition

It is easy for people to focus on their body weight and shape rather than what they eat. Focusing on body weight can often result in low self-esteem. To avoid this outcome, it is more beneficial to focus on healthy eating habits.

Hormones, such as testosterone, require appropriate nutrients in order to be created. Therefore, you must make sure all required building blocks are provided.

Adequate consumption of minerals and vitamins, which are essential nutrients, is vital for the proper functioning of the body.

Undoubtedly, in recent times, it has been difficult to achieve a diet that is up to standard.

Predominantly for this purpose, it is advisable to have adequate and proper nutrition. If by chance it is not adequate, external nutrients like Vitamin D and fish oil can be used to supplement your diet.

What you should also consider when nutrition is involved, is the fact that excess sugar intake is hazardous to the body.

Some effects of high sugar consumption include a stop in the production of testosterone, increase in fat storage, as well as visual disruption due to damaged blood vessels in the body system.

As much as possible, make sure you reduce or stop consuming sugar.

Feeding Properly

Feeding properly is a significant prerequisite to sustaining a healthy body.

By feeding correctly, it means you have a proper combination of various classes of food that includes carbohydrates, protein, and fats. To build testosterone, there is a need to increase the intake of eggs, butter, yolks, coconut oil, and other saturated fats in your diet.

Sugar intake should be avoided so that levels of testosterone will not decrease. Also, other activities that are attributed to low levels of testosterone are drug abuse and excessive alcohol intake. Whether for fun or due to prescription medication, the use of drugs can have a detrimental effect on testosterone levels. It is therefore important you consult with your doctor if you have a prescription to get more information.

Identify Your Well-Wishers and Build Relationships

Nobody knows or has it all. It means that as humans, there is no one capable of doing everything by him/herself. A compliment is all we require sometimes, and your well-wishers are the set of individuals that compliment you regularly.

Therefore, there is a need to know your preferred well-wishers, relations, playmates, and age groups who have always stood by you.

It is now up to you to channel your effort into strengthening your connections with these individuals. They are around us; therefore, develop those connections and make sure you can gain the necessary trust.

Let Your Mantra Encourage You
There are lots of mantras that you may have created over the years that you often repeat in situations where you experience self-doubt. The slogans go a long way in informing you of your past, the challenges you have faced, your accomplishments, and your outlook on the future.

These sets of mantras make you realize the need to take things slowly, comfortably, and receive guidance from your instincts.

"You are loved" is a great mantra to use often. Self-doubt may come up when you are not feeling too good, and it can result in you concluding that you have been deserted. By reciting this mantra, you can keep on believing in yourself, and in the fact that there are people who love you for who you are.

It is possible that all of us will experience self-doubt at some stage, as it is a part of life. It is easy to observe as you progress in life, that self-doubt comes into play when you think the love you receive does not align with your expectations.

If you have the people who love you around, appreciate them, and follow through on your goals, you can eliminate self-doubt.

Spend time in positive assertions and trust mantras. Exchanging pessimistic thoughts with an optimistic mindset is a significant step that you can adapt to eradicate self-doubt. It may look a bit weird in the beginning, but through practice and repetition, you can use optimistic assertions to develop your self-confidence.

Encouragement from Others

There are certain situations where you also fail to identify your toughness; instead, you dwell more on your faults.

In such situations, try as much as possible to consult with others. Advisers have experience and have a broad view of people. On your own, you may not be able to find out the things they are able to help you with.

You can also get inspiration from their trust, which can spur you into believing in yourself.

Pay Attention to Work

Focusing and paying attention to the most important work in front of you will assist in managing your self-doubt. Having too much free time and your inability to focus on important tasks often give room for self-doubt.

Low Testosterone and How It Affects Confidence

In a study titled "Single Dose Testosterone Administration Impairs Cognitive Reflection in Men," the study shows that testosterone influences confidence in men. Low testosterone levels can also result in low energy levels, fatigue, and depression.

These are some of the common reasons why people lack confidence. To address these issues, it is important to find some of the causes of low testosterone and then identify the means of addressing these issues.

The increase in confidence from the reduction in cognitive reflection and an increase in the reliance on intuitive judgment.

Testosterone Killers That Mar Your Social Confidence

Processed Sugar and Carbohydrates

When we talk about processed carbohydrates, we do not only mean sugars. We are also discussing other foods that transform into sugars after ingestion. These foods include bread, rice, and pasta. Your system is programmed to react to sugars by producing and releasing a hormone called insulin. The rise in insulin levels in one's body is a disaster to produce testosterone in one's body.

Additionally, when we eat highly glycemic food, lots of processed carbohydrates can knock down one's testosterone level for a couple of hours. Over time, it could be worse if one makes the consumption of these foods a habit, as the body could become entirely insulin resistant. Aside from the fact that this is related to prediabetes, it's also related to very low-level testosterone production.

Carbohydrates with less sugar are still a healthy and essential part of a balanced diet so much so that carbohydrates produce required building-blocks for testosterone. However, staying away from processed variations of carbohydrates and sticking with nutritionally beneficial ones will neither increase your insulin nor lower your testosterone production. One important source of healthy carbohydrates is chickpeas. They also make a good source of proteins, fiber, and a considerable percentage of vitamins and minerals for testosterone production.

Stress and Anxiety Levels

It's possible you understand that stress and anxiety take tolls on your health. At the same time, you may not know that it also possesses some chronic effects on the levels of your testosterone.

Objectively, there exists an inverse relationship between cortisone, the stress hormone, and testosterone. Anytime cortisone rises, testosterone falls. Also, cortisone is not only linked with one's testosterone levels, but it has an impact on anxiety levels depending on the amount present in the body.

Do you sometimes seem not to feel alive because you had a difficult day? It might just be that cortisone has started to toll on your testosterone levels immediately. It's important to know that when prolonged stress is involved, it can be more disastrous, as the body stores up cortisone as it tries to contain your stressors.

Biologically, one's body enters 'flight mode', and reproductive strength isn't an immediate concern. The body prioritizes other functions, which makes one unable to manufacture testosterone at the highest level.

Getting to reduce stress in one's day-to-day activities or trying to work on ways to cope with it, is a primary objective towards increasing the production of testosterone in one's body.

Excessive Alcohol Consumption

You may have listened to, or personally seen, the worrying consequence that a night spent binge drinking has on your ability to do and be at your best. Nonetheless, are you in the know that alcohol consumption also affects many processes in the production of testosterone? The reality is that storing excess alcohol in your system can reduce your testosterone.

Concisely enough, whenever you have a drink or two, you may not feel the effect of it on your testosterone. When one's system breaks down alcohol, the process involved makes use of some coenzymes called NAD+, which is a vital part of testosterone production. If one's system lacks required building-blocks to produce testosterone, then it cannot produce more of it. This spot is where the impact directly correlates with the quantity of alcohol taken. Hence, taking unquantified drinks will not possibly have a reasonable effect. One must be aware that the more one drinks, the less testosterone is produced. On occasions of having a beer or other mixed drinks, it's unlikely to affect the testosterone levels, but when one frequents them, it's worthy to note that one's testosterone production will plunge.

Consuming Water That Contains Chemicals

Given that you're someone who's predominantly aware of your health standards, it's possible that you drink a lot of water to stay hydrated and keep your body running smoothly. Undoubtedly, water is a valuable commodity we cannot do without and it's vital for biological processes. Nonetheless, it's equally important that you see to the quality of the water you ingest because the inadvertent high intake of water is a passage for testosterone damaging chemicals.

You may think that moving to bottled water is next, but the reality is that companies are being regulated and are not given the freedom to release the rate of contaminants in their products.

Additionally, many damaging chemicals like phthalates or bisphenol-A (BPA) that are usually seen in plastic containers can get back into the water. It is advisable to try to filter water before drinking it and ensure you make use of safe containers.

Too Much Body Fats

Everyone knows that being overweight comes with some health risks. One of them for men is that it severely reduces their testosterone levels. Human body fats contain aromatase, an enzyme in the adrenal gland, which transforms androstenedione and estrogen.

What Is the Implication?

The only meaning to this is that the more body fat you possess, the more your testosterone gets turned into estrogen. Another issue is that testosterone is a hormone that is fat soluble. This means that it could be stored in fat tissues instead of floating freely in the blood, thereby reducing your testosterone levels.

Testosterone acts in a critical role in one's body synthesis. Hence, as one starts shredding the excessive weight while testosterone levels are high, it will aid in burning off the fat.

Dealing with Low Testosterone Exercises

Engaging in routine exercise is advantageous to your general well-being. Your testosterone levels can be increased with the aid of routine exercise.

Some forms of routine exercise that can help increase levels of testosterone are lifting weights, high-intensity interval training (HIIT), and resistance training. In adherence to the tenets of weightlifting, squats, deadlifts, and bench press should be included during weightlifting.

Expose Yourself to The Sun

Vitamin D that is derived from the sun has been described by researchers to have great benefits. It is also very useful in naturally boosting levels of testosterone.

Exposure to the sun is the best way to increase levels of Vitamin D. However, in some countries, exposure increases the risk of developing skin cancer. Most people get used to sun exposure and make use of sunscreens to shield themselves, which translates to little or no sun exposure. Failure to expose yourself to the sun can pose a risk for deficiency in Vitamin D3, which can be a reason for low levels of testosterone.

Nevertheless, Vitamin D3 supplements can work some magic, since there are few foods that contain this vitamin.

Use Natural Ways to Increase Testosterone

Natural supplements such as testosterone boosters are of immense assistance in increasing your testosterone levels without any problem.

There are several supplements that have been tested and proven to work effectively. Here are some of these supplements:

Zinc

Zinc is an essential mineral that is vital to many substances associated with the body system. As with Vitamin D, Zinc is essential in building and maintaining adequate levels of testosterone.

Consistently consuming a diet that is low in zinc may have an adverse effect on testosterone levels in the body. Foods that are rich in zinc include seeds, legumes, and beans.

Some other natural ways testosterone can be increased include:

- Ginger
- Ginseng
- Magnesium
- Fenugreek
- Selenium
- Horny Goat Weed
- Tribulus Terrestre's

Write Down A List of Things That You Show Gratitude for Daily

You don't have to subject yourself to mediocrity. There is no need to be cautious of what you possess and what you do not. Only thinking about what you have been unable to achieve will make you feel inferior and might have a negative impact.

Rather than channeling your energy on what you do not possess, be concerned about what you currently possess and what you have achieved. It brings an affection of gratitude, and when you channel your energy to gratitude, the changes you require will arise, and your future will be guaranteed.

An affection of gratitude brings an optimistic spirit from you. When you are optimistic, you're relaxed. Naturally, the joy in you will turn around to bring good tidings.

Read One Positive Book A Day
One of my adapted habits to quickly increase my level of believing in myself is to read my favorite books. You can pick a book from your favorite author to read daily.

Don't Seek Consent from Outside
In a situation whereby you allow other people's judgment to cloud your thinking, you automatically give others control over your life. Lack of control over your life often results in self-doubt. It's an endless chain.

Seek advice from people you believe will give you the right answers. Nonetheless, it is crucial you remember that you will always remain in control, regardless of the decisions you make. Although there might be consequences, you must not regret your decisions.

Getting Over the Inner Critic
A couple of books found on shelves explain methods to get over self-doubt. Many people make use of the terminology 'conquering doubt' in a manner that looks dismissive.

Everyone has doubts about being their natural self. The role it plays is to keep you safe, although, that safety lifeline can turn against you if you fail to be aware of its negative consequences.

Take some time to check the concept of doubt in your life. Have you ever wondered what resources you use to get yourself out of self-doubt when it comes up?

Every time we attain little victories, our confidence gets a boost, which weakens our self-doubt. Your inner critic is often like a speed bump in the form of self-doubt. The very essence of speed bumps is to make you slow down while driving, never to put you to a complete halt. Hence, a similar approach can be copied to phase through self-doubt.

Self-doubt may be causing massive havoc in you. Try to realign with your purpose instead of letting the challenges of self-doubt overwhelm you. Blaming past failures will only result in further destructive mindsets. Take firm actions on set goals and approach your doubts with compassion. You have the sole responsibility to realign them peacefully without any feelings of guilt.

Your sojourn to internal tranquility and achievement is filled with numerous challenges. Stick to them and face them with attention and zeal for success with the necessary hard work required.

Let Go of Your Negative Mindset
Verily, many people's minds are filled with a lot of garbage while growing up. No one was an exception. Depending on their personal struggles, some people undergo a form of priming that causes them to keep shut in most situations. This is the case with a stutterer.

By assuming that no one wants to get into a discussion with a person that stutters, these individuals try to avoid conversations. By avoiding conversations, there will be negative impacts in the form of lost opportunities.

Self-doubts come from the reverse thinking plaguing the lives of many individuals. Now, it's time to reset this mindset. You can use a combination of counseling, therapy, and recovery to help get over self-doubt.

Most times, people are not willing to engage in the tedious emotional work of accepting that they were hurt, either due to too much dependence or a fear of getting abandoned. These dangerous mindsets still lurk around you, and it might become increasingly difficult to attain freedom and the much-required self-confidence you need. When one has a broken arm, reading, eating, sleeping, or exercising will never fix it.

To achieve your dreams, the need to sharpen your mind becomes non-negotiable.

Getting Out of Your Comfort Zone

In order to achieve personal development, you need to be ready to try something different, even if you feel awkward and uncomfortable. Have you ever thought about your first-time swimming? You kept harboring the fear of drowning, so you didn't exceed the shallow end for safety purposes. But now, you may have even considered swimming in an ocean. This applies to life. Little steps taken out of your comfort zone will push you inch-by-inch to take fresh challenges. This is the beginning of your progress.

Failure Is No Big Deal

Researchers have shown that the most prevalent factor that makes self-doubt creep in is the fear of failure. Although you may be caught awestruck, many successful people of this century have discovered a failure to be indispensable on their road to success. Elon Musk, the great tech-entrepreneur, maintains that failure is necessary for innovation. By being practical and accepting failure at different points in one's career, one will be making tremendous progress in overcoming one's fears.

The More You Learn, The Better You Feel

Ignorance makes you anxious and scared, whereas knowledge makes you confident and self-assured. The more skills you acquire, the better your chances of being successful in life.

The reverse is also correct. Your chances of succeeding are significantly reduced each time you misuse your resources.

It is not necessary to learn every minute, but the best way to learn is to have adequate rest in between your learning periods. You tend to feel better with every bit of knowledge you acquire.

Do not allow fear to dominate your life. Ignorance can only bring you fear and anxiety, so learn as much as you can during your lifetime.

Own Your Accomplishments

You must take matters in your own hands if you want to experience a great turnaround in life. You do not have to wait for people to compliment you for your success. Instead, congratulate yourself first. Praise yourself every time you achieve something, no matter how little.

Make Self-Doubt Work for You

This may sound crazy, but it has been observed that a certain amount of self-doubt can enable you to stay sharp, inventive, and focused on the task ahead. Self-doubt can help you stay on track and motivate you to put more effort into achieving your goals. However, if it is not correctly managed, it might drag you down. Therefore, you must not let self-doubt bring you down, rather see it as a stepping stone to going higher in life.

Intermittent Fasting and Its Benefits

Intermittent fasting is a pattern of eating whereby you skip certain meal hours during the day. This does mean you are restricted to eating a kind of food or encouraged to avoid others, but instead, it determines when you should eat.

The methods of intermittent fasting vary, but they all center on splitting your meals for the day or week into fasting and eating periods. Fasting is nothing new to most individuals because you fast while you are asleep at night, which is the reason the first meal of the day is called breakfast. However, this fast can be extended beyond typical breakfast hours.

You can choose to have your first meal of the day at noon and have your last meal by 8 pm. This means you fast for 16 hours a day and have an 8-hour eating window for the day. The 16/8 method is one of the most popular methods of intermittent fasting.

Of all forms of fasting, intermittent fasting is the easiest. A lot of people can attest to this as they reportedly do not struggle through it, but rather feel good during the process. Hunger is only a challenge during the beginning process, but the body adapts quickly, and hunger is then no longer an issue. During the fasting period, only liquids such as water, tea, coffee and other beverages with few calories are allowed; this means no food during this period. Supplements with no calories in them are also allowed during intermittent fasting.

How Does Intermittent Fasting Affect Testosterone?

The intermittent fasting facts might be overwhelming, but they will undoubtedly convince you to consider fasting regularly if you desire to boost your testosterone levels naturally.

Testosterone Is Positively Correlated with Insulin Sensitivity

Skipping breakfast is a good way of increasing testosterone levels. This is because the moment an individual wake in the morning, the circadian cycle of the body has a natural cortisol spike. This falls in the period when a lot of people have their breakfast. With individuals who are considered healthy and already have high insulin sensitivity, certain food intake causes a spike in their insulin level. This means a high level of cortisol is circulating the body at that period of the day, which causes a drop-in blood glucose. As a result, a phenomenon known as "false hunger" is experienced, which causes an increase in the consumption of calories.

Skipping breakfast helps regulate cortisol, insulin, and blood glucose levels at the time of the day when they are easier to produce.

Production of Adiponectin

The hormone called adiponectin can also be increased through intermittent fasting. Insulin sensitivity of the body is increased as a result of an increase in adiponectin during fasting. A study has shown that adiponectin is powerful, as it can reverse insulin resistance in mice.

Excess Body Fat Can Be Burned During Intermittent Fasting

The body uses excess body fat as a form of energy for daily activities, and this allows the body to get rid of toxins early in the day before carrying out activities such as glycogen synthesis and digestion. Burning excess fat is one of the fastest ways to increase testosterone levels in the body. There is an inverse correlation between the fat level of the body and common measures of insulin resistance like HOMA-IR, C-peptide, and insulin. The adipose tissue is responsible for the inverse relationship between insulin resistance and testosterone but has nothing to do with the sex hormone binding globulin (SHBG).

This means that an individual with a high level of body fat will only produce a low level of testosterone naturally.

Boost in Growth Hormones
Growth hormone levels in the body can be boosted by about 2000% by fasting for just 24 hours. Growth hormone and testosterone levels work hand in hand at increasing training capacity, improving protein synthesis, and increasing the uptake of glycogen into the muscles.

Chapter 5:
Charisma on Demand

Charisma is your ability to influence anyone that is around you. If you are a charismatic individual, people will naturally admire you. Some people are naturally charismatic while others need to make a conscious effort to develop their charisma.

To build your charisma, follow the tips below:

Building Up Your Self-Esteem
There is a lot to be said about the importance of having a sense of high self-esteem or being confident in oneself. An individual who exudes self-confidence is optimistic about his personality and is at ease amid other people.

You can build your self-esteem by attaining set goals, such as becoming an expert in your field, being the individual that brings pride to the family, being a true friend, or being a law-abiding member of your society.

The definition of self-esteem could mean different things to you, as it is a matter of opinion, but let your principles be shown by how you react to specific actions. Once you have a sense of self-worth, people will be ready to give you that iota of respect just as you respect yourself. Interacting with people from different backgrounds becomes child's play when you build up your self-esteem.

Develop the Skills of An Interested and Exciting Conversationalist

One of the most important habits to develop as a person is the skill of being a great conversationalist. This means being an active listener to the person you have a conservation with and knowing when to chime in with your questions and your suggestions. Develop the charismatic attitude of asking questions to people about themselves rather than making the whole conservation about you. It eliminates the chances of people considering you to be boring and pompous.

A charismatic attitude equips you with the skills to make your fellow conversationalist feel good while conversing with you.

Social Awareness and Body Language

When during a social gathering, be quite observant and take note of certain things. Things like what the main topic of conversation is amongst the people that make up the interactive circle, the topics that are too sensitive to bring up, or the way you should portray yourself in such a gathering.

Try as much as possible not to have body posture that is read as being on the defensive in the minds of other people. Put out an open, receptive body posture, and you will find yourself being at ease wherever you are, even in the company of people you do not know. These individuals will also be more comfortable and find it easier to relate to you.

Positive Mental Outlook

Society does not relate well with individuals who are stiff, who cannot have a good laugh, and who tend to make a big deal out of any slight issue. Individuals with this type of temperament do not get invited to social gatherings as they are boring, and probably too controversial.

An individual who is known for his jovial, humorous, and positive outlook is seen as a necessary asset in social gatherings.

If you are of the melancholy type, try to be more light-hearted, be more humorous, and take life easy. This will attract people who will come flocking to your side in a social gathering. With this type of attitude, you will see yourself getting more invites to gatherings, meeting new people, and making new connections.

Emotional Facial Expressions

Psychologists have made it known over the years that showing more emotion through your facial expressions is a great way to be a person with charisma. Learning the art of being more expressive with your face shows how much you empathize with your fellow individual. You can practice how to facially express different emotions in the confines of your room, and by asking people how well you portray such emotional expressions.

Of course, there is a downside to being more facially expressive with emotions. People will find it easy to identify situations when you are flustered or in a rage. To counter this, you can also practice working on keeping facial expressions in check. It is not all the time you want people knowing what is going on with you.

Be an Active Listener

Another skill seen as a must towards developing a charismatic attitude is the art of being an active listener in conversations. Some books on psychology have come up with different definitions of what it means to be an active listener.

In a nutshell, it means listening with rapt and undivided attention to what the other party is saying instead of planning out your reply.

Knowledge of Body Language Signs

Having a basic understanding of the giveaway signs a person is showing through their body language is a skill you also need to work on. You can garner this knowledge by reading books on body language, attending seminars on the subject, or by being a keen observer of people and their different body postures.

It helps in knowing if a person is comfortable with your presence or not. You can also develop methods through which you can let people become more relaxed around you when you can understand their body language.

Sharing Personal Experiences with Stories

Research by many intellectual bodies has shown that individuals with charisma connect more with their listening audience by telling captivating tales of their personal experiences. Managers in big conglomerate firms have been put through some charismatic attitude seminars to teach them the art of using storytelling to motivate people under them to boost productivity.

Rhetorical Questioning

People do not like answering rhetorical questions. They usually feel it is annoying and a waste of time. However, it is a charismatic skill worth learning. You can use rhetorical questions to motivate individuals to be better people, or to focus on what is essential.

Set Personal Goals That Can Be Confidently Achieved

Studies have shown that a charismatic leader is an individual who sets defined goals for his team of individuals and believes they can achieve them. He instills belief and passion in each member of his team through this winning attitude.

Team members would, as a result, work hard as a unit to achieve the set goals with lots of confidence.

Effective Use of Words in Communication

Individuals with charisma have been known to communicate effectively with the way they use words. They make use of words and phrases that make them connect on a personal level with the person they are having a conversation with. This can be quite soothing, especially in cases where an individual is very emotional.

Social Risk-Taking

As you build up confidence in your social interaction skills, you realize you can read social flows quickly. You become much more comfortable and positive in interacting with people on a social level with ease. You can further enhance your confidence by engaging in the act of testing yourself in uncharted waters by engaging in actions you would never have thought of doing socially.

What Really Is Social Confidence?

Self-confidence is, in simple terms, a personal examination of your abilities when it comes to engaging in an activity with utmost success. Think back to the first time you had to perform an activity like driving, skiing, or flying a plane. At first, you are going to be afraid because you know these activities can result in serious injuries or death. But with time, as you practiced these activates, you gained more confidence in your ability to handle these situations.

But it should be noted here that self-confidence and social confidence should not be misconstrued to mean the same thing.

While self-confidence is your trust in your abilities or skills generally, social confidence refers to your trust in your social skills and your ability to gain acceptance in a social setting. It is a targeted form of your confidence.

Being socially confident is a different thing entirely. The way you build your self-esteem is also applicable when you decide to improve your social confidence levels.

In a social gathering, you have many options available to you in terms of how you react, and what you say in any scenario. These options will seem daunting if you are not confident in your social interaction abilities, especially in matters of physical intimacy with the opposite sex or when you try too hard to fit in.

When you are socially confident, you tend to take more social risks. This is because as you face these social risks often in your daily social interactions, you become bolder and have no anxiety in taking such risks.

One must work on cultivating a charismatic attitude by working on personal social skill levels to a considerable extent. This makes for easily fitting in with any social function you find yourself.

Phrases That Kill Your Charisma

We just discussed some things you can do to become a more charismatic individual. These are tips you can incorporate in your daily life. Since those are things to add, did you think of the things you need to stop doing?

Pre-Emptive Disqualification

Most people make use of such phrases frequently. It is a method of setting the bar for the assessment of a speech or performance.

If you want to sing and then start a phrase with, "I am not very good but..." you are trying to tell people that they can judge your singing poorly. The truth is that you are putting a bias in the minds of your listeners. As a result of the bias you have set, it will be impossible to get an honest opinion from your listeners.

Saying "No Problem"

This is usually the easiest reply people come up with anytime someone says, "Thank you." This reply implies that you're helping them only because it doesn't have any impact on your life. It means that if it would have cost you something to make yourself available to help, you would not have been available.

There are various situations where this may become apparent. It may be a case where your friend asks for your help in moving to another apartment, or another in which your assistance is required in setting up a piece of new equipment.

You should make people understand that you are assisting them mainly because you value the friendship you share with them. Every time you get a thank you from your friend, it is an opportunity to develop your relationship further. Try not to waste this opportunity.

You can decide to change this phrase to another much more effective phrase like, "I am always happy to help." People will understand that you are trying to make your relationship with them much stronger. As a result, more people will be attracted to you as a person.

There are other situations where saying, "no problem," is not an issue. It may be a scenario where you help someone get a product from the top shelf in a grocery store. Here you are merely doing them a favor.

Saying, "You Messed Up."

Do you understand what it means to point accusing fingers? That is precisely what you are trying to do when you use this phrase. There are situations where you can use this phrase and get away with it, but in other cases, you are asking for a fight.

If you are in a grocery store and there is an error on your receipt, you may get away with telling the cashier, "You messed up my receipt." The only reason why the cashier will let it fly is that as the customer, you are always right.

When you say this same phrase to someone with whom you have a relationship, like your family members, friends, or partner, then you are asking for trouble. No one in this category is going to let you off easily.

A better option to avoid confrontation is to use a phrase that does not point an accusing finger. If there is something wrong and you want to correct it, you can use another phrase.

A phrase like, "There may be an error in the inventory. Could you assist me in fixing it?" is a better option.

In the first part of the phrase, you avoid blaming anyone. The error may have come from someone else entirely, so you don't want to blame the person delivering the records.

You can easily blame a person, and after rechecking, you find out there was no error to begin with. Using this phrase still gives room to accept that there is no mistake in the inventory records.

To avoid confrontation, the concluding part of the phrase forces the person you are discussing with to work with you. When you are both working towards the same goal, there will be no room for confrontation.

The second phrase minimizes resistance and makes the work go faster.

The Use of Negative Absolutes

Most situations where people use negative absolutes is during an argument. The use of a negative absolute can escalate the debate into a big fight. It is essential you take note of such instances in order to avoid them.

A phrase that depicts a negative absolute is the use of, "You never..." or, "You always..." before saying something negative. It is essential you avoid these statements as it can cause a considerable strain on a relationship.

Some typical examples of negative absolutes include the following:

- "You never have time for me."

- "You are always talking about your ex."

- "You never do the dishes."

- "You always think you are right."

Chapter 6:
Instantly Persuade People

Learning to persuade people is an important part of everyday life. There are times when you need things to happen in a way and getting people to do it is the only option.

Developing the right skills will help you persuade individuals and influence their decisions.

How to Persuade People

How Do You See This?
Remember that whoever asks the question whenever persuasion is involved is in control. This means the direction of any persuasive conversation lies in your hands if you are the one asking the questions. This is a great tool that helps you persuade the other person into agreeing with you.

This is essential, as it helps you connect with the other person, as it gives the impression that you understand them.

It is no secret that most people love to be heard and they enjoy doing the talking and sharing their opinion. Hence, you will have something to say when people ask us about themselves.

Therefore, asking this question allows you to understand other people's point of view concerning a certain point. As a result, a connection is built between you and them. You can utilize other people's opinions when passing across your point.

The moment you become able to see the things from the perspective of others; you will realize how you can use it to persuade others actively.

Accept Being A Data-Driven Individual

Although most people like to consider themselves as data-driven people, the majority are not. Whenever you ask a person whether they are data-driven, they most often say yes to this question.

The moment you get them to admit to being data-driven they are going to try to prove it to you. This is because they wouldn't want to be inconsistent or confused. There are six principles of influence that control decision making in humans and one of them is consistency.

This is an essential tool; the moment you get a person to agree to something, it becomes even easier for you to persuade them using the data you have.

Use Silence.

This is a powerful tool in persuasion.

When you keep quiet, you automatically force the other person into filling the silence. They may eventually slip up on something useful to you the more they talk.

Deliberately choose to not respond during a conversation when it's your turn to speak to find out what the other person would say. The chances that they would bring up something useful that would keep the conversation going is high.

This was a technique created by Esquire great Cal Fuss man and later adopted by Tim Ferriss. Although it might seem counter-intuitive, it is an excellent way to establish a connection between you and other people.

One of the reasons why silence is an excellent tool in persuasion is that it is unexpected, and something that most humans like without even knowing it.

The next time you get into a serious conversation with someone, you can try it out. Give them the freedom to talk, nod and smile in agreement to whatever they are saying. This makes them believe you are following and would motivate them to keep talking. You will be amazed at how well this works in a persuasive situation.

Have You Thought Of...?

Always remember that humans are very emotional beings. We do not like to be doubted or disregarded. This is the reason a more subtle approach should be used when you want to question a personal judgment.

There is a possibility that the other person has thought about it but doesn't take it seriously when the question is asked; therefore, you can move on to making your thoughts known. If they haven't thought about it, you trigger them to consider it before voicing out their opinion.

Such a question is related to Pre-suasion. This means that if they haven't given prior thought to your question, the tendency that they would pay more attention to whatever you have to say is high. This puts you in control of the conversation, and you steer it in the direction you want, making it easier for you to convince the other person.

Sentences You Should Always Avoid

Now let's talk about the two phrases you should avoid during a conversation. We all find ourselves guilty of using them at one point or another. To avoid them, you must first be aware of them.

"Listen to Me!"

This is a statement that must be avoided in a conversation as it is in no way persuasive. Very often when we find ourselves in a heated discussion with friends or loved ones, we find ourselves making use of this sentence.

This hardly works because rather than appeal to the subconscious mind of the other person with a more convincing point, you come off as forceful because you have nothing new to offer, which is counter-productive.

"You Are Wrong!"

During an argument we most often find ourselves making use of this phrase just because we feel we are right, while the other person is wrong. But the thing is, the other person also feels the same way.

The best way to get across to someone is to have in mind that facts are never persuasive. If the other person has made up their mind on something, no matter how convincing your points are, you can never get them to agree with you.

Words That Can Persuade Customers to Visit Your Business

You

Using the word "you" makes whatever you are writing personal. It is one of the easiest ways to persuade your customers. Simply hearing the word "you" has a subtle effect on how your customers react to your requests.

In your writing, this word makes it seem like a conversation on a friendly level.

Free

One word that attracts a lot of people is "free". Who doesn't love to get free stuff?

Providing something for free can influence the decision of an individual. It doesn't matter if there is no change in the actual value of the product.

To understand the power of the word, consider two similar products, like two different brands of cookies. Assume the original price of the first brand, A, is $2 while the other brand, B, is $10. Also, assume that B is a much better option than A.

If there is a sale in which A is going for $1 while B is going for $5, you will notice a lot of customers opting to purchase B. It means that people will prefer to go for superior quality at half the price than low-quality cookies at a meager amount.

Consider another scenario where A is free while B is $4. You will observe that most people will opt for the free option, which is of lower quality.

Now, the thought running through the minds of individuals will be to get a box of cookies at no cost than losing $4 on the same box of cookies. When A becomes free, it becomes more valuable than B, even though there is no change in quality.

This behavior is referred to as loss aversion.

Because

The use of "because" offers a reason why you want someone to do something for you. It is easier to get someone to perform a task if you give them a reason to do so. Following natural human behavior, regardless of how authentic the reason, you can get people to do what you want by adding an idea to your request.

How to Use Because

When conversing with people, using "because" in your sentences is an easy way to persuade them to like you more. Simply make a request or a statement and then connect a reason using "because".

First, create a request or statement.

The following are simple ways to make a request or statement, and then connect them to a reason:

- I would like you to come with me because

- Try this shirt because

- Let's do it at your house because

- I want to go to the concert because

Then, add a reason.

Once you know the request you want to make, the next step is the reason for the request. If you want the reason to work like a charm, it must be convincing. This includes adding a reason that provides specific benefits.

Here are some sentences that show how effective it can be:

- "I hope you will come over to my house."

- Now add a reason to the sentence, and it becomes:

- "I hope you will come over to my house so we can work on the fort."

Including a reason and benefits may look like this:

- "I hope you will come over to my house so we can work on the fort. We will have our private area to hang out once it is complete and you can stay longer without feeling like you are intruding."

You can combine "because" with another crucial persuasive word, such as "you". By combining these two words, you can improve the compelling power of your statements.

There is a reason why these two words are stronger when used together. Using only "because" in a sentence makes the reason for a request objective. To make the reason for a request personal, you must add "you" to the reason.

How Your Business Can Benefit from The Use of Because

The use of 'because' in your business is a simple way to get your customers to comply with your requests. They react instinctively to a request once they hear this powerful word.

As a business, there are times when you will get requests from a customer. In some cases, you may be unable to handle such requests. In your reply to the customer, use this word to explain the reason you are unable to meet the expectations of the customer.

Giving a reason for turning down a job will provide more understanding between you and the customer. It will help maintain a good relationship into the future.

You can also use it to give more insight to your mission. Your goal of setting up a business is not just to make money. There should be a mission that influences business operations. If you can explain your mission and give reasons for the business, you are going to attract more willing sponsors and angel investors.

You can use "because" to explain the reason behind a free product, discount, and special offer. We have all been victim to a hidden catch during some special offers or free product offerings. For this reason, a lot of people are skeptical about taking part. If you want more of your customers or audience to become a part of what you are offering, then give them a clear, honest reason why you are offering free products or discounts.

Explain any issues with product delivery or product damages using the word "because". If your customers will not be getting a product on the promised date, it is their right to know why. You can also make a client more relaxed and understanding when you choose to explain. It will help prevent requests for refunds since the customers know they will be getting their products.

Instant

Human beings are unpredictable in most situations. In some cases, you may find people looking for delayed gratification while others may prefer instant rewards.

There are different situations where these apply. To become a successful business owner, you will need to understand and accept delayed gratification. You also need to realize that your customers prefer instant rewards.

Certain words stir up the part of the brain that deals with instant rewards. These words include immediately, fast, and instant.

Business owners who are into online product sales can provide instant rewards to their customers with immediate access to the product.

For those that run businesses in the traditional setting, the best way you can provide instant rewards is to deliver the product as soon as possible. In case they make a complaint, you should also get in touch as quickly as you can.

Rapid response can significantly influence the decisions of a customer. There a lot of customers that will not buy your products regularly. Merely including "instant" in a product description can change their opinion.

If you are going to use this word, there is a specific rule you always need to follow. The rule is to ensure that you keep your promise to your customers.

If you know you cannot keep a promise, it is better you don't make such a promise. Your customers will be more comfortable if you under-promise but deliver beyond expectations.

Chapter 7:
Get Respect Immediately

The aim of this chapter is to make you become a better person that people will appreciate more. You don't have to be perfect. Everyone makes mistakes. Your ability to own up to your mistakes and care for others are some of the things that earn you respect.

If you are respectful, people will know through your value of yourself, your love for others, your ability to look beyond people's flaws, and your composure. These attributes are respected in any individual.

You want to do unto others the same things you would accept as a person. You will want to be treated with respect and kindness if you are in a pinch. Showing others this type of attitude will make them reciprocate these actions and respect to you.

How to Earn Respect

Your Presentation
This is the easiest way to double the respect you receive.

People are always moved by what they see, and what they hear. Before they get to know your personality, they always get the first impression through your appearance. This is how they will determine if they will accord you respect or not.

What is the best way to present yourself?

Dress to Suit the Occasion
It is quite embarrassing when you are invited to a dinner party, and you dress looking like you are heading to the mall. This speaks volume. You don't have to wear expensive clothes to dress appropriately for an occasion.

All you need to do is to make sure your clothes fit, you look smart, and you look nicely groomed. Consequently, you have given people the impression that you are an upstanding citizen, even before you utter a word.

Some people believe that it is vain to attach any importance to your appearance. This is not true. It is generally advisable not to be excessive about anything, including the way you look, as simplicity gives the aura of sophistication.

This, of course, will involve money (not too much), your ability to take a good bath, have a good hair and body groom (if you are of that type), and looking smart. The simplicity of this trick will get people to respect you.

How You Stand Your Ground on Your Beliefs in A Respectful Way
This scenario presents an opportunity for people to air their differences without offending one another. It is seemingly impossible, as, during the heat of the moment, people are usually not composed. It is utterly wrong to impose your opinion on others. Similarly, it is misguided to reshape your belief to impress people, that is you being disrespectful to yourself.

Take, for instance, you are the only rock lover in the mix of people that prefer classical music. If they gave their opinion on their belief, you will be accorded more respect if you don't impose your belief on them, but generally, agree to disagree about others opinion.

Temperament

If you are easily angered, there is a big possibility that you will not be respected. This is because you will come off as too emotional and irrational. People are more likely to avoid engaging with you in any form of interaction.

It is important to air your opinion, suggestions, or contributions. It is very wrong, however, to be mad if things do not go the way and method you envisage them to be.

There are different ways to approach debatable matters without coming off as angry:

- You should be deliberate or intentional in providing solutions before you engage in a conversation about the problem.

- Things tend to get out of hands quickly when you are in a public environment, so you might want to take the conversation somewhere private.

- Never approach people when you are emotional about something; there is a 70% chance it will go negative. Give it time before you speak.

- Your tone when you talk matters a lot. If you sound accusatory, you might fan a fire to the flame. Instead, construct your words more carefully by using statements like, "I believe you don't…" rather than saying, "You never go out of your way…"

- It always pays to be composed and collected.

- Try to exercise empathy. This way, you put yourself in the other person's situation, and you might relate better to the circumstances.

- Never be on the defensive. Admit when you are wrong.

If you can successfully remain calm through things, people will trust you to handle situations and will respect you.

Acknowledge Your Mistakes

This might not be a popular trick, but it brings results. People who refuse to own up to their mistakes are considered prideful. To be prideful means you believe you are better than others. This does great harm to any relationship.

Here is an example of a scenario. Imagine a friend's mistake cost you money and instead of owning up to it, they try to justify it. They continuously display this bad behavioral pattern. Such persons will quickly lose any form of respect from his/her peers.

To be prideful is not an appealing attribute in a person, and this can cost you good relationships, be it business, personal, or casual. To earn respect from people, it is advisable to be humble. Nobody is known to be perfect, and as a result, people relate more to you when you admit your wrongs and consider your mistakes.

If you can't think about what to say when you make mistakes, start by saying this, "I am so sorry I came off as offensive, not my best attribute, it won't happen again," or you can say, "I apologize for the wrong I have done." Very easy!

Owning up to your mistakes gives you respect and doesn't make you seem like a difficult person to deal with. This will go a long way in strengthening your relationship with others, as they will feel appreciated and relevant

How You Respect Others to Get Respect

To be respected, you also must respect others. Respecting the next person has a significant impact. Don't limit your respect to people of high influence or positions of importance.

Respect should come from a more natural ground. As humans, the end goal in life usually is to attain a place of peace, happiness, and wealth. We are all going through a different route to accomplish that.

So, irrespective of one's opinion or belief, at the end of the day, we all want the same thing. Instead of treating people cruelly because they don't fit your definition or standard of anything, it is better to extend an act of kindness and genuine love.

You may wonder how this relates to earning respect. If you are to describe the most disrespectful people you have ever come across, it will be those who felt they were better than others, either because of their wealth, position, race, beliefs, or class. It always goes back to being full of pride. These are the people that get the least amount of respect.

Act in A Respectful Manner

Being respectful goes way beyond words; it is also how you act. Your body language can show that you are disrespectful. For instance, your boss is talking to you, and you don't give him your attention. Instead, you are concentrating on your laptop screen. That is considered rude, or if you roll your eyes or walk away during a conversation.

There are various attributes that can show how disrespectful you are to a person. Agreement is not the only sign of respect. Differing opinions makes us unique.

If you are known to act in ways and manners that are considered disrespectful, people will generally want to avoid you, and that can create damage to your relationships.

Stop Insulting Others

To act in a disrespectful manner is not only when you are addressing the person himself, but it could also be you talking bad about another person without them being present. This act is rampant in social gatherings, workplaces, and organizations.

The person you are talking to will never respect you. They are most times careful, knowing that you will probably talk about them in the same manner as well. You are termed as the gossip and the one who creates rifts between people.

To earn respect, you need to be an open person. Don't talk bad about people. That way, you are considered trustworthy and respected.

How to Handle People Taking You for Granted?

If you feel like people often get to know you so they can exploit you, then you really need to go through this section with full attention.

The best way to prevent people from taking you for granted is to set boundaries and stick to them. This tells people that you would not tolerate them taking you for granted and that you deserve to be respected.

Before you set your boundaries, you need to consider those things you can control.

Do not set boundaries you cannot enforce. For instance, you have friends who continuously loan money from you but never bother to pay you back because they probably feel you can afford to let it go. You can decide to limit the amount of money you give out to them on loan or make them sign an undertaking to pay you back.

It is also important to tell the person who is guilty of such acts. This is because people have a reason for how they act the way they do. Hearing from them will help you to assess how best to enforce your boundaries. You can also figure out ways to help them out without giving them room to take advantage of you.

For instance, ask them when they intend to pay you back and insist, they pay you back before loaning them more money. Setting boundaries does not mean they will not be crossed. As humans, doing things in the same manner repeatedly can make it seem like there is nothing wrong.

When this happens, the next action to take is to talk about it again with them. Make them understand:

- That you do not like their actions
- What your boundaries are

- The reason why you chose to set those boundaries

If they keep violating your boundaries, then you need to take drastic actions to bring about the changes you desire. The sad truth is that you might have to cut yourself off from them to maintain peace.

A lot of people who find it difficult to command respect from others feel like nobody ever listens to them.

- Do people overlook your opinions, or do you feel like no one takes you seriously?

- Are you constantly being interrupted or ignored?

- Is no one listening while you are speaking?

Your presence will be felt, and you are heard when you apply the tips below. These tips will make people have more respect for you. Tips on how to speak so people will listen to you include the following:

- Address people by their names during a conversation.

- Avoid talking in parables or using jaw-breaking words for easy comprehension. People will tend to keep away from you if they struggle through understanding what you are saying.

- Let your conversations also involve the other person's interests. Do not make the mistake of talking about only your interests.

- Gesticulate more often to drive your point across and keep their interest.

- Ask the other person a few questions. It makes them more involved and interested in the conversation.

- Do not avoid eye contact. Making eye contact with a person during a conversation shows them how interested you are in the conversation. If it is a group conversation, give everyone equal eye contacts to make everyone feel valued.

- Work on making your voice clearer and more audible for everyone to hear.

- Complaints and negativity should be minimized. Otherwise, people will lose interest in talking to you.

- Avoid bragging. No matter how hard you try to conceal it, people will see through you and keep their distance.

- Ask people how they think you can improve your communication skills.

- Use effective pauses. Silence sometimes plays an important role in communication.

- Change your tone and speed when talking. This has a way of making the conversation lively. You can practice this at home before trying it out in public.

Get Respect with Your Body Language

Body language can describe how a person feels about himself even without saying it.

You will come off as shy or insecure if you continuously walk around with your eyes fixed on the ground and your shoulders hunched. You will barely be respected with such body language.

If you walk around with your head held high, you portray confidence. People will respect you because you respect yourself and they sometimes believe that you have something worth being proud of. Below are some characteristics of confident body language:

- Walking with a purpose

- Good eye contact during a conversation or when addressing a group of people

- Good posture, avoiding slouching or crossing of your arms

- Gesticulate more often when speaking

- Keep your chin up and eyes forward instead of looking down

Always remember that there is a difference between confidence and arrogance. Arrogance rids a person of respect.

Chapter 8:
How to Analyze People

For one to decipher the hints people give off, either spoken or unspoken, one must see beyond the facade. It is impossible to know the entire story of anyone through rational thinking. To properly analyze an individual, you must become knowledgeable on other means of human communication such as body language.

It is also required that you let go of any preconceived ideas, sentiments (like indignations), or any reservations that could cloud your vision of people. The most important thing is to stay open-minded and absorb knowledge without bias.

It doesn't matter if the subject of study is your superior, colleague, or companion; it is crucial that you remain neutral and open-minded to get a correct result. Also, you need to discard any previous belief you may have about a person in order to perform a great analysis. Those who study people are taught to study even the latent. They know how to use the essential senses which help them to see beyond what is typically seen in order to properly analyze an individual.

What Is Body Language?

This is a type of communication which is nonverbal. It is dependent on the various movements of the body including minor and major movements. These minor and major body movements include changes in facial expressions, posture, and gestures.

Sometimes, the use of body language may be in combination with speech, or in other cases it may replace the use of speech. Body language can be used in a conscious or subconscious manner.

What Does Body Language Tell You About A Person?
Although speech may be your most important means of communication now, you used body language for communication when you were younger.

Understanding the message an individual is trying to pass is often dependent on your ability to analyze the body language of the individual. You may be able to assess if a person is lying or if they are trying to gain more understanding of a presentation.

Below are some easy ways that body language can help you understand the emotions of an individual:

Determining A Lie or Anxiousness in An Individual
In western cultures, a clear sign of nervousness is the inability of an individual to make eye contact. It may also signify fear or nervousness.

An individual that is not confident in the information they are giving will typically try to cover their mouth or eyes while speaking.

Lack of self-assurance will often lead to anxiousness. There are other apparent indications of anxiousness, and they include sweating, licking of the lips, and shaking.

It Shows Interest
Body language that indicates interest includes proper eye contact and nodding. A person that is interested in the topic of discussion will avoid fiddling with a pen, checking the time, or using their smartphone.

It is essential you don't mistake someone who is listening passively for an active listener. A passive listener will not be able to attain any of the information you are trying to convey. A proactive body language is also a good indication of a person paying attention to you.

It Is an Excellent Means of Identifying A Bored Individual
Depending on the body language of an individual, it is possible to determine if they are bored or not. There is one significant reason why it is difficult for an individual to mask boredom. It is because their desires do not align with their experiences now.

A person who is successful will possess charisma, energy, and strong body language. In addition to all these qualities, this individual will also know how to maintain eye contact. Combining all these qualities will make an individual capable of using body language to communicate with others effectively.

You will notice that such an individual will be in total control of the gestures they make while speaking and will also be capable of drawing the attention of others. If you can meet such an individual, you will be able to sense their confidence through the perfect handshake.

It Is an Easy Way to Identify Submission

Signs of helplessness from an individual can imply that the person is submissive. Such a person will often have their head downwards. Nervousness and an active effort to avoid criticism and conflict are signs of submissiveness. A face that is devoid of emotion also helps to prevent drawing too much attention.

Analyzing Body Language

As a form of nonverbal communication, body language replaces the use of words with physical motions. The physical actions are used to express the necessary information.

Gestures, facial expressions, body posture, touch, and eye movement are some of the physical motions that help in analyzing body language.

Analysis and interpretation of the body language of human beings are known as kinesics. Sign language is not the same as body language. There are significant differences between sign language and body language.

The features of sign language include grammar systems and other properties that are present in other standard languages. There is no grammar system in body language, and there is no general interpretation of body movements.

What Is Nonverbal Communication?

Nonverbal communication is a method of communication that doesn't depend on the use of words. There are similarities between nonverbal communication and body language. Body language is a branch of nonverbal communication.

People can use nonverbal communication in various ways including the following:

- Speech rate
- Personal space
- Hairstyle
- Touch
- Volume of voice
- Gestures
- Clothes
- Facial expressions
- Hygiene

The Role of Nonverbal Communication

The role of nonverbal communication in the life of an individual is often undermined. This is a skill that assists individuals in relating to others. Your nonverbal communication skills often determine your ability to solidify your relationships with others.

Different cultures interpret nonverbal communication in various ways. In some cases, the lack of a nonverbal communication cue has a specific meaning.

In nonverbal communication, each movement and combination of various movements such as eye movement, facial expressions, hand gestures, and postures has a meaning. Nonverbal communication cues may either be subtle or overt. Depending on how it is used, it is open to misinterpretation.

It is one of the easiest ways to assess the emotions of an individual. A person that intends to be deceptive will often make a nonverbal communication cue that has a meaning different from their body language. It is because nonverbal communication is not easy to fake.

Types of Nonverbal Communication

Nonverbal communication is present in different forms. The way people interpret nonverbal communication will vary for everyone. The message they pass regarding the thoughts of an individual is also broad.

The different types of nonverbal communication you will experience daily include the following:

- Eye movement and contact that represent the direction of a person's eyes
- Facial expressions that represent changes in features of the face
- Posture indicates the body of an individual as it relates to the body of other individuals
- Body movements that show how the body of an individual moves
- Tone of voice is an indication of the variance in voice pitch, such as the use of sarcasm
- Gestures that signify the movement of the head and limbs

Nonverbal communication is essential to emphasize, support, or contradict a verbal message.

Importance of Nonverbal Communication

When running a business or making new relationships, understanding and analyzing nonverbal communication can give you an upper hand. Using your knowledge of nonverbal communication, it is possible to investigate the reactions of clients and what influences their decisions.

If you can read nonverbal communications quickly, it is possible to avoid making any mistakes in front of clients, coworkers, family, or friends.

Ways of Analyzing People

The first way has to do with hints given off by body language.

It has been discovered that words make up for about seven percent of communication, while body language makes up fifty-five percent, and tone of voice is responsible for the remaining thirty percent. For this, it is pertinent to let the art of analyzing body language hi come naturally to you. Don't force it or get logical, be calm and let it flow. Be at ease, relax, and pay attention.

Be Observant of People's Outlook

There are key things to observe when analyzing people which include what they are wearing, how they are dressed, what their dress sense depicts. Each dress sense could be a sign of casualty, ambition, sexuality, or spirituality.

Be Attentive to Poses

There are questions to ask yourself concerning the posture of people, which are: Do they exude confidence with the way they raise their heads? Do they carry themselves with an unsure posture or fidget, which could mean their self-worth is low? Are their chests pushed out, which could mean arrogance or pride?

Pay Attention to Shifts in Body Parts

Bending and Space
People naturally stay close to people they like as opposed to the people they don't like. It is important to take note of a person's proximity to others.

Folded Arms and Legs
This posture portrays annoyance, self-justification, or self-defense. The crossing of the legs is usually accompanied by pointed toes in the direction of another person of interest.

Concealed Hands
Hands on laps, in pockets, or at the rear is usually a sign of people keeping a secret.

Biting of The Lip or Picking of The Finger Nails
This is usually a sign that people are anxious about something, or they are in a compromising position. These acts serve as an avenue for relief.

Decode Countenance
Feelings of people can easily be displayed on people's faces. One is assumed to be worried or of an overthinking nature with the appearance of deep frown lines on the face. Laugh lines depict happiness. Puckered lips portray annoyance, resentment, or disdain. Grinding of the teeth and jaw clenching portray anxiety.

The second way has to do with listening to your instincts.

Aligning with people is not just about words or body language; instincts take you a step further. Being intuitive requires your guts rather than what is on your mind. It helps in better identifying and analyzing every unspoken word by paying attention to depictions, sounds accidentally let off, or expressions, instead of relying on rational thinking.

What helps when getting to know someone deeply other than what's beneath their facade is your instinct, which enables you to go beyond what can be seen physically to obtain a desirable result.

List of Instinctive Hints

Acknowledge Insight
These bursts of visions come so quickly when discussing with people that it might be easy to overlook them and replace them with other thoughts in an instant. It helps to be sensitive, so you don't miss out on them.

Respect Your Instincts
That initial awakening you get during a new connection, even before you have the chance of gathering your thoughts is your instinct tugging at you. It suggests inner peace or discomfort to you. These emotions happen quickly and help you measure the sincerity of people upon first contact.

Be on Guard for Impulsive Compassion
Take note of your emotions when studying people. Your emotions can get so intense that you begin to experience the same emotions your subject is exhibiting. Be sensitive to how you feel after each session with people. Check if you experience body pains or feel downtrodden. A professional examination is necessary to be sure you are empathetic.

Goose Pimples Sensitivity

That mild stinging sensation we get when we meet those we look up to or when they say something, we can relate to is known as goose pimples. They also occur when you sense that you know someone even though they have never crossed your path.

A Third Way of Analyzing People: Respond to Strong Feelings

Feelings resonate well with our instincts, and one of the ways we get sensitive around people is through feelings. While being around some people can put you at ease, being around some others could be exhausting; it makes you want to look for a way out. This careful nudge is usually sensed somewhere around the body although it can't be seen. Medically, it is called "chi" in Chinese, a sensation that is very important to overall health.

Tactics for Studying Strong Feelings

Be Aware of People's Presence
This does not necessarily have anything to do with words or actions; it is the energy we generally give off. It hangs over us like a cloud. When analyzing people, pay attention to nature. Do they have an attractive nature? This does not necessarily have anything to do with words or actions; it is the energy people generally give off.

Pay Attention to How People Sound and Their Laughter
Feelings can be deduced from how loudly or softly we speak, or how we otherwise sound. Variations in sound make up a reverberation. Be observant of how the sound of people's voices makes you feel as you study them. Are their voices relaxing or calm? Do they sound harsh, resentful, or fretful?

Be Observant of People's Eyes

The eyes tell you a lot of things if you pay attention to them. It has been discovered that the eyes send a lot of signals just like the brain does to the body. Pay close attention to the eyes of people and look out for what they are saying. Do they look sensual? Calm? Are they filled with rage? Do they express cruelty? Also, can you decipher a love life from those eyes? Or are they evasive?

Observe the Response to Body Contact

Body contact can cause us to emit strong emotions that feel like a surge of energy. Be aware of how a handshake or a hug makes you feel. Do you feel relaxed, or uncomfortable? Does the person's hand feel damp, which could signify agitation, or does it feel flaccid, which could signify distraction or inferiority?

Chapter 9:
How to Think Under Pressure and Crush It

There are different times when we find ourselves under pressure. It may be the moment after your presentation when you must answer questions. The same also applies to selling a product to a prospective buyer.

To be successful under pressure, you must think of ways to pass your message across clearly. You must be confident. Having adequate knowledge can also help you to get through a high-pressure situation.

Learning to think on your feet is one of the few techniques that can get you to overcome any high-pressure situation. Below are some of the methods you can implement:

Avoid Jumping into Your Response
One of the mistakes people make in a high-pressure situation is responding too soon. It is often due to anxiety. As a result, they begin the response without a clear idea of where it will lead.

To give the best response when under pressure, you can start by taking a deep breath. It is a technique that provides an opening for you to put your thoughts in order. It works in both conversations and in interview settings.

Since you are taking your time to give an appropriate response, you also reduce the chances of getting flustered.

Ensure That Your Body Is Functioning at Its Normal Pace

A simple sign that you are under pressure is an increase in your heart rate. Your speech is also much faster than normal, and your brain will also be performing faster than usual.

A combination of these is sure to have a negative impact. If your brain is working at a faster pace, it means you are generating thoughts faster than you can analyze them. With an increase in the rate at which you speak, you may end up saying things that may make you seem weird or get you into trouble.

By slowing down the pace of your speech, your brain will be able to plan how you should present your thoughts accurately.

Develop A Concise Response Based on The Question

If someone is asking you a question, the answer that the person is expecting should be specific. The problem with answering under pressure is that you may end up giving answers that contain excess information, or answers with minimal information. Each answer has its demerits.

If the response contains too much information, you may take a long time to answer. People quickly lose interest once a reply starts getting too long. In addition to blurting out things that should be kept secret, people will see you as a blabbermouth who is also boring.

A short answer also has its downsides. If you are trying to get out of a high-pressure situation, short answers will only lead to more questions. Since this type of answer will not reveal the necessary information, you are giving the other person full control of how the conversation should go.

To deal with these issues, giving a concise answer is best. Such an answer will be short enough to reveal the answer to the question and avoid giving out too much information. To develop the perfect answer, you must ensure that you are focusing on only what the question has asked.

There will be so much information available in the form of thoughts, but you need to select only what is most important. Attaching a supporting fact to the response is another excellent way to give more insight.

Stalling

The response to some questions requires more than a deep breath to formulate. In such cases, there are specific tactics you can implement to stall for time. Below are some of the tactics you can apply to get more time to think of a proper response:

Create A Focus

Some questions may have a vast scope. A good tactic is to narrow the question down to a smaller scope. This will make it easier to answer the question.

Request for A Definition of Terms

Some questions may contain terminology that you are unfamiliar with. Before you start coming up with an answer, ask that the other person define these terminologies. You are only doing this to make sure that your answer will align with what they want to hear.

Say the Question to Yourself

As you repeat a question you are asked, you will be able to gain clarity on certain parts of the issue. You can rearticulate the question to make it simpler for you to tackle.

Practice Various Questions That Cause High-Pressure

Specific questions commonly come up in high-pressure situations. Practicing such questions will help in developing better ways to answer such questions.

The questions in this list may differ for each workplace environment, business, or friends circle. Identifying questions that cause an increase in the pace of your speech and your thinking is essential.

Sometimes, a person merely asking how your business is doing may put you in a high-pressure situation. It may also be a question about your vision for the business.

Don't Take A Defensive Position

High-pressure situations often put you in a defensive position. There are various reasons why you may want to get into a defensive position. It is often due to criticisms.

If you come up with a proposal or a strategy for growth, it is often a good idea to have someone look at the strategy or proposal. Anyone looking at your documents may have found some areas where you have made certain errors. Getting criticism for such mistakes may often cause you to take the defensive position.

A typical reply to criticism that shows you have taken a defensive position is the use of, "No, but…" as your response. A better reply that gives room for creative thinking and sharing ideas is to reply with, "Yes, and…"

Make Moments Where You Are Under Pressure Seem Like Fun

The way you look at a high-pressure situation will affect how you perform. If your interpretation of a high-pressure situation is terrible, then you will have issues dealing with it.

The same also applies if you see such a situation as a threat. Your interpretation of this situation will lead you to a place of fear and result in a loss of self-confidence. Fear, in this case, can interfere with your judgment, thought process, and memory. It is what causes you to act on impulse.

Change your view of a high-pressure situation. Consider it a fun challenge you need to overcome. As a result of your new outlook, you can eliminate fear and gain more control of the situation.

Falling Apart Under Pressure

When you find yourself under pressure, certain things may cause you to fall apart. If you find yourself in a situation like a previous moment when you failed, you may begin to worry. It is normal human behavior to worry about failing again and making the wrong choice. If you are not careful, you may end up overthinking every decision.

It doesn't matter how well you usually perform a task. Once you start overthinking, it will cripple your ability to work effectively. It will often result in your inability to take a step forward.

When you want to avoid failure, it is common to keep telling yourself not to fail. If only you understood that this action only increases the chances of doing whatever you are trying to avoid. Also, you also lose a lot of willpower in the process.

Merely focusing on the task at hand is an easy way to avoid failure when you are under pressure. If you are in a high-pressure situation but retain your positive outlook, you can see the case as a challenge you need to overcome.

Chapter 10:
How to Sell Anything to Anyone All the Time

The growth of your business often depends on your ability to sell your products to your customers. The truth is that not everyone is a great salesperson. Nonetheless, you can train yourself to become better at selling anything to anyone.

One of the great things about making sales on your own is that you are in control of your business growth. Your profits at the end of the month are often a reflection of your sales performance during the month. As a result, you can assess your skills and appreciate your efforts more.

To ensure you are making enormous profits at the end of each month, you need to develop yourself. There are specific methods and techniques you can implement to get better at selling anything to anyone.

Below are some methods you can follow:

Show That You Are an Authority
Solidifying your position as an authority in a niche is the easiest way to sell your products to people. It is the same reason why consumers are willing to spend thousands of dollars on an iPhone or a Samsung device.

Have people seen a demonstration of your knowledge or skills? Is there a reason for people to trust your words?

If you can solidify your image as an authority in your target market, it becomes easier to get people to buy from you. Product sales are often dependent on trust. Your customers are sure to keep buying your products if you can make them trust you explicitly.

Becoming an authority in a specific niche has never been as easy as it is in recent times. Access to social media offers you the opportunity to share relevant information and create quality content. Blogs also have a significant impact depending on how you use them.

Connect with Your Customers
A lot of sales are often a result of the connection between the seller and the buyer. It may not be due to the quality of the product available. Making sales will be easy if you have the best product on the market, but customers will be more willing to buy from a seller they feel is like them in many ways.

Forming a connection with your customers is quite easy. You need to connect on an emotional level. Your use of words, analogies, and anecdotes can be of immense help. When people decide to purchase a product, their emotions often cloud their logical reasoning. Things like a simple greeting and compliments go a long way when connecting with a customer.

Comprehensive market research can set you up for great relationships with customers. It also helps you to create a profile of the customer you are meeting for the first time. Following the results of your market research, it is easy to identify the problems your customers face, and the solution to these problems.

Making sales is essential, but being human comes first. It is important you show your human side before trying to make sales.

Don't Be Obnoxious

Just because you are trying to sell your product doesn't mean you should become intolerable. Your first impression on your prospective buyers matters a lot. Don't be the blabbermouth during the conversation.

You should have a filter for anything you say to your prospect. This filter should help decide what information is relevant to the prospect and what is not.

Let the focus of the conversation be your buyer. Tailor the interaction to revolve around the buyer. This extends to any voicemails you leave, any emails you send, and more.

Emotions are important

When trying to make sales, a lot of people underestimate the impact of emotions. We often place our hopes on prospective customers making decisions based on logic. This is not true in most cases.

Making decisions based on emotions is what makes customer behavior very unpredictable. If you are unable to take the emotions of your customers into account, you won't be able to make consistent sales.

To make the most of the emotions, the first step is to understand the various emotions that can influence a decision. They include the following:

- Pride
- Anger

- Greed
- Shame
- Fear
- Joy

During your conversation with a prospect, you may be able to draw out certain emotions. Connecting with a prospect will make them happy. It then results in an emotional bias during the decision-making process.

To make sure you can make sales whenever you want, you should be able to influence at least two positive emotions in a prospect. It should be done subtly, without the prospect noticing. If you draw out too many emotions, both positive and negative, you will end up compounding the process.

Not All Customers Are Good for You

A good salesperson always ensures that their impact on the customer will make them return another time. Nonetheless, it is vital you understand that not all customers are good for the business.

There are specific interactions with customers that will turn out badly no matter how hard you try. The earlier you understand this, the better it will be. Keeping a lousy customer around will have a negative influence on you, other customers, and the business.

You may find yourself in a dicey situation sometimes. The customer that may be ruining your brand may be your highest-paying customer. It is for situations like this that you need to come up with new ideas each day.

What Value Are You Selling?

Customers usually have an interest in the value a product offers. The cost is what makes the product unique. That is how you survive the competition.

The value of your product can also be the dream that you are selling. In some cases, it may be an opportunity for your customers to turn in more profits.

Explaining the value of a product to a customer before trying to sell the product will have a positive impact. You are giving the customers time to visualize the outcomes and opportunities they can get from the product.

If you rush into trying to sell your product, it will take less than 5 seconds for a customer to assess the product thoroughly. It is not enough time for them to get a good understanding of the product.

A product value that promises high returns on investment is always attractive to customers.

Do Your Research but Remain an Active Listener?

Getting information on your prospects is a lot easier with social media. It is the least you can do if you expect your prospects to also learn about your products.

Various social media platforms make it easy to do your research. They include the following:

- Facebook
- LinkedIn
- Blogs

- Google

- Twitter

Performing your research provides all the information you need regarding a prospect. It doesn't mean you will get all the information you need.

To fill in the gaps of your information, you need to remain an active listener. If you ask critical questions, you can get the relevant answers from your prospects. It is then possible to better understand their problem and proffer the best solution.

Come up with a list of questions to ask your prospects before you meet. These are to serve as a guide. You don't have to force the conversation.

As an active listener, remain quiet while your prospect answers each question. Don't ask too many questions at once. You want to get as much information as possible.

Create A Profile of Your Prospect

There are lots of reasons why a profile is essential if you want to make sales. A profile helps you identify what products meet the requirements of a prospect.

If you want to be able to sell anything to anyone, you need to understand that not everything is suitable for everyone.

In selling anything to anyone, you must define the prospect that fits into your definition of "anyone". Once you define this prospect, you can manage your time and increase your chances of successfully closing a sale.

Set Your Mind on Closing the Sale

From the moment you meet a prospect, your mind should already be on closing the sale. A sale is not complete unless you can close it. Everything you are trying to do is for this final moment.

You can significantly improve your chances of closing a sale if you are consciously working towards it. This is the moment when you make the sale, so it is vital. It is also vital you learn how to close a sale to increase your success rate.

How to Close A Sale?

Closing a sale involves negotiating the best deal for your product. It is a skill that you master through practice. The only way you will get practice is to close sales with your customers frequently.

As you develop your skills as a negotiator, you will become more assertive and tactful when dealing with your customers. It doesn't matter if you are not a natural at negotiating; the potential is present in everyone.

Specific tips can help you develop your negotiating skills to make you better at closing sales. Below are the essential tips you need:

Prepare for The Process

There are some necessary steps we often take for granted. Preparation is often one of those steps. It is easy to overlook this step when you feel you have all the necessary information you need.

To boost your chances when trying to close a deal, you need to know everything about your customer. It is also crucial you identify the services and products that align with their needs.

Due diligence is critical in this situation. It is through this process you can determine the amount your prospect is willing to spend on the product. Personal information on your customer can also be helpful. This may be the area they live, favorite restaurants, and other preferences that can help gain trust when you mix it in subtly during the conversation.

Research on other products available on the market can also help you determine your product information that should remain a secret until trying to make the sale. Dropping such information as a surprise is sure to throw the customer off balance, which you can use to your advantage. It makes it easier to close the deal.

Create A Balance Between Being Nice and Being Firm

If you are not willing to compromise at some points, you may end up losing the sale. As a negotiator, understanding situations that require firmness and those that require you to be nice.

Why is this important? Closing a sale is not the end of your business with a customer. You always want customers to come back another time. Being nice while trying to close a sale will ensure that your relationship with a customer remains positive.

Your Body Language and Tone

During a conversation, your body language always speaks the loudest. Combining your body language with an excellent tone of voice will set the mood for a great conversation. A lot of the messages that you wish to pass across during a conversation is often done using body language.

Body language and tone of voice in a formal environment is usually different from what you use when trying to make a customer feel comfortable. You need to smile more and try to talk at a much slower pace.

Don't Undersell

It can be difficult to get a good deal when negotiating with a customer that has more experience. Sometimes, you end up making the wrong decisions. This may be to avoid getting rejected.

A counter-offer is usually necessary after a customer refuses to accept your terms. To make a suitable counter-offer, it is vital you ask the customer for an explanation. The explanation should give you clear reasons why they are not accepting your terms. You can then create a counter-offer that is beneficial to both you and the customer.

In some cases, it is better to have the client come up with the counter-offer. Remaining silent after a refusal will often prompt a counter-offer from the customer.

Avoid Giving the Initial Offer

A good thing about closing a deal with a customer is the limitless opportunities that are available. A simple step that opens the door of opportunities is to avoid making the first offer.

If your customer makes the first offer on what you are selling, you have a higher chance of receiving a great deal. As a good negotiator, you will still make a counter-offer at a higher price.

After a period during which there will have been various counter-offers, you will be able to settle on a price that provides an excellent return on investment (ROI).

Learn to Manage Your Time Wisely

If you want to make lots of sales, you should know how to manage your time effectively. To manage your time, you should be able to tell if a person is going to buy your product or not.

You should also have a limit on the amount of time you spend with one customer. Taking too much time talking to a single customer will eat into the time you would have spent convincing another prospect.

To be successful in making sales, you should be able to determine a prospect that will buy your product within the first minute of your interaction. In most cases, when a customer starts asking too many questions, it is often a sign that they have no interest in making a purchase.

You can also observe the trends in your previous sales attempt. You may notice that it has been difficult making sales after four minutes of conversing with a prospect. In future interactions, you can set your limit to four minutes. As soon as this time elapses, you know it is profitable to move on to the next prospect.

Implementing Psychological Tricks

If you are trying to sell something to someone, there are certain tricks that can influence the response of the other individual. Using these tricks effectively will have an impact on your sales.

Some of the psychological tricks you should know include the following:

Confirmation Bias

This implies that people will choose a piece of information that is like their belief rather than another option with accurate facts.

Rhyme-As-Reason Effect

People tend to accept rhyming sentences as facts compared to sentences that do not rhyme.

Decoy Effect

If you have two options you want people to choose from, adding a third option can improve the possibility of your customers picking one of the two real options. The third option usually has some benefits over the first option but is inferior to the second option.

Peak-End Rule

If you decide to make a presentation, a high point during the presentation and the end of the presentation remain fresh in the memories of your listeners.

Anchoring Effect

People use the initial information they get to compare any other information they receive about the product.

Sales Techniques You Should Know

Use the Silent Treatment

Silence when trying to make a sale is a powerful tool that can work for you or against you. The silence can make people feel very uncomfortable, and that makes customers make decisions in your favor. To take advantage of this technique, you must be strong willed. If you end up breaking the silence, you may end up underselling. Merely state your price and go quiet. Now, wait for your customer to break the silence.

The Free Trial Technique

This is a popular technique in making sales. It is suitable for both online and traditional sales methods. It allows the customer to get a feel of the product and its features before they decide to purchase.

There are different ways through which you can apply the free trial technique. You can choose to run a 3-day trial for free or offer a money back guarantee for a certain duration. As customers get attached to the product, it becomes more difficult to send it back.

Through the free trial, customers can assess the functionality of the product you are selling. There are a few skin care products that offer 30-day money back guarantees. If you don't notice any significant improvement in your skin while using the product, you can return it for a refund.

If you offer music tutorials online, you may decide to offer a 7-day free trial period. It gives your customers the time to assess your teaching and how much they gain during this time.

Using Offers and Discounts to Promote Sales

This is another technique that a lot of sellers use. You can also observe it on Amazon. Discounts are also available when buying from street vendors. It may be difficult to notice because you must work for your discount by bargaining.

In supermarkets, grocery stores, and online stores, you can find some discounted products at a very high price. The discount will make the deal very attractive and almost impossible to pass up. This is when a lot of people give in to impulse spending habits.

Implementing offers is another excellent way to make it difficult for customers not to purchase your product. You can create an offer by including another product whenever a customer purchases your product. It is also possible to invest in a sales promotion, such as a Christmas sales promo, or Black Friday sales.

Scarcity Marketing
Scarcity refers to the unavailability of a product. If you need a product but cannot find it anywhere, then it is scarce. Scarcity marketing is a technique that prompts customers to make immediate purchases.

The trick behind the effectiveness of this simple strategy is how it works on the minds of buyers. Customers believe that if they fail to take advantage of the opportunity at that moment, they may never get the chance again. As a result, sales increase when a product is scarce.

In some cases, a ban on imports on a commodity will cause customers to stock up on that commodity.

There are different ways you can implement scarcity marketing. Labeling a product as an "Exclusive Product" or a "Limited Edition" is a form of scarcity marketing. It may not look like a scarcity marketing strategy, but customers react because they don't want to miss out on this deal.

You can better understand how to implement scarcity marketing strategies below:

Rare Items

If you are a seller of rare items, then you will always find collectors who are willing to pay a reasonable price for your products. Any rare item is unique and almost impossible to find. It can be the original edition of a favorite book or a coin from the 18th century.

The thought of being one of the few people in the world to own an item often prompts customers to purchase rare items.

Limited Quantity Products

Any product available in limited quantity means that only a specific number of these products were made. Also, the company will not manufacture this product at any time in the future.

Other limited quantity products are only available depending on the season. Limited quantity products may be a remastered game or a game console with a unique design that differs from the original.

Chapter 11:
Use Psychology to Get What You Want

Persuading someone to do what you want is a process that must be subtle. This makes it a bit complex to achieve unless you can harness the right skills. If you lack basic persuasion skills, it may be difficult to get someone to do something as easy as lending you a pen.

There are various tricks you can use in getting people to do what you want. These tricks will help improve your ability to sway opinions in your favor.

Psychology is an area that provides all the necessary tips and tricks that help in persuading others. If you know how to influence the function of the brain, it is possible to get people to do what you want.

Politicians and salespeople are a part of many individuals who have discovered easy methods of swaying opinions. It is the same way a company advertises a new product and convinces its customers of the benefits of that product.

What are some of the psychological tricks you can use? Below are some of these excellent tricks.

The Bandwagon Effect

It is easier to get someone to accept a belief if there are lots of other people who also accept this belief. This is what the bandwagon effect describes. Just because people accept this belief does not imply that it is the right belief.

By implementing this psychological trick, you can persuade people to do something you want. The first step is to get a few people to accept or do whatever task you need. These may be your friends or family members.

Once you have people who are doing the task, you can then easily persuade another person to join in. If you are trying to sell a product, you can give your friends and family free products to try out. When your prospect sees others who use your products, it becomes easier to get them to buy the product.

Priming

This is a technique that can subtly influence the decision-making process of an individual. There are different types of priming. Some of the most accessible types of priming you can use to get what you want include repetition priming, associative priming, and conceptual priming.

Associative priming is the use of an object that is closely associated with another object. By introducing the first object, it triggers the memory of the individual to another similar object.

Conceptual priming involves the use of a stimulus that has a conceptual relationship with the response. An example of objects in the same conceptual category will be a gaming console and a gamepad.

Repetition priming is the use of a specific stimulus to prompt a response at a faster rate. The faster response is due to the repetitive pairing of the same stimulus and response. An example will be asking an individual to repeat the word 'silk' ten times and then asking, "what do cows drink?" Due to the repetition of the word silk, the fastest response to the question will be milk.

The priming process of an individual is usually subtle and impossible to notice. Priming an individual to make a decision that will benefit you is quite easy if you set up the environment properly. If you want someone to decide to eat a bowl of cereal in the morning, placing a bowl, a milk jug, and a cereal carton will make the decision easy for them to make.

Don't Say A Word

This is very effective if you are trying to get information out of an individual. If you ask a question, you might get an unsatisfactory answer. Just saying nothing and staring will often get the individual to keep talking.

It is essential you maintain eye contact while remaining silent. If you are lucky, you may get the person to tell the truth about a situation. However, the direct eye contact and the pause can often be misinterpreted as you already having the accurate information.

Use Tiredness to Your Advantage

Tiredness can affect people both mentally and physically. At this point, you can quickly get what you want out of an individual. A good time to use this trick is after a workday.

If you have a demand or request, you can put it across at this moment when they are not mentally alert. Due to their level of tiredness, they will lack the energy to argue with you over these requests.

Contrasting

This is a technique that a lot of people know about. When you want to get something from someone, you start by asking for something bigger than your real request. Since the demand is too high, there will be a need to lower your demand.

While you negotiate with the other person, you will reach an agreement of lower demand. While this will appear as a win for the other person, you know that you have obtained your original demand.

Reciprocity Norm

The reciprocity norm is a simple trick that has been in existence for a very long time. It is the primary desire of humans to repay their debt to others. It implies that you will be more inclined to help someone if they have been of help to you in the past.

Now that you understand this simple trick, how can you make it work for you?

It is straightforward. If you want to get someone to do something for you, do something nice for the person first. You don't have to go overboard; a simple box of doughnuts will suffice.

As a result of your kind gesture, they will be willing to accept a request from you when the opportunity arises.

Show Them What They Stand to Gain

When bargaining with someone, getting them to focus on what they will gain will make it easier to influence their decision. The way you phrase your sentences is vital in this situation. Let the emphasis be on what they will receive and not what they will lose.

When phrasing your sentence, your offer should come first before your demand. It should look like you are providing something of value so you can get their attention. Once they show interest, you can then make your request.

Let People Watch

It is easy to persuade someone if there are other people around watching. This is only effective if you are persuading them to do something that is right. It is a technique that works almost all the time.

If it feels like you are being watched, you will be more inclined to do the right thing. Doing the right thing in some cases may be difficult. The feeling that others are judging you is always a good motivation.

It is common to find pictures of eyes in places like toilets or public areas. If you have a feeling that you are being watched, it is easy to avoid littering the environment. It also persuades individuals to always clean up after using a public toilet.

If you find this book helpful in anyway a review to support my endeavors is much appreciated.

www.ingramcontent.com/pod-product-compliance
Lightning Source LLC
Chambersburg PA
CBHW031055080526
44587CB00011B/695